FROMMER'S
SAN FRANCISCO
MARY RAKAUSKAS

□

1989–1990

Published by Prentice Hall Trade Division
A Division of Simon & Schuster, Inc.
Gulf + Western Building
One Gulf + Western Plaza
New York, NY 10023

ISBN 0-13-047504
ISSN 0899-3254

Text Design: Levavi & Levavi, Inc.
Manufactured in the United States of America

*Although very effort was made to ensure the accuracy
of price information appearing in this book,
it should be kept in mind that prices
can and do fluctuate in the course of time.*

CONTENTS

MAPS

To Alex and Patricia Yakutis,
Leone and Kris Fladeland,
and Donna Valerie D.V.M. who
kept the circus on the road

INFLATION ALERT: I don't have to tell you that costs will rise regardless of the level of inflation. In researching this book I have made every effort to obtain up-to-the-minute prices, but even the most conscientious researcher cannot keep up with the changing pace of inflation. Even if prices have risen above those quoted, I feel sure that these selections still represent the best value for money in San Francisco and environs.

CHAPTER I

AMERICA'S DREAM TOWN

□ □ □

What is the secret of San Francisco's continuing attraction? Ask anyone who has fallen in love—the city is romantic, breathtaking, classy, bohemian, frequently unpredictable, a bit eccentric, exciting, gutsy, stunning, and very much a survivor. The appeal of this collection of intriguing attributes exists even for those who have never seen Nob Hill and never eaten sourdough bread.

In a national sampling taken a while back, the vast majority of adult Americans questioned named San Francisco as the city they would most like to live in.

The odd part about this is that a large number of the respondants had never even been to San Francisco! They'd merely heard about it. And this love affair still seems to persist.

No other spot in the U.S.A. has managed to project such a universal image into the hearts of its compatriots. Washington may have the White House, New York City may have Broadway, and Los Angeles, Hollywood, but none of them exerts a fraction of the sentimental pull still wielded by the "cool, gray City of Gold" more than a century after the gold has petered out.

Why?

It's no use asking San Franciscans for the reason. They are so narcissistically enamored of their city that they merely grin and say "Well . . . naturally . . ." and let it go at that.

So it has to be left to non-natives—like myself—to try and find the answers. And I've found several.

A SINGULAR CITY

For a start, San Francisco is absolutely unique, not merely in America, but in the world. Superficially it's shaped like a compressed accordion. It's almost a conglomerate of tiny self-contained cities.

Yet San Francisco is enchantingly beautiful. But not in the way

Rome or Paris or parts of Washington are beautiful. Her beauty has a humorous, rakish, slightly zany air, a certain cartoon quality that doesn't leave you awestruck but makes you smile with your eyes and fills you with warmth deep inside and—yes—makes you want to stay there for the rest of your life.

Maybe it's the way those gingerbread houses cling to the steep hillsides like displaced alpine cottages. Or it's the glitter of sunshine on the golden pagoda roofs of Chinatown. Or it's the sudden unexpected glimpses of ocean when you stop climbing and look back over your shoulder. Or it's the bouncing, bell-clanking onrush of a toy-like cable car that seems to have escaped from Disneyland.

For over 200 years, what was to become San Francisco was passed, unseen, by the Portuguese, the Spanish, the English, even the Basques. It hasn't let itself be ignored since. The city moves up and down. So do its residents. San Franciscans are people of strong opinions and action. They'll take a stand, even if it's tilted. They're outspoken; they're winners. To their continuing credit, indifference is not part of the makeup of this charming city, nor its residents.

SOPHISTICATION

"Cities," the late and great Will Rogers once said, "are like gentlemen. They are born, not made. Size has nothing to do with it. I bet San Francisco was a city from the very first time it had a dozen settlers."

Which puts a big slice of San Francisco's charm in a nutshell. For despite its delightful quaintness, the Bay City has an aura of cosmopolitan sophistication, of metropolitan style and elegance, that makes far larger communities seem like hick towns in comparison.

Figures, in her case, *don't* tell the story. San Francisco has about 745,000 inhabitants, of whom about 16% are Chinese, 20% Italian, 3.9% German, 5% Filipino, 3% Irish, 2.9% British, and some 2% Japanese. The black population is over 13% of San Francisco's inhabitants.

Which amounts to a pretty average American mixture.

Yet, somehow, this middling mass of people (fewer than Houston, Texas, for example) conveys an instant Big City impression, the picture of an urban world center quite out of proportion to its actual size.

One reason for this is the San Francisco chic.

The commercial hub of the city around Union Square and the window displays of the department stores and little boutiques match some of New York's finest shops for style and attractiveness.

But beyond these surface symptoms, San Francisco's urban sophistication is based on its tolerance. An easygoing broadmindedness combined with an eminently stretchable moral code.

No other city in the U.S. looks so benevolently on saints and sinners alike.

But perhaps the real test of San Francisco's maturity is the manner in which it copes with its past.

San Francisco has a very murky past indeed. As a matter of fact, it once ranked along with Shanghai and Marseilles as one of the wickedest ports on earth.

But whereas Chicago leans over backward to make visitors forget its hell-raising heritage, San Francisco does the opposite. It carefully preserves and enshrines its scarlet yesterday, dusts it off, mounts it on a pedestal—and then charges you admission to see it!

On the east side of Union Square you'll find a quiet, sedate, two-block mall opening, lined with sycamore trees and little deluxe shopfronts. Until the turn of the century this thoroughfare was known as Morton Street, the most infamous section of the Barbary Coast red-light district, with an undraped female beckoning from every window.

Today it has been rechristened . . . **Maiden Lane!** And every March or April it becomes the flower-wreathed bower of the annual Daffodil Festival. Which makes it a fairly typical sample of San Francisco's sense of humor.

SPANISH BACKDROP

The city began life under the name of **Yerba Buena** ("good herb") as a mission post founded by Spanish monks in 1776.

In 1821 it became Mexican territory but remained very much what it was—a sleepy little village of 30 or so families, grouped around an adobe Customs house, guarded by a "company" of nine cavalrymen who were rarely paid.

Today the original site, at Kearny Street between Clay and Washington, is called **Portsmouth Plaza.** Nothing Spanish has remained. The place is the hub of Chinatown.

REBELLION AND GOLD: In June 1846 English-speaking Californians launched the so-called Bear Flag Rebellion against Mexican rule, fighting under an emblem that was supposed to represent a grizzly bear; the Mexicans mistook it for a hog.

The Anglos won hands down and promptly founded what was possibly the shortest-lived republic on record. It lasted precisely 26 days. Then the Big Brother Republic absorbed it, and California became part of the United States.

Yerba Buena, occupied by 50 sailors and marines from the U.S.S. *Portsmouth,* was renamed San Francisco a year later.

There's no telling how long the place might have remained a drowsy village if it hadn't been for the cry of "Gold!" It was the signal that sent the "Forty-Niners" rushing to California from every point of the compass.

Few of them found any gold worth shouting about. In San Francisco, disappointed diggers were soon committing suicide at the rate of 1,000 per year. But the gold rush transformed the town into a roaring, roistering, wide-open, boom metropolis, where literally anything went, providing you could pay for it.

SIN CITY

The town was swarming with assorted gangs of thugs calling themselves "Hounds" or "Sydney Ducks," but collectively known by the local tag of "hoodlums."

One of the most flourishing trades was that of supplying unwilling sailors to windjammers bound for the Far East. This was usually accomplished by slipping the seamen doped whisky in some waterfront tavern, then rowing their unconscious bodies out to a ship whose master paid COD.

Because of the victims' most frequent destination, this game was dubbed "shanghaiing"—and has since become an established dictionary term. King of the profession was a gentleman named Calico Jim, who shanghaied—one after another—six policemen sent to arrest him on a murder charge.

At irregular intervals groups of irate citizens formed vigilance committees for the purpose of ridding the town of some of the worst cutthroats. These committees were little more than rapid-order lynch mobs, and they hanged as many innocents as hoodlums.

And, almost invariably, they degenerated into thuggery themselves. Whereupon a new batch of vigilantes had to be raised to get rid of the previous lot—and so the process went on ad infinitum, always leaving San Francisco with just as many hoodlums as before.

Together with the gangsters came the women. They came from New York and New Orleans, from Paris and Rio, from Vienna and Liverpool—the cream and the gutter scrapings of the world's harlots. They did a roaring business in the town where eggs sold for a dollar apiece, some of them building mansions that left Easterners pop-eyed with wonder.

But only some. For along with the white pleasure sisters came shipload after shipload of half-starved Chinese girls. They were little more than terrified children, sold by their parents to slave dealers and kept virtually imprisoned in Chinatown cribs to earn fortunes for their owners.

Every attempt to "clean up San Francisco"—and there were dozens—ended in failure. The cribs, mirror houses, opium dens, and gambling parlors went right on operating until. . . .

THE EARTHQUAKE

The morning of April 18, 1906. On the previous night, the immortal Enrico Caruso had sung at the Opera House. All but a handful of San Francisco's 400,000 inhabitants lay fast asleep when—at 5:13 a.m.—the ground beneath the city went into a series of convulsions. As one eyewitness put it: "The earth wasn't shaking—it was undulating—rolling like an ocean breaker."

The quake ruptured every water main in the city—and simultaneously started a chain of fires which rapidly fused into one gigantic conflagration. The fire brigades were helpless. Militia troops finally stopped the flames from advancing by dynamiting entire city blocks.

For three days the fire burned on and finally out. Then 28,000 buildings lay in ruins and 500 people lay buried beneath them. As Jack London wrote in a heart-rending newspaper dispatch: "The city of San Francisco . . . is no more."

The city that Jack London knew was indeed no more. For the San Francisco that rose from the ashes—bigger, healthier, and more beautiful—was a different town. The fire had accomplished what the reformers had failed to do—seared the vice and violence out of her bones.

The old and ill-famed Barbary Coast and opium-reeking Chinatown became mere memories, whispered legends. The new San Francisco expanded into a reasonably law-abiding, cultured, though still somewhat rakish, metropolis.

San Francisco has shed the viciousness of its lurid past, but it has retained some intriguing aspects of it.

It's still a hard-drinking town, in spite of the fact that bars must close at 2 a.m.—two hours before those in New York City.

It's still a very internationally minded port, more at ease with foreigners than any other place in the U.S. with the exception of New York City. And it's intensely proud that it was chosen as the birthplace of the United Nations in 1945.

It still views with tolerant amusement certain human tastes and foibles that would mobilize the vice squad elsewhere.

It is this last quality that has made it the cradle and focal point for every bunch of individualists, oddballs, and outsiders that ever felt out of step with Main Street, U.S.A.—the bohemians of the '30s, the beatniks of the '50s, the hippies of the '60s, the gays of the '70s. And although the movements have changed, the easygoing atmosphere on which they thrived lingers on.

All of us who love this town hope that it will keep right on lingering. For the day the spirit evaporates, San Francisco will cease being San Francisco. And we will have lost our Dream City.

CHAPTER II

INTRODUCING SAN FRANCISCO

□ □ □

San Francisco occupies the tip of a 32-mile-long peninsula between the San Francisco Bay and the Pacific Ocean. Her land area measures about 46 square miles—comparable to Manhattan, but minute by the standards of, say, New York City or Los Angeles.

But don't be misled by this. For although the downtown section is wonderfully compact, and Chinatown compacter still, the rest of the city meanders over and around, and occasionally through, 40 hills, some of which become positively mountainous when you're in the process of climbing them. Twin Peaks, at almost dead center, is over 900 feet high.

The hills, however, count among the city's chief charms. They offer sudden, breathless views of moving ships and creeping fog banks on the harbor below, or rolling stretches of open brown countryside at what seems arm's length.

As somebody once put it: "When you get tired of walking around San Francisco, you can always lean against it."

For a really spectacular view, visit **Coit Tower,** which rises a gleaming white 210 feet on the crest of Telegraph Hill. For $1 an elevator whisks you up to the observation room at the top. Pick a clear day and you'll never forget the sight.

But for our orientation point, I'll choose:

UNION SQUARE

This is the true heart of the city, the hub of her shopping district, and, incidentally, one of the smartest, most restful, and most beautifully groomed plazas in the world.

The square was named for a series of violent pro-Union mass

demonstrations staged there on the eve of the Civil War. Today it's an impeccably manicured 2.6-acre park, planted with palms, yews, boxwood, and flowers, centered on a towering memorial to Admiral Dewey's victory at Manila Bay.

The square is rather like an oasis. Flanked by jammed, traffic-humming **Geary, Post, Powell,** and **Stockton Streets,** it has a curiously tranquil air, ideal for meeting a date, feeding a pigeon, or just drowsing in the sun.

You'd never know you were sitting on top of a huge underground garage, capable of housing 1,085 automobiles.

THE LAYOUT

Across the road from the square, you'll see the front of Macy's department store. Stand with your back to it and you're facing due north.

This is the direction, first of all, of **Chinatown,** the very scrutable ethnic capital of Chinese-Americans and one of the most marvelous shopping and eating territories in San Francisco. (See the special section on it.)

Adjoining Chinatown is **North Beach.** You'll find no beach there, but an extremely hectic nightclub region, home of the topless establishments that have made it a mecca for people-watchers who don't believe in having their vision obstructed. Favored far more by visitors than by blasé locals, it, too, gets a section of its own.

Still farther north rises **Telegraph Hill,** topped by Coit Tower. Once San Francisco's Bohemia and the cradle of the beatnik cult, it has gone the way of so many Bohemias and become a high-rent region of "cute" luxury apartments, populated by clean-cut advertising and insurance execs and stock brokers.

Head on in the same direction and you run into the **Embarcadero.** This is the port area of San Francisco, and one of the world's largest and busiest. Across from the waterfront piers is the Levi Strauss headquarters complex directly under Telegraph Hill. Be sure to visit the park surrounding the buildings; it's complete with a running brook, fountains, and places to sit and enjoy the view.

Slightly to the west, however, lies **Fisherman's Wharf** and the neighboring **Aquatic Park.** This is one of the town's great fun areas, and I have devoted a separate section to it.

For the moment, let's get back to Union Square.

Northeast from where you're standing stretches the **Financial District,** the teeming rectangle between **Kearny** and **Sansome Streets,** swarming with conservatively garbed people brisk with purpose, a reminder that San Francisco—among many other things —is one of America's great banking and brokerage centers, much like New York's Wall Street area.

Farther northeast stands the old **Ferry Building,** once the great focal point of city transportation—before the bridges were built when ferries crisscrossed the bay—recently experiencing a revival of activity. The ferries to Sausalito and Larkspur leave from this point; the building under the tower houses the World Trade Center; across the way is the Embarcadero Center. This 8.5-acre complex includes the controversial Vaillancourt Fountain, noontime shows by San Francisco's variegated street people, sidewalk cafés, some remarkable buildings and outdoor sculptures, and the futuristic Hyatt Regency—all of which are covered in detail in subsequent chapters.

The Ferry Building forms the tip of **Market Street,** San Francisco's seemingly endless, 120-foot-wide main artery. Although millions of dollars have been expended on brick sidewalks, ornate lampposts, and elaborate street plantings, sections of Market Street remain relentlessly unfashionable. Cutting diagonally across the entire northeast portion of the city, it represents an unofficial boundary line. Virtually all points of interest to visitors are to be found north of it.

Running down from Aquatic Park and bisecting Market Street is **Van Ness Avenue,** another boundary line. Where the two streets cross stands San Francisco's magnificent **Civic Center.** This is a classically handsome group of buildings set around a landscaped plaza, containing the domed City Hall, the Opera House, the main library, and the strikingly beautiful **Louise M. Davies Symphony Hall.** It is also the scene of San Francisco's frequent demonstrations for and/or against—well, you name it—just about everything.

The area I have just described forms a rough triangle, with Van Ness Avenue as its western, Market Street as its eastern, and the waterfront as its northern boundary. Within this triangle lies nearly everything that could be termed the tourist's San Francisco. Nearly, but not all—for her bridges are among San Francisco's greatest spectacles.

GOLDEN GATE BRIDGE

In 1987 San Francisco celebrated the 50th birthday of what is possibly the most beautiful—certainly the most photographed—bridge in the world. It spans tidal currents, ocean waves, and battering winds. With its gracefully swung single span, spidery bracing cables, and sky-zooming twin towers, it looks more like a work of abstract art than the practical engineering feat it is—among the greatest of this century. Half-veiled by rolling fog clouds, it becomes a dream image.

The mile-long steel link between the city and the Redwood Empire to the north reaches a tower height of 746 feet above the water. The bridge, oddly enough, was first visualized by the self-styled "Emperor" Norton, but wasn't constructed until May 1937, at the then-colossal cost of $35 million. Contrary to dire predictions, it neither collapsed in a gale, or in an earthquake, nor proved a white elephant. It changed the economic life of the Bay Area by allowing development of areas north of San Francisco, and was a symbol of hope when the country was awash with joblessness.

It's an awesome bridge to drive across (the round-trip toll is $1 on weekdays, $2 on weekends), or you can join the millions of pedestrians who choose to stroll across, gazing up at the bridge's red towers, out at the vistas of San Francisco and Marin County, and down into the stacks of oceangoing liners.

Bridge-bound **Golden Gate Transit** buses depart every half hour during the day for **Marin County,** starting from the Transbay Terminal at Mission and 1st Streets and making convenient stops at Market and 7th, at the Civic Center, and along Van Ness and Lombard Streets. Consult the route map in the Yellow Pages of the telephone book or call 332-6600 for schedule information. You can ride to the toll plaza on the city side of the bridge. East of the plaza is a parking and observation area. **Vista Point,** at the bridge's northern end, offers one of the great views of San Francisco.

You can walk out on the bridge from either end. Be prepared: it's usually windy and cold, and the bridge vibrates. But walking even a short way is one of the best ways to experience the immense scale of the structure.

GOLDEN GATE FERRIES

On July 24, 1938, the ferry that plied the bay between downtown San Francisco and the Marin shores went out of business. Competition with the magnificent new bridge was too great for it; it was rendered obsolete. On August 14, 1970, that ferry went back into action. The commuter pressure had proven too great for the bridge, and an auxiliary shuttle was needed.

The ferry service, while enthusiastically greeted by drivers willing to forgo the morning and evening crush and leave the car at home, is just as much a delight to carless tourists or penny pinchers who want a tour of the bay without paying guided-tour prices. On weekdays the fleet dashes back and forth between the San Francisco Ferry Building, at the foot of Market Street, and downtown Sausalito and Larkspur, keying its pickup and dropoff to commuting worker schedules. On weekends and holidays it gives the tourist a leisurely ride at reasonable intervals throughout the day. In the morning it offers a snackbar with coffee; in the evening it features bar service.

For those going farther into Marin County, a ferry goes all the way to Larkspur's ultramodern ferry terminal, offering some good views of the upper bay and even San Quentin Prison, almost as famous a landmark as Alcatraz. There are shops and restaurants a short walk from the ferry terminal, but there's not a lot to do unless you wish to explore Marin County by public transportation.

The fare for Larkspur is $2.75 weekdays, $3 weekends; there's a 25% discount for children 6 to 12 when accompanied by an adult. The Larkspur ferry operates a Monday-to-Friday commuter service, with weekend service only in summer. There is frequent daily service on the Sausalito route. The fare is $3.50 both weekdays and weekends. For information and schedules call 332-6600.

SAN FRANCISCO–OAKLAND BAY BRIDGE

This immense, silvery giant links San Francisco with Oakland, her neighbor city across the bay. With a total length of 8¼ miles, it's the world's longest steel bridge.

A double-decker structure, with five lanes for automobiles traveling one way on each level, it is joined in midbay—at Yerba Buena Island—by the world's largest-diameter tunnel. The bridge, in fact, is really a superbly dovetailed pattern of bridges, the west crossing comprising two separate suspension bridges joined at a central anchorage, the east crossing consisting of a 1,400-foot cantilever span followed by a succession of truss bridges. And it looks even more complex than it sounds.

You can drive across the bridge (toll is 75¢ coming back to the city, nothing going out). Or you can catch a bus at the **Transbay Terminal** (Mission at 1st Street) and ride to downtown Oakland.

CLIMATE

A guidebook published in 1877 stated: "The climate of San Francisco is peculiar and cannot be described in a few words."

And this, at least, is one fact that hasn't altered over the years.

San Francisco's climate is very peculiar indeed. The local tourist agencies like to describe it as "almost perpetual spring," but I'm afraid it's a bit trickier than that. It can be freezing cold in summer and pleasantly balmy in winter. It can also be both these things on almost any given day, summer *or* winter.

Still, despite this notorious changeability, San Francisco never experiences climatic extremes. The mercury rarely dips below 40°, and on the few occasions it dares rise above 70° the natives shuffle about muttering darkly of a "heat wave."

Mark Twain is reported to have said, "The coldest winter I ever spent was a summer in San Francisco." So bear in mind that San Francisco weather is usually cooler than what you might expect, if you've not been here before. Pack at least one warm sweater and a light jacket; an all-weather coat is a good idea for both men and women. Light-weight summer clothes should *not* constitute the bulk of your wardrobe for a visit here.

Throughout most of their history, San Franciscans spurned mechanical heating devices of any sort, preferring to warm up internally with stiff doses of whisky, brandy, or rum. They seemed to cherish the illusion that their city never got chilly, all evidence to the contrary notwithstanding. Only in the past 40 years or so did they begin to install heating in their buildings.

But the Bay City does have a natural air conditioner, which renders the artificial kinds unnecessary. It's the fog. Two or three warm days are all it takes to turn it on.

San Francisco Average Monthly Temperatures (in degrees Fahrenheit)			
January	50.7	July	58.8
February	53.0	August	59.4
March	54.7	September	62.0
April	55.7	October	61.4
May	57.4	November	57.4
June	59.1	December	52.5

Northern California's summer fog bank is produced by a rare combination of waters, winds, and topography. It lies off the coast waiting to be pulled in by the rising air currents when the land heats up. Held back by coastal mountains along a 600-mile front, it probes for any passage it can find. And the access most readily available is the slot where the Pacific Ocean penetrates the continental wall—the Golden Gate.

Thus San Francisco seldom gets more than a couple of hottish days in a row. Then the milky-white mass seeps in, blanketing the bay, stretching a solid sheet across the sky and blocking off the sun. And a familiar trumpeting fills the air, a sound that Herb Caen—San Francisco's columnist laureate—described as the "Fugue for Five Foghorns."

The penetrating basso blasts of the foghorns are San Francisco's municipal anthem, a sound so characteristic that it's difficult to conjure up any vision of the city without that background concert.

Yet the fog contributes to the almost-magical atmosphere that is the essence of San Francisco. Because of the intervening hills, the mist will cloak one neighborhood but leave the blue sky intact over another. You can climb a hill wrapped in moist grayness, then suddenly find yourself looking down at a sun-sparkling scene on the other side.

TOURIST INFORMATION

If you have any questions about what to do and where to go in San Francisco, the people to see for answers are the cheerful experts at the **San Francisco Convention and Visitors Bureau, Visitor Information Center,** 900 Market St., on the lower level of Hallidie Plaza at Powell and Market (tel. 415/391-2000). They can render answers in German, Japanese, French, and Spanish, as well as English. They're open weekdays from 9 a.m. to 5:30 p.m., on Saturday to 3 p.m., and on Sunday from 10 a.m. to 2 p.m. When planning your trip in advance, write (their mailing address is P.O. Box 6977, San Francisco, CA 94101), enclose $1, and they will send you an invaluable 90-page magazine, including maps and a three-month calendar of events. When in town, dial 391-2001 any time of the day for a recorded description of current cultural and special events; this information is also available in German (tel. 391-2004), French (tel. 391-2003), Japanese (tel. 391-2101), and Spanish (tel. 391-2122).

A second source of assistance and information, especially for those heading north into the Big Trees, is the **Visitors Information Center** of the Redwood Empire Association, One Market Plaza, Spear Street Tower, Suite 1001, San Francisco, CA 94105 (tel. 415/543-8334), across the street from the Hyatt Regency. Racks hold informative brochures, and the very knowledgeable desk staff is willing to plan out tours both in and north of the city. Their free annual *Redwood Empire Visitors' Guide* is crammed with detailed information on everything from San Francisco walking tours, to museums, to visiting Marin, to the timetable of the Super Skunk train through Mendocino County. Stop by and pick one up, or write for one in advance of your trip, enclosing $1.

On the newsstands, any of the following will give you a detailed description of what's coming up in the day or week ahead: the pink **Date Book** section of the Sunday *San Francisco Examiner and Chronicle* or the **Calendar** page in the daily *Examiner* (features offbeat and local events). Two excellent free weekly publications are **Key** and the **San Francisco Guide.** Both cover what to see and what's doing in detail. Either publication can be found at most hotels.

ONE FINAL WARNING

Whatever else you choose to call this city, *never* call it Frisco. Here, that's a demeaning diminutive, and every native within earshot will wince if you do.

CHAPTER III

GETTING AROUND

□ □ □

As I have said before and will say again, San Francisco is the walker's city par excellence and should be explored on foot—in comfortable walking shoes and in good health. Most of her attractions are within easy strolling distance: Chinatown is adjacent to the downtown shopping district and runs into North Beach, which in turn encompasses Fisherman's Wharf, as well as the nightlife belt.

But for the sake of those hills and your arches, plus the necessity of getting to more distant points like Golden Gate Park or the zoo, here's a quick rundown on the transportation system.

Most of San Francisco's public transport is operated by the Municipal Railway, better known as **The MUNI,** which crisscrosses San Francisco completely. For detailed information, phone 673-MUNI, or consult the bus map and routings at the front of the Yellow Pages in the San Francisco telephone book. MUNI sells a map of its routes for $1.25 at newsstands.

Its streetcars and buses service an area of about 700 square miles, and fares are a reasonable 80¢; cable cars cost $1.50 (exact change only). Express buses, which stop at major intersections only, also charge 80¢. Transfers are free on all rides and are good in any direction for 1½ hours.

San Francisco bus and streetcar drivers are usually cheerful, courteous, and helpful, but they're not equipped to make change; have correct fare ready when you board.

STREETCARS

Riding San Francisco's wonderfully comfortable and feather-sprung streetcars may turn you against gasoline vehicles for life. They make buses feel like oxcarts. There are five lines, lettered J, K, L, M, and N, and they all run up and down Market Street past the Civic Center, where they branch off in different directions. The streetcars, however, are gradually being replaced by the MUNI metro, a subway that will eventually run alongside and under BART in the downtown area.

BUSES

Some 70 different bus lines go to virtually every point on the San Francisco map, as well as over the bridges to Marin County and Oakland. See the Yellow Pages for a concise summary of routes. For information on city bus routes, call **MUNI** at 673-MUNI. Other useful bus information is available from **Golden Gate Transit** (tel. 332-6600) and **AC Transit** (tel. 653-3535).

CABLE CARS

In addition to being a (moderately) practical means of transportation, cable cars are San Francisco's rolling symbols, mobile museum pieces, and favorite toys. They are, in fact, official historic landmarks, designated as such by the National Parks Service in 1964.

They owe their existence to the soft heart and mechanical genius of a London-born engineer named Andrew Hallidie. In 1869 Mr. Hallidie watched a team of four overworked horses hauling a heavily laden horsecar up a steep San Francisco slope. One horse slipped and the car rolled back, dragging the other poor beasts behind it.

There and then the engineer decided to invent some contraption that would replace live horsepower with the mechanical kind. And four years later, in 1873, the first cable car—promptly christened "Hallidie's Folly"—made its maiden run from the top of Clay Street.

One Irish onlooker voiced the general opinion by exclaiming: "I don't believe it—the damned thing works!"

A good many visitors have difficulties believing it even now, because the design of these rolling fossils hasn't changed in over a century—and they have no engines!

Each weighing about six tons, they are hoisted along by means of a steel cable, enclosed in a center rail and therefore invisible, but you'll hear its characteristic slapping sound whenever you cross the tracks.

The cars move when the gripman (*not* driver) pulls back a lever which closes a pincer-like "grip" on the cable. The speed of the car is therefore a constant 9½ mph—never more or less. This may strike you as a hectic snail's pace, but it doesn't feel that way when you're cresting an almost perpendicular hill and look down at what seems a bobsled dive straight into the panoramic valley. Or if you're slamming around a horseshoe curve on what you'd swear are two wheels.

The conductor contributes to the scenic railway sensation by hollering "Heeeeeeere we go!" and "Hold on tight for the curve!" at the appropriate moments.

In spite of the nerve-tingles they produce, cable cars are eminently safe. They have four separate braking devices, and most of the crew's time is spent applying them. The gripman operates the wheel brakes and the track brakes. The conductor frequently helps him by turning the hand lever of the rear brakes on the rear platform. And in real emergencies, there's a lever that rams a metal wedge into the cable slot, stopping the car so effectively that it takes a welding crew to dislodge it.

Because some of the cars have only one-way controls, they have to be reversed on a turntable. This, too, is done by the crews—manually. But there's always a crowd of willing helpers standing around the Powell and Market Streets turntable, giving a hand with the pushing.

Cable-car crews may be hard-working, but they're also an elite corps—the marines among the MUNI Men. They positively bask in the admiration of local kids and tourists alike, and never cease polishing their image as "characters."

Cable-car bells were intended as warning signals, but the crews wouldn't dream of doing anything so mundane as simply clanging them. No, siree; they jazz it up, one car intoning "ding-dering-ding" while the other replies in passing "ding-ding." It's as essential a part of the San Francisco symphony as the hooting of the foghorns.

The two types of cable cars in use hold a maximum of 90 and 100 passengers respectively—but only in theory, because San Franciscans regard cable-car capacities as a matter of elasticity. To them, a cable car will shift as many people as can grab a toe-hold somewhere. And the tourists (about half of all riders in summer) immediately join the game. So you'll see beehive clusters of people inching uphill, with a cable car tucked away somewhere in their midst.

By the turn of the century there were cable cars running in most parts of the globe. But, one by one, other cities scrapped theirs in favor of less antiquated transport—Melbourne, Australia, was among the last to give up its trolleys.

On several occasions the San Francisco municipality wanted to follow suit. But each time this resulted in such a citywide uproar and outrage that in 1955 the perpetuation of the three existing lines was written into the City Charter.

The mandate cannot be revoked without the approval of the majority of voters. Which doesn't look like it will ever be forthcoming.

San Francisco, therefore, boasts the world's only surviving system of cable cars.

There are three lines in all. The most scenic—and exciting—is

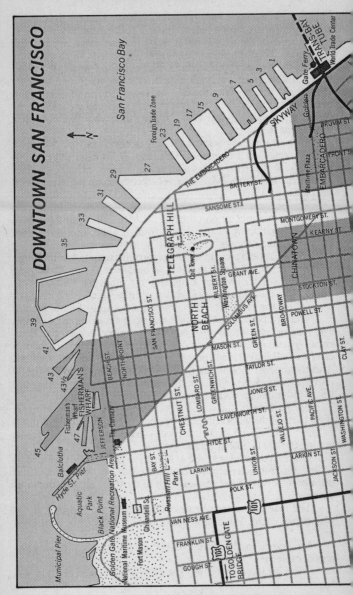

DOWNTOWN SAN FRANCISCO

San Francisco Bay

N→

Foreign Trade Zone

THE EMBARCADERO

SKYWAY

Golden Gate Ferry

World Trade Center

TRANS-BAY TUBE

Maritime Plaza

EMBARCADERO

BATTERY ST.

SANSOME ST.

MONTGOMERY ST.

KEARNY ST.

FRONT S

DRUMM ST.

TELEGRAPH HILL

Coit Tower

Filbert St.

Grant Ave.

Washington Square

CHINATOWN

STOCKTON ST.

BROADWAY

POWELL ST.

COLUMBUS AVE.

NORTH BEACH

SAN FRANCISCO ST.

BEACH ST.

NORTH POINT

GREEN ST.

GREENWICH ST.

MASON ST.

TAYLOR ST.

JONES ST.

LEAVENWORTH ST.

CLAY ST.

CHESTNUT ST.

LOMBARD ST.

HYDE ST.

UNION ST.

VALLEJO ST.

PACIFIC AVE.

WASHINGTON S

JACKSON ST.

FISHERMAN'S WHARF

Fisherman's Wharf

JEFFERSON

The Cannery

BAY ST.

LARKIN ST.

Russian Hill Park

LARKIN

POLK ST.

101

Municipal Pier

Balclutha

Hyde St. Pier

Aquatic Park

Black Point

Golden Gate National Recreation Area

National Maritime Museum

Ghirardelli Sq.

Fort Mason

VAN NESS AVE.

FRANKLIN ST.

GOUGH ST.

TO GOLDEN GATE BRIDGE

101

the Powell-Hyde line, which follows a vertical and lateral zigzag course from the corner of Powell and Market Streets over both Nob Hill and Russian Hill to a turntable at gaslit Victorian Square in front of **Aquatic Park,** near the Maritime Museum.

The Powell-Mason line starts at the same intersection and climbs over Nob Hill before descending to Bay Street, just three blocks from **Fisherman's Wharf.**

The California Street line begins at the foot of Market Street, cuts through Chinatown, crests **Nob Hill,** and continues to **Van Ness.**

The fare on the cable-car system is $1.50 for adults, 75¢ for students (ages 5 to 17), 15¢ for seniors. There's a special $5 one-day MUNI adult pass that allows you unlimited rides. And there's a 40¢ transfer that lets you switch to a non-cable-car line. The cable-car system operates from approximately 6:30 a.m. to 12:30 a.m. Call 673-MUNI for more information.

To watch how San Francisco's wheeled mountain goats are stabled, pampered, and maintained, see the visit to the cable-car barn in the kids' chapter later on.

TAXIS

San Francisco has plenty of cabs, but they're hard to waylay at any time—and more so on rainy nights. They're also fairly costly. The rate begins at $2.90 for the first mile ($1.40 when the meter starts, and $1.50 for the mile), then grows at $1.50 for each mile. Plan on a $28 fare from the airport.

There are plenty of street phone boxes on which to call a cab, at no extra charge. Here with a few sample numbers: **Veteran's Cab** (tel. 552-1300), **Desoto Cab Co.** (tel. 673-1414), **Luxor Cabs** (tel. 282-4141), **Yellow Cab** (tel. 626-2345), **Allied Taxi** (tel. 826-9494), **City** (tel. 468-7200), and **Pacific** (tel. 986-7220).

ON DRIVING AND PARKING

Here are just a few pointers which may help you to avoid some frequently encountered problems in driving throughout the state as well as in San Francisco.

TIPS FOR DRIVERS: For a start, California law requires buckling up seatbelts. This applies to both driver and passengers.

Be sure to pay attention to signs and arrows on the streets and roadways or you may find that you're in a lane which requires exiting or turning when you wanted to go straight on. What's more, San Francisco's profusion of one-way streets can create a few small difficulties—in going around the block, say, or getting from point A to point B. However, most road maps of the city indicate which way traffic flows.

You'll be pleased to know that you can turn right at a red light (unless otherwise indicated), but be sure to come to a stop first.

Driving around San Francisco requires a few pointers for visitors from less cluttered and more level regions.

Remember that cable cars are like sailing ships—they *always* have right-of-way. What's more, their gripmen see to it that they get it. So don't argue with them; they're damned sturdy vehicles. Also, on wet days their tracks tend to be slippery and are best avoided.

Pedestrians are *supposed* to have right-of-way in most U.S. cities, but in San Francisco they actually insist on it. And the cops back them to the hilt. So for the sake of your pocketbook, follow the example of local drivers and wait courteously while the foot-sloggers cross the road.

Never underrate the pull of gravity on San Francisco's hills. It's mighty. When parking on a grade, put on the hand brake, put the car in gear, and *always* turn your wheels toward the curb when facing downhill; when facing uphill, always turn them away from the curb (in either case you'll be using the curb as a block). This practice is law in San Francisco. Otherwise your car may join the hundreds of yearly runaways, or at the least you'll get a parking ticket. And when driving downhill, always use low gear.

ON-STREET PARKING:

Street parking is a tough business (the local cops are the quickest towaway lot I've ever seen). Parking lots abound in all the difficult-to-find-a-spot areas, but they're quite expensive. Where street parking is not metered, signs will tell you when you can park and for how long. Curb colors indicate reserved parking zones—and they mean it! Red is don't stop, don't park. Blue is for the disabled with California-issued disabled plates or a placard. White is a five-minute limit. Yellow and yellow/black are for commercial vehicles. Once again, the San Francisco Police Department does not regard parking regulations lightly. Violate the law and you may be towed away, and that will cost you dearly: in total, the tab to retrieve your car may be as much as $90, plus daily storage fees. So resist temptation and don't park at a bus stop or at a fire hydrant; watch out, too, for street-cleaning signs. No matter how rushed you are, keep in mind that parking in a garage is almost always cheaper and less stressful.

PARKING GARAGES:

As long as I've brought up the topic of garages—short-term parking is expensive. It can run from $3.75 to as much as $5.25 for the first hour ($1.75 for 20 minutes). For 24 hours, prices are more reasonable and usually range from $12 to $15. Apart from meters, however, there are some exceptions to the high cost of short-term parking. In **Chinatown** the best (and cheapest) place to park is the Portsmouth Square Garage at 733 Kearny (enter between Clay and Washington). Between 10:30 a.m. and 2:30 p.m. you may wait in line to enter. The price is 50¢ for the first hour, 75¢ for the second hour, $1.75 for the third hour and each hour thereafter, for a maximum of $12 for 24 hours. At the **Civic Center,** try for the Civic Center Plaza at Taylor and O'Farrell, where parking is 50¢ per hour, $15 for 24 hours. **Downtown,** head for the Sutter-Stockton Garage at 330 Sutter, where it's 50¢ for the first hour, $1 for the second hour and each thereafter, to $14 for 24 hours. At **Fisherman's Wharf / Ghirardelli Square,** try the North Point Shopping Garage at 350 Bay St., where the tab is $1 per half hour, $8.50 maximum; or the Ghirardelli Square Garage at 900 North Point, which charges $1 per half hour, $6 maximum. On **Nob Hill,** the least costly I've found is Park & Lock at 877 California St., where the fee is $1.50 per hour, $5.75 maximum. On **Union Street,** in the area of high-traffic shopping, try for the Cow Hollow at 3060 Fillmore for $2 per hour, $7 maximum.

CAR RENTALS

You certainly don't need a car to explore San Francisco proper. In some areas, like Chinatown and the Financial District, a car is a positive handicap. But if you plan to tour the Bay Area, you may find it practical to utilize one of the scores of car-rental firms competing for your favors.

If you have an unusual-size vehicle in mind—for example, a van—your best bet is to go with one of the big rental-car companies. You'll find **Avis** at 675 Post St. (tel. 415/885-5011, or toll free 800/331-1212); at the San Francisco Airport (tel. 415/877-6780); and at the Oakland Airport (tel. 415/562-9000). **Budget Rent-A-Car** is at 321 Mason St. (Union Square) (tel. 415/775-5800, or toll free 800/527-0700); at the San Francisco Airport (tel. 415/875-6850); and at the Oakland Airport (tel. 415/568-4770). **Hertz** is located at 433 Mason St. (tel. 415/771-2200, or toll free 800/654-3131); at the San Francisco Airport (tel. 415/877-1600); and at the Oakland Airport (tel. 415/568-1177). **National Car Rental** locations are 531 Sutter St. (tel. 415/788-4941, or toll free 800/328-4567); the San Francisco Airport (tel. 415/877-4745); and the Oakland Airport (tel. 415/632-2225). No matter which rental company you use, it's always a good idea to check out the car before you leave.

Note: If you plan to drive very far outside the city, you might want to call about California road conditions (tel. 557-3755) or weather (tel. 936-1212).

A WORD ON "BART"

BART is an acronym for the **Bay Area Rapid Transit system,** San Francisco's much-touted answer to the growing congestion of private motor vehicles. It is a high-speed, rapid-transit rail network that connects San Francisco with Oakland, Richmond, Concord, Daly City, and Fremont—a distance of 71 miles.

BART's cars are 70 feet long and designed to represent the last word in public transport luxury, with carpeted floors, tinted picture windows, automatic air conditioning, and recessed lighting. They hit a top speed of 80 miles per hour (average is 42 mph including stops), while a computerized control system monitors and adjusts train speeds and maintains safe spacing. At least it does now. For the first year, before the bugs were worked out, the trains had to wait while a stationmaster called ahead to the next stop to make sure the way was clear!

The part of the route between San Francisco and Oakland runs through the longest underwater transit tube in the world. This link opened in September 1974, six months after the then general manager resigned under fire, and two years after it was supposed to have opened.

Today commuters and shoppers whiz under the waters of the bay, and underground through the downtown region, in a comfort they had only dreamed of after the demise of the ferries.

If you'd like to see whether or not you agree with residents that this recently completed rail transit system was worth the wait and the cost, take a BART trip. An excursion ticket allows you, in effect, to "sightsee" the BART system. For $3, for instance, you can buy a three-county tour ride, returning to the point of departure within three hours. You can ride anywhere, get off and tour the stations, and even see the countryside once the train surfaces. *Save your ticket,* as you need it to operate the exit gate. Exiting at any stop invalidates your excursion ticket, so see all you want to before you leave. Regular point-to-point fares vary according to distance. You can travel from downtown metropolitan San Francisco and be in the lush countryside of Contra Costa County in a matter of minutes. From BART's Embarcadero Station, you can make an easy connection with a Golden Gate ferry for a trip across the bay to Sausalito in Marin County, or wander around the Embarcadero Center, a modern, high-rise, office-and-shopping complex with several restaurants. Also, from this station you may exit and immediately enter the magnificent atrium lobby of the Hyatt Regency Hotel.

For other rides and details on connections with other public transport, call 788-BART. Or pick up a free copy of the "Fun Goes Further on BART" brochure at any station. Fares range from 80¢ to $3.50, depending on distance and time. Children 4 and under ride free.

Currently, BART trains operate from 6 a.m. to midnight Monday to Saturday, and from 9 a.m. to midnight on Sunday.

CHAPTER IV

THE ABC'S OF SAN FRANCISCO

□ □ □

   Whether you're a regular visitor to the Bay Area or a first-timer, there are likely to be some basic bits of information that prove oddly elusive. I offer here some bottom-line facts, arranged in alphabetical order for handy reference, to help make your trip as enjoyable and frustration-free as possible. Remember, too, that San Francisco prides itself on its hospitality to tourists. Don't hesitate to make use of the numbers given in the "Tourist Information" section of Chapter II should you need help with something not covered in this brief survey.

AIRLINES: Domestic carriers serving the **San Francisco International Airport** include Air Cal (tel. 433-2660), Alaska Airlines (tel. 931-8888, or toll free 800/426-0333), American (tel. 398-4434, or toll free 800/433-7300), Continental (tel. toll free 800/258-1212), Delta (tel. 552-5700, or toll free 800/221-1212), Eastern (tel. 474-5858), Northwest (tel. 392-2163, or toll free 800/225-2525), Piedmont (tel. toll free 800/251-5720), Southwest (tel. 885-1221, or toll free 800/531-5601), TWA (tel. 864-5731), United (tel. 397-2100), and USAir (tel. toll free 800/428-4322).
   Domestic carriers serving the **Oakland Airport** are Alaska Airlines, Alpha Air (tel. toll free 800/421-9353), America West (tel. 839-1292, or toll free 800/247-5692), American, Continental, United, and USAir.

AIRPORTS: There are two airports within striking distance of San Francisco—the **San Francisco International Airport** and the Oakland International Airport. The former has the higher volume of traffic and is located 15 miles south of downtown San Francisco on U.S. 101. Travel time to the downtown area during morning and afternoon rush hours is about 40 minutes, 25 minutes at other hours.

Airporter coaches ($5 for adults, $2.50 for children under 17 accompanied by an adult) serve the Downtown Terminal at Taylor and Ellis Streets (near the Hilton) with frequent departures throughout the day. For information, call 673-2433. SAM-TRANS buses serve downtown as well as the peninsula. For information, call 761-7000.

There's a 24-hour Super Shuttle (tel. 558-8500) airport service which, with three hours' notice, will pick you up at your door (hotel or residence) and take you to the airport 45 to 60 minutes before departure. Or you can arrange to be picked up at the airport. The fare is $9 for adults; $4 for those under 5 years.

The **Oakland International Airport** is about five miles south of downtown Oakland on Calif. 17 (Interstate 880) at the Gegenberger Road exit. It primarily serves East Bay communities, though some San Francisco travelers do use it. There's lots of parking space and bus service is available from various Bay Area locations. Shuttle buses from the Oakland Airport connect with BART trains. The SFO helicopter operates between Oakland and San Francisco Airports.

No airport or departure tax is levied on international visitors.

If you need to know the location of the terminal at the airport from which you will be departing, the Smart Yellow Pages of the San Francisco telephone directory gives a handy illustration at the front of the book under the "Airports" heading.

AREA CODE: The telephone area code for San Francisco is 415.

BABYSITTERS: If you're staying at one of the larger hotels, the concierge can usually recommend organizations to call. Be sure to check on the hourly cost (which may vary by day and time), as well as any additional expenses such as transportation and meals for the sitter. One such service is **Temporary Tot Tending** (tel. 355-7377, 871-5790 after 6 p.m.), which offers childcare by licensed teachers, by the hour or day, for children from infants on up. Open 6 a.m. to 9 p.m., Monday through Friday only (except for convention times, when weekend service is available).

BANKS: As with most cities, banks are generally open from 10 a.m. to 3 p.m. Monday through Friday. However, if you need to cash a check, your hotel may be your best resource, depending on the amount involved.

BUSES: Greyhound Bus Lines serves San Francisco from most cities in California. Greyhound is located at (you guessed it) the Greyhound Depot, 50 7th St. between Mission and Market Streets (tel. 433-1500). For general information and schedules, call your nearest ticket office.

CHARGE CARDS: Please note that not all restaurants, stores, or shops in California accept all major credit cards, and some accept none. So check first if you expect to use plastic for a large expenditure—it can save annoyance and possibly some embarrassment. Unlike many states, purchases of package liquor can be charged in California.

CLIMATE: See the "Climate" section of Chapter II.

CRIME: As in all cities having a considerable influx of tourists from within the U.S. and abroad, crime is always a problem. San Francisco is no exception. To avoid an unhappy incident or an end to what might have been a pleasurable trip, use discretion and common sense. One sensible option is leaving valuables in the hotel safe, if you are staying at one of the larger hotels.

CURRENCY EXCHANGE: Foreign-currency exchange services are provided by the Bank of America and Deak International, among others. **Bank of America** has offices at 345 Montgomery St. in the Financial District (tel. 622-2451), open from 9 a.m. to 3 p.m. Monday through Thursday, till 5 p.m. on Friday; and at the Central Terminal International Building, San Francisco International Airport, for the convenience of in- and outbound passengers, open from 7 a.m. to 11 p.m. daily. **Deak International** is at 100 Grant Ave., downtown (tel. 362-3452), open Monday through Friday from 9 a.m. to 5 p.m. for foreign-currency exchange.

DENTISTS: Hotels usually have a list of dentists should you need one, but they are also listed in the Yellow Pages. The **San Francisco Dental Society** can be reached at 421-1435.

DOCTORS: Here again, hotels usually have a list of doctors on call. The **San Francisco Medical Society** number is 567-6234.

EARTHQUAKES: There will always be earthquakes in California —most you will never notice. However, in the case of a significant earthquake, there are a few basic precautionary measures to take, whether you're inside a high-rise hotel, out driving, or just walking. When you are inside a building, seek cover; do not run outside. Move away from windows in the direction of what would be the center of the building. Get under a large, sturdy piece of furniture, or stand against a wall or under a doorway. When you do exit the building, use stairwells, *not* elevators. If you are in your car, pull over to the side of the road and stop—but not until you are away from bridges or overpasses, and telephone or power poles and lines. Stay in your car. If you are out walking, stay outside and away from trees or power lines or the sides of buildings. If you are in an area with tall buildings, find a doorway to stand in.

EMERGENCIES: For police, fire, highway patrol, or medical emergencies, dial 911. Otherwise, you can reach **ambulance service** at 931-3900; the non-emergency **police** number is 553-0123. To reach the **Poison Control Center,** call 476-6600.

EVENTS AND FESTIVALS: See Chapter II, "Tourist Information."

HOSPITALS: CliniCARE at **St. Francis Memorial Hospital,** 900 Hyde St., on Nob Hill (tel. 775-4321), provides drop-in outpatient services from 8 a.m. to 5 p.m. Monday through Friday. No appointment is necessary. The hospital also has 24-hour emergency service.

INFORMATION: See Chapter II, "Tourist Information."

LIQUOR LAWS: Liquor and grocery stores, as well as some drugstores, can sell packaged alcoholic beverages between 6 a.m. and 2 a.m. Most restaurants, nightclubs, and bars are licensed to serve alcoholic beverages during the same hours. The legal age for purchase and consumption is 21, and proof of age is required.

If you are in the wine country and decide to make some larger-than-usual purchases of a vintage or two, unlike many other states (including New York), California permits you to purchase liquor with a credit card. The store may also handle the shipment of wine and relieve you of what might otherwise be a weighty problem.

NEWSPAPERS: The *San Francisco Chronicle* and the *San Francisco Examiner* are widely distributed throughout San Francisco. The Sunday edition of the *San Francisco Examiner and Chronicle* will fill you in on happenings in the upcoming week.

SPORTS (SPECTATOR): As of this writing, San Francisco has a major-league **baseball** team, the San Francisco Giants (tel. 392-7469 or 467-8000); an NFL **football** team, the San Francisco 49ers, locally known simply as the "Niners" (tel. 468-2249 or 467-8000); and a **basketball** team, the Golden State Warriors (tel. 638-6000). Both the Giants and the 49ers roost at Candlestick Park (where no one can hold a candle to the wind), located on Giants Drive at Gilman Avenue. The Warriors reside at the Oakland Coliseum Arena at the 66th Avenue or Gegenberger Road exit from Interstate 880. You'll find a complete schedule of games at home and away under *"Sports Schedules"* at the front of the Yellow Pages.

And, finally, there's the Sport of Kings. **Bay Meadows thoroughbred racing** season runs through the latter part of January. The track is located at the intersection of Hillsdale Boulevard at Bayshore Freeway (U.S. 101) in San Mateo (tel. 574-7223).

STORE HOURS: Stores are usually open from 10 a.m. to 6 p.m. Monday to Saturday; closed Sunday. Stores in Chinatown are generally open from 10 a.m. to 10 p.m. daily.

TAXES: California State Sales Tax is 6%.

TRAINS: Amtrak service to Los Angeles and Seattle operates out of Oakland. Regularly scheduled connecting buses leave San Francisco from the Transbay Terminal (tel. 982-8512).

Southern Pacific has train service from San Francisco to the towns of the peninsula. The depot is at 700 4th St., at Townsend (tel. 495-4564).

USEFUL NUMBERS: For San Francisco **weather** information, phone 936-1212; for the **time**, 767-8900; and for information on **highway conditions,** 557-3755.

CHAPTER V

WHERE TO STAY

□ □ □

In an average year over eight million tourists and convention visitors flock into the "Paris of the West" or "Baghdad-by-the-Bay," as San Francisco is variously known.

The Bay City maintains a universally high standard of tourist accommodation that extends from the deluxe to the modest family establishments in the economy price ranges. I'm willing to stick my neck out and claim that in terms of courtesy, civility, and creature comfort, San Francisco's hotels probably offer the best dollar's worth in the nation.

San Francisco boasts at least 14 hotels in the international luxury class—which is remarkable for a city of less than a million inhabitants. And, as expected, these charge international luxury rates. A cross section of these "platinum towers" heads up the hotel discussion.

After these, under the heading "Upper Bracket," come the slightly less expensive and less posh hotels that offer a great deal of luxury at prices a bit lower than the superstar hostelries. This is where you'll find "Inns and Such," describing some of the best of handsome old buildings turned into super-luxurious, charming inns with European-style accommodations.

The hotels that follow, under the title "Moderately Priced," are representative of the bulk of San Francisco lodging places: attractive, well-located hotels geared to the majority of San Francisco's visitors—people like you and me who want comfortable accommodations but are willing to dispense with the royal frills. The many described here are merely a selection; if space allowed I could easily add another dozen that are equally good values.

In the final grouping of "Budget" hotels, you'll find some excellent choices. Several of these hotels offer rooms with shared bath, especially handy for students and younger travelers on a limited allowance.

But all these hotels have one thing in common: they come up to my pretty exacting standard of comfort and cleanliness. Most (though not all) are within walking distance of both downtown and each other. So if one of them should be filled, the next will be close by. This is an important point, because during peak season— from late May to late September—even San Francisco bulges slightly at the seams with tourists and conventioneers.

Remember, there is an 11% tax on all hotel bills in San Francisco, which must be added to the price.

LUXURY HOTELS

San Francisco has a history of preserving and restoring buildings, and one example of this is the **Four Seasons Clift,** 495 Geary St. (at Taylor), San Francisco, CA 94102 (tel. 415/775-4700, or toll free 800/332-3342). There is a gaggle of pricey hotels in San Francisco—huge, with every type of shop, cities within a city—but few of them have the warm elegance, finesse, and sophistication of an era once associated with tuxedos, pearls, and polo: in summary, "class." This is a very special place. Built in 1918 as The Clift, the property was purchased by Four Seasons in 1977, and the interior was completely restored leaving 329 rooms, about one-quarter of which are sitting room–bedroom combinations. The rooms are tastefully and individually decorated and their color schemes include pale blue, rust, and cool beige accented with subdued stripes and floral patterns; furnishings are plush. Amenities include TVs with remote control, clock-radios, mini-bars, baths with a phone, and such extras as a hairdryer, padded hangers, shampoos and bath gels, and a scale and bathrobe in your dressing room. Should you wish to purchase a robe the proceeds are donated to charity. By the way, these amenities are as much in evidence in and around the lobby as they are in the rooms. When did you last find notepaper and a sharpened pencil for your use in the phone booth?

For families, the Four Seasons Clift has prepared a folder listing the many items the hotel can provide for children, from baby blankets to teddy bears, baseball cards, and coloring books. Room service stands ready with a supply of Oreo cookies and milk, popcorn, and a long list of other goodies.

Both the Redwood Room (a true art deco beauty) and the French Room are open for breakfast, and at lunch locals crowd the rooms. The French Room offers dinner nightly and features such delicacies as sautéed scallops in gingered orange sauce or lamb loin with roasted garlic cloves, in the $25 to $35 range. At lunch, there's veal piccata, and smoked salmon and prawns, for $12 to $25. In addition, the hotel is home to the only American chapter of the

British-based Society for the Promotion of Christmas Puddings, a band of devotees of the King George Christmas Pudding that Charles Dickens wrote about so vividly over 150 years ago. For the curious, the pudding is featured on the hotel's holiday menu. The Lobby Lounge offers a light lunch and English tea service Monday through Saturday.

Rates range from $165 to $235 single, $165 to $255 double, with suites from $525 up.

Boasting the largest guest rooms (over 500 square feet) in the city is the **Donatello** (formerly the Pacific Plaza), 501 Post St. (at Mason), San Francisco, CA 94102 (tel. 415/441-7100, or toll free 800/227-3184, 800/792-9837 in California). It opened in late 1980 where a motor inn once stood, but there is no confusing the two. The simple elegance of the Donatello's intimate lobby is the perfect prelude to the spacious rooms decorated with cool colors, tapestries or paintings, and live plants. The feeling is one of a private residence impeccably groomed.

Besides the traditional amenities there are special touches such as extra-length beds, remote-control TVs, clock-radios, free local calls (a true bargain in San Francisco), robes for each guest, and nightly turndown service.

Developing a superior reputation among local restaurants is the Ristorante Donatello. The à la carte menu at dinner features classic northern Italian cuisine with such dishes as crisp duckling with Italian spices, boneless squab, quail, and of course, pasta. Entrees range from $20 to $28. The restaurant is open for breakfast and dinner. Cocktails are served in the lounge daily from 11 a.m. to 1 a.m.

Parking is available for $17 a day, with in-and-out privileges. Rates are $175 to $250 single, $195 to $250 double. Suites range from $345 to $550.

The **Campton Place Hotel,** 340 Stockton St. (between Post and Sutter), San Francisco, CA 94108 (tel. 415/781-5555, or toll free 800/647-4007, 800/235-4300 in California), is a small (126-room) hotel that offers big-hotel luxury. It occupies the early-20th-century buildings of the former Drake-Wiltshire Hotel. It was opened in 1983 after $25 million worth of renovations and improvements. The results are terrific—intimate, luxurious, modern, gorgeous.

The guest rooms are beautifully appointed, with king-size or double-double beds, concealed color TVs with remote control, AM/FM clock-radios, direct-dial phones, air conditioning, and luxurious bathrooms with marble floors, vanity and tub, brass fixtures, bathrobes, telephone, and goodies like soaps, shampoos, and bath gels.

The Campton Place has a concierge to arrange for theater tickets, restaurant reservations, and travel plans. There are even maids and valets available to unpack and pack your luggage.

On the premises is the Campton Place Restaurant, serving three meals a day. It's become a very popular luncheon spot, with entrees like brook trout with black walnuts or veal medallions with farmer's cheese, priced at $14 to $20.

Rooms at the Campton Place rent for $200 to $260, single or double; suites begin at $550. Overnight parking is available for $20.

The newest of San Francisco's luxury high-rise hostelries, the **Ramada Renaissance Hotel,** 55 Cyril Magnin St. (at Market and North Fifth Streets), San Francisco, CA (tel. 415/392-8000, or toll free 800/228-9898), is ideally situated in the heart of the city—two blocks from Union Square and a half block from the Powell Street cable car. Built at a cost of $103 million, the hotel is palatial in scope and appearance. It occupies an entire city block and has 1,015 rooms and all the extra services and conveniences even the most sophisticated traveler might expect.

As you enter the hotel, you'll see an imposing seven-panel bas-relief mural of the history of San Francisco by Ruth Asawa. Two stone lions hold court in the travertine marble lobby. Ahead is the main staircase covered in a rich beige-pink-blue Tai Ping sculpted carpet woven in China. Above this an oil by Tony Chimento depicts the Renaissance woman.

The second-floor lobby looks upward into a three-story atrium. Here you can enjoy a leisurely drink at the Piazza while listening to contemporary and classical music played on a grand piano, somehow fitting in a room this size. Mushroom-colored velvet sofas and beech chairs done in seafoam green are interspersed throughout. Two eight-foot-high gray marble statues of a Roman couple accent the height of the atrium, as do the huge vases of fresh flowers.

The guest rooms reflect the same subdued elegance, from the beige carpeting and furnishings of bleached ash to the floral and city prints of the area. Each room has the conveniences and attention to detail that make a stay pleasurable: king-size beds, bathroom phone, well-lit makeup mirror, shower massage, even French milled hand soap on the marble vanity, and window vents that open if you want fresh air! The ultimate in security provides a computer-coded guest-room key card which is changed at the end of each stay. And there are rooms with special facilities for handicapped persons.

Should you need special cosseting, check into the Renaissance Club, which occupies the top four floors and features the amenities one might expect of a private club. Personal check-in and concierge service, a continental breakfast and afternoon hors d' oeuvres, and access to the health club are included in the basic charge. Guest rooms are supplied with terrycloth robes, hairdryers, the daily newspaper, and evening turndown service. Seven suites contain private whirlpool baths.

You will be pleased by the Ramada Renaissance's helpful staff and the number of services provided. You would expect a concierge and bell captain, but there's also a foreign-language information desk, currency exchange, a tour desk, and, on request, acoustic couplers linking personal computers to off-site computers. And all guests are offered complimentary morning limousine service to the Financial District.

As one might expect, the hotel has not stinted in its restaurant facilities. There are two areas for dining, both on the second floor—the Corintia Ristorante and the Veranda. The Corintia specializes in northern Italian cuisine, and what cuisine! I've covered the restaurant in detail in Chapter VI. It's worth a visit.

The Veranda's menu features both traditional favorites and some innovative specialties for breakfast, lunch, and dinner. If you yearn for salsa piquante at breakfast, the guacamole omelet will satisfy your innermost craving. For less exotic tastes at lunch, the tostada grande with chicken, avocado, tomato, cheese, and refried beans is delicious. For dinner, sautéed pork medallions with chanterelles might be appealing, or there's always the reliable barbecued veal short ribs. Luncheon entrees range from $8 to $14; at dinner they run $10 to $19 (lobster, $30).

Single rooms at the Ramada Renaissance range from $135 to $195, the higher price for a junior suite; doubles run $160 to $220, and suites, $240 to $380. Rates for the Renaissance Club range from $185 for a single and $210 for a double; suites are $400 and $950. Children 18 or under stay free in the same room with their parents.

If you're in town for a grand evening of theater or a personal celebration, the hotel has special packages you might want to check into. Some include complimentary champagne, continental breakfast, even limousine service.

The French-owned **Meridien San Francisco,** 50 3rd St. (at Market), San Francisco, CA 94103 (tel. 415/974-6400, or toll free 800/543-4300), is ideally suited for the leisure as well as business traveler. It's located at the center of the city's entertainment, business and shopping triangle—Moscone Convention Center, the financial district, and Union Square with its world-famous shops, historic cable cars, and neighboring theaters.

The Meridien has 700 luxuriously appointed guest rooms and 26 suites on 32 floors of its 36-story tower. The rooms are all modern and elegant, with expansive floor-to-ceiling windows, decorated in understated pastels, and decked out with every possible amenity, including king-size or double-double beds, remote-control color

TVs with in-house movies, direct-dial phones, AM/FM clock-radios, air conditioning, mini-bars, luxurious tub/shower baths, and 24-hour room service. Each evening your bed is turned down and mints are left with the next day's weather report. The views of San Francisco, especially from the upper floors, are breathtaking.

In true French fashion, the Meridien has two excellent restaurants. The first, Café Justin, reminiscent of an authentic French brasserie, is decorated in forest green, salmon, and cream, with floral accents. Breakfast, lunch, and dinner, with a menu including regional French specialties, are served here daily from 6 a.m. to 11 p.m. On Sunday from 11 a.m. to 2:30 p.m. Café Justin offers a champagne and seafood jazz buffet brunch with over a dozen seafood selections plus brunch standards like omelets and eggs Benedict, as well as desserts and salads, for $25 per person.

Pierre at the Meridien is the hotel's gourmet restaurant. It's a relatively large place, but it's laid out as a series of small dining areas, so it feels intimate and cozy, and is graced with the soft jazz sound of Merl Saunders at the piano.

Pierre's carefully prepared menu is a superb marriage of gourmet French technique and California's seasonal best. A dinner at Pierre might begin with sautéed duck foie gras with port gelatin, proceed with an entree of sea bass or rabbit and lamb with roasted garlic cloves, and finish with homemade pastries or roasted peaches. The food is complemented by a richly diverse wine list and presented impeccably. Entrees average $25 to $35. Pierre's is open for dinner Monday through Saturday from 6:30 to 10:30 p.m. Reservations are recommended.

Room rates at Le Meridien are $155 to $200 single, $180 to $225 double.

The **Hyatt Regency,** 5 Embarcadero Center, San Francisco, CA 94111 (tel. 415/788-1234, or toll free 800/228-9000), is, architecturally speaking, San Francisco's most unique hotel. Its 17 modern stories rise from the rose-brick edge of the Embarcadero Center at the foot of Market Street, where the rococo clock tower of the Ferry Building provides a contrast in themes. The structure is shaped like a vertical triangle, with two sides forming a right angle and the stunning third sweeping inward from ground level like the side of an Egyptian pyramid, serrated with long rows of jutting balconies.

Two escalators take you up to the lobby level where you step into a vast central court. Ringed with ivy-hung balconies that double as corridors, this space reaches 17 floors toward the glass roof at the top. Daylight filters down in an eerie soft glow. The centerpiece is a huge circular sculpture (*Eclipse* by Charles Perry) atop a smooth black trough of a fountain. Containers of flowers, birds in cages, seating areas for various functions—from drinking to snacking to just relaxing—are scattered everywhere. Live music is featured almost constantly in the atrium lobby. Guests in the 803 rooms, which open onto the corridors above, live in their own "world within a world."

The rooms themselves are comfortably furnished and richly hued in browns and earth tones set off by bold splashes of color in the fabrics. Each has color TVs and digital clock-radios, built-in closets, and separate dressing areas with both makeup and full-length mirrors. The king-size beds are misnamed—they are fit for emperors. Rooms with two double beds are supplied with sofa, easy chair, and cocktail table. In every room you get a choice of six first-run movies on your television set. Room service is available 24 hours daily.

The hotel's 16th floor houses the Regency Club, with 52 deluxe guest rooms, private bar and game room lounges, complimentary continental breakfast, after-dinner cordials, and private concierge.

Restaurants range from the flower-dotted Mrs. Candy's in the lobby to the Market Place, and the haute-cuisine Hugo's to the rooftop Equinox—a revolving lunch-and-cocktail spot that gives you a complete sweep of San Francisco scenery every 45 minutes. Friday nights there's tea-dancing in the lobby. But perhaps the most charming place for lunch is the street café outside the Market Place, where on sunny days you can watch the shifting panorama of brokers, bankers, secretaries, and artists while listening to street musicians in the Embarcadero Center.

Parking is available in the plaza for $18 per 24 hours, with in-and-out privileges.

Rates are $189 to $240 single, $215 to $260 double. Rooms on the Regency Club floor cost $210 single, $240 double.

The **Stanford Court,** 905 California St. (at the corner of Powell Street), San Francisco, CA 94108 (tel. 415/989-3500, or toll free 800/227-4736), stands at the corner where the cable-car lines cross. Once the luxurious Stanford Court Apartments, constructed in 1912 and considered a historic landmark, the eight-story building has been preserved outside, but the hotel inside is $20 million-or-so worth of newness.

A lofty stained-glass dome highlights the entrance of the hotel. The furnishings throughout the hotel consist of antiques and period pieces. Many of the 402 guest rooms have canopied beds, and all have large oak armoires that cleverly conceal the TV set, a writing desk, marble bedside tables, and etchings of old San Francisco on the walls. Appointments include two television sets (a small one in the dressing room), two telephones (one in the bathroom), heated towel racks, overhead heat lamps—everything right down to hand-milled soap.

The Stanford Court has two restaurants. The Café Potpourri, with beamed ceilings, high-backed booths, and white filigree tables and chairs, serves breakfast and lunch. Its main restaurant, Fournou's Ovens, with walls adorned with terracotta and limestone bas-relief panels, terracotta tile floors, and substantial mahogany-beamed ceilings, is open for dinner nightly featuring traditional and nouvelle French cuisine. Fournou's copper-roofed, multiterraced conservatories, modeled after the winter gardens of 19th-century Europe, house Fournou's Bar, with views in all directions and nighttime piano music. Dinner here might begin with a terrine of fresh duck liver with pistachio and proceed to the likes of roast rack of lamb, roast glazed filet of pork with gingered orange sauce, or fresh cracked Dungeness crab with dill butter and white wine sauce, ranging from $20 to $35. Desserts such as soufflé glacé Grand Marnier top things off.

Rates are $175 to $235 single, $205 to $265 double, with suites beginning at $425.

Discreet Nob Hill elegance is also the hallmark of the neighboring **Huntington Hotel,** 1075 California St. (between Mason and Taylor), San Francisco, CA 94108 (tel. 415/474-5400, or toll free 800/227-4683), so exclusive that room service emanates from the prestigious L'Etoile restaurant. Each of the 145 luxurious rooms is uniquely furnished in tasteful and elegant fashion with ample custom-made and antique pieces, as well as all modern amenities—color TVs, direct-dial phones, etc. Some rooms have wet bars and small refrigerators; some look out over Huntington Park, which was the original site of the Huntington mansion. Baths are equipped with imported Irish linen hand towels bearing the Huntington crest, nightly turndown service is one of the many ways guests are pampered, and a record of guests' preferences is kept. The Huntington accepts no convention trade.

Dining options include the Big Four, serving breakfast, lunch, and dinner in a walnut-paneled interior enhanced with beveled-glass panels and mirrors, and photographs of the mansions of the "big four" (Mark Hopkins, Charles Crocker, Leland Stanford, and of course, C. P. Huntington), as well as authentic period prints. The substantial, clubby décor features comfortable green leather-upholstered furnishings and white-clothed tables lit by green-shaded candle lamps. Hunting prints adorn the walls of the cocktail lounge. The continental fare is excellent, with entrees ranging, at dinner, from $22.50 to $35.

The Huntington's gourmet restaurant is L'Étoile, one of San Francisco's premier restaurants. The full details are in Chapter VI.

Single rooms at the Huntington range from $155 to $210,

doubles run $175 to $235, and one- and two-bedroom suites are $250 to $700.

The elegant **Mark Hopkins,** 1 Nob Hill, San Francisco, CA 94108 (tel. 415/392-3434, or toll free 800/332-4246), at the crest of Nob Hill, stands 20 stories tall—an open-winged tower with a view from every one of its 400 gracious rooms, recently renovated at a cost of $9 million. Guests can take their choice between classical or contemporary décor, and the appointments and service are of the high level one expects in this caliber of hotel. All the rooms have views (the higher, the better), sumptuous baths, color TVs, alarm clocks, and radios. And 17 of the suites offer the ultimate in luxury and comfort as with the Jacuzzi Suite where you have a spectacular view of the Golden Gate Bridge.

The Mark opened in 1926 on the spot where railroad-millionaire Mark Hopkins's turreted monster of a mansion once stood. It gained global fame during World War II when it was considered *de rigueur* for Pacific-bound servicemen to toast their goodbye to the States in the Top of the Mark cocktail lounge. Today the Mark hosts conventions and the traveling well-to-do. Locals still stand toasts at the Top of the Mark.

Dining and drinking facilities include—in addition to the famous Top of the Mark—the oak-paneled Nob Hill Restaurant, serving breakfast, lunch, and dinner daily. Its menu is best described as classical French with a California flair. The Lower Bar, under a skylight roof, is a delightful setting for cocktails and piano bar entertainment nightly.

Rooms at the Mark are priced from $175 to $235 single, $205 to $265 double or twin; suites range from $350 to $1,100.

The **Fairmont Hotel and Tower,** atop Nob Hill, 950 Mason St. (at California Street), San Francisco, CA 94106 (tel. 415/772-5000, or toll free 800/527-4727). Just across the cable-car tracks stands the magnificent edifice of the Fairmont, a block-square marble palace often referred to as "a city within a city."

With a total of 600 rooms, including numerous suites, it shelters six restaurants, several cocktail lounges, the city's leading nightclub, and every convenience from a bank branch to a liquor shop and 24-hour room service.

The original seven-story building—all gold, marble, and plush carpeting—withstood the 1906 earthquake, although it was gutted and had to be refitted. In 1961 the 24-story Tower was added—a slender, modern shaft of white and gold. The Tower is topped by the Crown Room, the lavish counterpart of the Mark's "Top," a cocktail lounge with an outstanding city view that is reached by an outdoor elevator known as the Skylift.

Those staying at the Fairmont will revel in such details as a maid to turn down your bed at night, large color TVs, luxurious baths, custom-made soaps, clock-radios, electric shoe polishers, and huge walk-in closets.

Dining options at the Fairmont include the lattice- and mirror-walled, dome-ceilinged Squire Room, an elegant setting for French/continental lunches, dinner, and weekend brunches; the informal 24-hour Brasserie; the Crown for lavish buffet meals with a view; the Cänlis for international fare served in an Oriental setting; the Venetian Room, a supper club featuring such top-name entertainers as Ella Fitzgerald and Tony Bennett; and the exotic Tonga for Chinese specialties in a South Seas ambience with dancing on a boat deck. In addition, you can enjoy drinks and piano music at the elegant Cirque Bar, music and cocktails nightly in the New Orleans Room off the lobby.

Rates in the Fairmont's main building are $140 to $180 single, $170 to $210 double and twin; suites begin at $400. In the tower singles go for $180 to $200, doubles and twins run $210 to $255, and suites start at $500.

Located in the heart of the city—facing out on verdant Union Square—is the elegant *grande dame* of San Francisco's hotels, the **Westin St. Francis**, 335 Powell St. (between Geary and Post), San Francisco, CA 94102 (tel. 415/397-7000, or toll free 800/228-3000).

The main building is a handsome, pre-earthquake edifice. There is a splendid rosewood-paneled, wine-draped, and crystal-hung lobby that extends back to the carpeted foyer of the new straight-walled, 32-story tower building. It is here that the main desk and an open cocktail area are located. Rooms in the main building have unusually high ceilings; they've been recently redecorated. All 1,200 rooms in the hotel are attractively furnished, and supplied with lots of luxuries and amenities like color TVs and direct-dial phones.

High above the city, on the tower's top floor, are Victor's, featuring excellent California nouvelle-cuisine dinners, and the adjoining Oz, one of the city's choicest dance clubs.

Additional dining facilities include the Dutch Kitchen, a 24-hour restaurant. Fresh seafood is offered at the handsomely oak-paneled English Grill, open for lunch and dinner Monday to Saturday. Soup-and-sandwich fare is served daily at the hotel's Dewey's Union Square Bar & Monument Saloon. The Compass Rose is open for lunch weekdays and is the perfect spot for an afternoon drink in a plush, nostalgic setting.

The St. Francis has its own garage, charging $18 per 24 hours with in-and-out privileges.

Room rates range from $140 to $230 single, $170 to $270 double, $350 to $1,500 for suites.

The largest of San Francisco's noted hotels is the 1,910-room **San Francisco Hilton on Hilton Square**, 333 O'Farrell St. (at Mason), San Francisco, CA 94102 (tel. 415/771-1400, or toll free 800/445-8667), a streamlined rectangle of beige concrete that merges with the evening fog. It's the complete luxury hotel, a city unto itself, composed of three connecting buildings. Hilton Square includes the original 19-story main building with 955 rooms, a 46-story, 569-room tower topped by a panoramic restaurant, and a new 23-story landmark with an additional 386 rooms.

The Hilton is ideally located across the street from the terminal where you arrive by bus or shuttle from the airport. As a matter of fact, the entire Bay Area is easily reached from the Hilton since the hotel is within easy walking distance to the cable cars, buses, and the city's MUNI and BART transportation systems.

There's a beautiful, sweeping grand entrance to the lobby. Inlaid marble defines the 16-bay registration area with a separate concierge desk. An elegant sidewalk café—the Café on the Square—provides a lovely spot for spectators to eye the passing parade and the promenade of hotel shops.

One of the Hilton's unique features is its internal parking system. Notify the hotel that you are bringing a car and it will book you into a room that is directly accessible to the parking levels. (There's a daily parking charge.) And at the 16th-floor level of the original tower, is an inner courtyard outfitted with a heated swimming pool and cabaña/garden rooms.

Hilton Square offers several characteristically San Francisco restaurants to choose from. Henri's, on the 46th floor, serves classic California cuisine in a breathtaking setting I promise you won't forget for as long as you remember San Francisco. The magnificent 360° view displays the Golden Gate Bridge and the Bay Bridge, Sausalito, Telegraph Hill, and the East Bay. And the retractable skylight exposes the night sky in all its grandeur. Kiku of Tokyo, an intimate corner of Japan itself, presents authentic Japanese cuisine. And Phil Lehr's Steakery has been a unique San Francisco tradition for over 40 years, offering prime cuts by the pound.

All guest rooms are spacious and modern in typical Hilton style. Memorable floor-to-ceiling views are available from many of these spacious and grandly appointed rooms, as well as color TVs with first-run movies, mini-bars, radios, marble bathrooms, and 24-hour room service to pamper each guest during her or his stay.

Room rates range from $150 to $215 single, $170 to $235 double; suites are $365 to $640.

At another of the older, quietly elegant hotels, a brightly costumed welcoming Beefeater immediately identifies the **Sir Francis Drake**, 450 Powell St. (at Sutter), San Francisco, CA 94102 (tel.

415/392-7755, or toll free 800/227-5480, 800/652-1668 in California). The very hospitable hotel lays accent on unobstrusive service and serene detail in the guest rooms. The hotel faces Powell Street, one block up from Union Square.

In Crusty's Café, which has been recently redecorated, the menu features all manner of dishes, accompanied by San Francisco's famous sourdough bread.

The 415 tasteful rooms have tub and/or shower baths, color

TOKYO-BY-THE-BAY. Just a mile from the heart of downtown, the **Miyako Hotel,** 1625 Post St. (at Laguna Street), San Francisco, CA 94115 (tel. 415/922-3200, or toll free 800/533-4567), is located in the Japan Center that borders Nihonmachi, the city's Japanese quarter. The center was opened in 1968 and the hotel's 15-story tower and 5-story annex overlook a fascinating complex of shops and restaurants.

From the moment you enter the peaceful lobby with a beautiful flock of origami birds at the bell desk, you know you are in a building where East has merged successfully with West. Of the 208 roooms, 202 are equipped with American-style beds and chairs, carpets, color TVs, and Japanese baths. But there are shoji screens opening onto balconies and tokonoma niches for flowers, bowls, or Buddhas. There are 14 luxury suites with private saunas.

Six of the Miyako's accommodations (four rooms and two suites) are very popular among Occidentals. They are done in all-Japanese décor, which means you sleep on the floor laid with tatami mats and spread with huge down quilts called futons. A bamboo and rock garden runs the length of the wall and can be contemplated in peace from your sunken bathtub. Or you can watch color TV from the comfort of your futon.

The hotel provides you with an instruction sheet and some especially relaxing bath salts for your Japanese-style furo bath. The only thing they don't supply is a bath girl, but most couples seem to manage on their own.

A new elegant lobby restaurant serves a combination continental-Japanese cuisine. The waitresses dress in kimonos, and service is swift and smiling.

So happy an experience is the Miyako that Bay Area people often come in for the weekend, hire a Japanese suite, settle into the bathtub, and leave it only for forays to Nihonmachi.

Rates are $100 to $150 single, $130 to $170 for doubles and twins; suites are $215 to $350.

TVs equipped with first-run movies available, and classically refined furnishings featuring quilted coverlets and floor-to-ceiling drapes. On the 21st floor, the Starlite Roof is a popular downtown spot for dancing, complimentary hors d'ouevres beginning at 4 p.m., and drinks.

Rates are $110 to $180 single, $130 to $200 double or twin, and, $280 to $550 for suites. Parking is available at $18 for 24 hours with in-and-out privileges.

One of the most enjoyable hotels in town is the extremely well-located **Hyatt on Union Square**, Stockton Street (between Post and Sutter), San Francisco, CA 94108 (tel. 415/398-1234, or toll free 800/228-9000). Although not as startlingly innovative as the Hyatt Regency, it is a handsome, modern hotel with an elegant old-world courtyard façade graced by Ruth Asawa's bronze fountain sculpture. The 693 rooms, renovated at a cost of $5 million, are ultramodern in décor, utilizing mirrored walls, beige rugs, and gold, brown, or royal-blue drapes and spreads. Every modern amenity is on hand, including first-run movies on your color TV.

The Hyatt boasts a plush rooftop restaurant, One-Up, on the 36th floor of the tower, serving high-quality continental-cuisine lunches weekdays, dinners nightly, and brunches on Sunday. The One-Up Lounge is open for cocktails, served with piano music until 2 a.m.

Equally lovely, and one of my favorite downtown spots for lunch, is the Plaza Restaurant. Floor-to-ceiling windows offer a beautiful view of Union Square, and a garden ambience is created by green rugs, bamboo furnishings, a fountain, and many potted palms. Overhead is a stained-glass skylight dome. Breakfasts, lunches, and dinners are served, and a wide range of fancy teas and coffees is featured.

You can also enjoy casual dining and deli fare at Napper's, Too During the summer Napper Valley serves lunch at an outdoor patio.

Guests at the Hyatt can use the facilities at the luxurious San Francisco Tennis Club, which include 12 indoor and 12 outdoor tennis courts, sauna and steambaths, a health club, two squash courts, a restaurant, lounge, and pro shop. And business people will appreciate the free limousine service to the financial district weekday mornings. Joggers can also get early-morning limo service to a track in the Embarcadero.

Rates at the Hyatt are $155 to $205 single, $180 to $230 double, with suites from $500.

The **White Swan Inn**, 845 Bush St. (between Taylor and Mason), San Francisco, CA 94108 (tel. 415/775-1755), has the charm and serenity of an English garden inn in an Evelyn Waugh novel. At the same time, the inn affords a unique combination of warmth, service, and style geared to fit the needs of the most discriminating traveler. It's a delightful and romantic discovery in a city filled with hotels often offering only cool efficiencies.

The White Swan Inn is a handsome, quietly tasteful four-story hotel constructed in the early 1900's and renovated by Four Sisters, Inc. A handsome reception area boats a cheery fireplace, a carousel horse (Sir Winston) with a handsome but nameless teddy bear astride, an antique oak breakfront, plants, soft chairs—all surrounded by rich, warm woods.

There are 27 rather spacious rooms in all, each with its own teddy-bear companion. Softly colored English wallpaper and floral-print bedspreads add to the feeling of warmth and comfort. As for the more utilitarian details, each room has a wet bar with a refrigerator, a working fireplace (especially welcome on crisp San Francisco days), private bath with fluffy oversize towels, color TV, and bedside telephone. There is turndown service in the evening, a morning newspaper at your door when you arise, and if you put your shoes outside the door at night, you will wake to find them polished.

Each morning a generous breakfast is served in a lovely common room just off a tiny garden. High tea is also served, and includes hors d'oeuvres, sherry, wine, and home-baked pastries. You can have your sherry in front of the fireplace while you browse through the books in the library.

The White Swan Inn will also arrange reservations for restaurants, theaters, sports, and special events, and for limousine service, if needed.

Just 2½ blocks from Union Square, two blocks from Nob Hill, and 1½ blocks from the Powell Street cable car, the inn is excellently located. Rooms are $150 to $165, double occupancy; $15 for an extra person. The Ashleigh suite is $260 and offers a large separate sitting room in addition to the sleeping quarters. Valet parking can be arranged at $15 per day.

UPPER BRACKET

The **Monticello Inn,** 127 Ellis St. (between Cyril Magnin and Powell), San Francisco, CA 94102 (tel. 415/392-8800, or toll free 800/669-7777), opened in September 1987—a renovation of a 1906 building—and is a first-rate addition to the neighborhood. The only Early American influence near Union Square, it's attractive, beautifully decorated, and moreover, exceptionally reasonable.

The Monticello Inn re-creates Colonial American charm at the San Francisco frontier. Thomas Jefferson, whose bust is displayed in the lobby, would have been pleased with the inn's simplicity and elegance. The spacious lobby is replete with Early American reproductions hanging on Williamsburg-blue walls, a Federal-period desk, a stately grandfather clock, fresh floral displays, and to the rear, a charming parlor where you can enjoy a late-afternoon glass of sherry by the fireplace.

Each of the 91 rooms features the country-colonial luxury and elegance of canopied beds, with spreads in light-blue, pale-yellow, and peach floral prints, and upholstered chairs to match. Baths are spacious and afford all the amenities one expects in a fine hotel. And for the peace and quiet of a superb night's rest, the rooms are thoroughly soundproofed. There's also a stocked honor bar and refrigerator in each room, color TV with remote control, and digital clock/radio. In-room videos are available.

The inn provides complimentary continental breakfast and evening wine service at the cozy fireplace in the parlor, as well as complimentary limousine service to the financial district. Same-day laundry and valet service are available. For those with cars, the in-house parking is a real blessing in this section. Nondrivers will find the inn quite conveniently located—it's two blocks from Union Square and half a block from the Powell Street cable car.

Guest rates are $94, single or double occupancy; suites are $114 to $123. Should you need information, directions, or reservations, the young, friendly staff is very helpful.

The Corona Bar & Grill, adjacent to the hotel and at the corner of Ellis and Cyril Magnin, opened in November 1987. You will find this extraordinary restaurant discussed in Chapter VI—don't miss it.

It would be hard to find a more convenient place to stay than the **Villa Florence,** 225 Powell St. (near Geary), San Francisco, CA 94102 (tel. 415/397-7700, or toll free 800/553-4411, 800/243-5700 in California, 800/345-8455 in Canada). It's ideal for anyone who wants to be in beautifully appointed surroundings in the center of the downtown area, near Union Square.

On the Powell Street Cable Car line with easy access to Fisherman's Wharf, the hotel lies two blocks in any direction from the heart of the financial district, the Moscone Convention Center, or the BART and MUNI stations. It's adjacent to Saks Fifth Avenue, Macy's, Neiman Marcus, and enough specialty shops to satisfy the heart of the most dedicated shopper.

The Villa Florence, opened in May 1986, is the superb result of a $6.5-million renovation of what once was the turn-of-the-century Manx Hotel. As soon as you enter the hotel, you'll have an idea of the magnificent refurbishing job done throughout: the arched entryway, graceful palms, marble columns, murals of Florence, huge marble fireplace, rich maroon upholstered chairs, Etruscan-style table lamps, giant urns on pedestals, fresh flowers, and maroon-and-tan floral carpet all reflect an aura of Italian grandeur.

The beautiful, elegant bedrooms feature pink-and-blue floral chintz drapes and matching spreads, as well as white furnishings including very comfortable chairs. Though the rooms are a bit smaller than most, the décor and the high ceilings afford a feeling of airiness. All modern amenities grace the rooms—color TVs and pullout writing tables concealed in the chest of drawers, direct-dial phones, and well-stocked honor-bar/refrigerators. The bath has make-up mirror lighting, overhead heat lamps, hand-milled soap—some of life's little pleasures for your convenience and comfort.

There are 177 rooms in all, including junior and deluxe suites. Rooms are $97, single or double occupancy. Junior suites are $114; deluxe suites, $154.

If there were nothing more to be said about the Villa Florence, its price and location would be enough to consider it an exceptional buy. However, as you enter the hotel, you'll notice a dining area to your left separated from the main body of the hotel by glass walls elegantly etched with simple shell designs. Beyond the dining area is Kuleto's, the northern Italian restaurant with specialties from Tuscany. See Chapter VI for details of this gem of a restaurant.

The Inn at the Opera, 333 Fulton St. (near Franklin), San Francisco, CA 94102 (tel. 415/863-8400, or toll free 800/325-2708; 800/423-9610 in California), is a unique part of San Francisco's cultural heritage. Originally built over 50 years ago to cater to visiting opera stars, the inn recently was transformed into a small luxury hotel (48 rooms) in the heart of San Francisco's creative center—only steps from the Opera House and Davies Hall. The inn still caters to many performing artists.

As you approach the inn you'll see the trappings of a more gracious age—a portico, flower boxes, polished brass, curtained windows, and a carpet leading to the door. The interior of this jewel, every bit as handsome as the entry, greets visitors in a reception area light and airy with European furnishings, soft pastel colors, and a floral French area rug in warm, delicate browns, pink, and greens. A hospitable bowl of apples along with fresh flowers and old brass inkwells adorns the desk. There's an elegance, classic beauty, and intimacy here and a concerned attention to needs that are difficult to find in the best of luxury hotels.

Each room in the inn reflects the same feeling of warmth. Subtle tones of green with beige complement finely checked drapes and huge stuffed pillows in floral prints, some edged with the drapery design. But the comfort of the room is only the beginning. There's a well-stocked refrigerator with wines, pâtés, soda, and other gourmet items, and there are wine glasses at the wet bar. Other pleasant amenities are the terrycloth robes you'll find in the armoire and the chocolates placed on your nighttime pillow.

The Act IV Restaurant at the Inn at the Opera is a special place for dining or lounging or having a drink at the handsome mahogany bar. The broad and deep-brown, teal, and green Rousseau-like floral wall tapestry enhances the warm woods and green velvet and leather chairs. And the plump matching tapestry-design throw cushions can induce you to spend the whole evening in total comfort on overstuffed sofas. In the evening the fireplace and the music of the pianist at the grand piano give the restaurant a quiet intimacy. Act IV is open daily for breakfast from 6:30 to 11 a.m. and for dinner from 5:30 to 10 p.m., an après-theater menu is served until 1 a.m. Or you can go for Sunday brunch from 10:30 a.m. to 3:30 p.m. The continental menu is excellent, offering a good range of moderately priced entrees.

Whether you're a romantic or one who simply enjoys the attention, charm, luxury, and quiet of an elegant, small hotel, the Inn at the Opera is highly recommended. Guest rooms range from $105 to $135 for single or double occupancy; suites are $145 to $195. The inn will obtain tickets to the Opera, symphony, or ballet.

INNS AND SUCH: In recent years a marvelous trend has evolved in the San Francisco accommodations scene. Old buildings have been taken over and turned into quaint inns, charming bed-and-breakfast hostelries, and super-luxurious, European-style accommodations. Most are in the Luxury or Upper-Bracket categories, and all are immensely popular and have limited rooms. Reserve as early as possible.

First on the scene, and most unique of them, is Bob Pritikin's Victorian **Mansion Hotel,** 2220 Sacramento St. (between Laguna and Buchanan), San Francisco, CA 94115 (tel. 415/929-9444), with 20 rooms, which in its few years of operation has become San Francisco's most chic, celeb-studded hideaway, attracting the likes of Robin Williams and Barbra Streisand, among many others.

Set in a terraced garden adorned with Bufano sculptures (the hotel houses the largest collection of Bufano works on display anywhere), the Mansion delights guests with an abundance of luxury and whimsy. To wit: First you are greeted by a host or hostess in Victorian attire and offered a glass of wine or sherry. You'll then discover a fine selection of classical music in your room. There's a game room with billiard tables, its walls painted with a mural of *Pigs Playing Pool* (murals of turn-of-the-century San Francisco enhance most of the walls in the public areas). In the Victorian Cabaret Theater, complete with a live parrot, Claudia the Ghost, sitting at the grand piano in a wheelchair, plays requests with invisible fingers; other nights she performs extraordinary feats of magic, and Pritikin, "America's foremost saw player" also entertains.

CITY ELEGANCE, COUNTRY STYLE. For a touch of the French countryside with modern comforts in the heart of San Francisco, you can't do better than the **Petite Auberge,** 863 Bush St. (between Mason and Taylor), San Francisco, CA 94108 (tel. 415/ 928-6000), 2½ blocks from Union Square, two blocks from Nob Hill. It's a tiny place, with 26 rooms of varying sizes, all decorated in French country style with floral wallpapers, antiques, quilts, and lacy throw pillows. Eighteen rooms have fireplaces and bathrooms with tub/showers; one of these is a suite with Jacuzzi tub, wet bar, private entry, and private deck. The other eight rooms have shower bathrooms (some of these rooms are quite small). All rooms have direct-dial phones, and cable color TVs concealed in armoires—so they don't disturb the quaint décor when not in use. There's shampoo, hair conditioners, bath gels, and special soaps in each bathroom. At night you'll find your bed turned down, and a rose, imported chocolate, and good-night poem placed on your pillow. Each morning you'll find a newspaper at your doorstep. And if you want your shoes polished, you leave them outside your door in the evening, and they're returned, gleaming, by morning.

Every day at the Petite Auberge begins with a delicious home-made breakfast. You can partake of eggs, cereals, muffins, croissants, breads, yogurt, granola, fresh fruits and juices, coffee, and tea in the tiny dining room downstairs. In the afternoon, there's wine, sherry, cakes, and hors d'oeuvres in the lounge; it's a great time to relax and get to know the other guests. And anytime during the day or night, there's coffee, tea, and sodas for the asking. There are other special touches here as well: in the lounge, there's a basket of menus from local restaurants for your perusal, as well as a book with restaurant recommendations jotted down by previous guests. There's a flower sachet in the elevator. And there are teddy bears everywhere that you can cuddle. (They're available for purchase; everyone falls in love with them.)

The Petite Auberge staff is young, friendly, helpful, and attentive; for all its charm, they are what makes the inn as special as it is. You'll always find someone around to advise on where to visit, make reservations, or just chat. They can even arrange valet parking at a nearby security garage for $17 a night. And unlike some small inns, there's someone on call 24 hours a day, seven days a week.

Rooms at the Petite Auberge cost $110 to $170 for single or double occupancy; the suite rents for $205. Occupancy by an extra person costs an additional $15.

As for the rooms, each is different, but they're all furnished with well-chosen antiques—brass beds with handmade quilts, velvet drapes, Victorian memorabilia, etc.; all have direct-dial phones, but no TV, and most look out on a rose or sculpture garden. Each is named after a famous San Franciscan—Bufano, Coit, Huntington, or Pritikin—but the ultimate indulgence is the opulent French, Empress Josephine Room which is furnished with priceless antiques. There's even an all-glass (including spectacular stained glass) Garden Room. Baths, by the way, though all private, are in the rooms or a step away. Fresh-baked croissants and coffee are served at breakfast. The Mansion restaurant, presided over by Master Chef David Coyle, is open to guests of the hotel only.

But the best thing about the Mansion is its total and oft-theatrical originality, reflected in Pritikin's philosophy that "The Mansion is only as good as its last performance."

Rates range from $75 to $150 for one person, $90 to $200 for double occupancy; those rates include continental breakfast.

Billed as a luxury pensione, the **Bed & Breakfast Inn, 4** Charlton Court (off Union Street between Buchanan and Laguna), San Francisco, CA 94123 (tel. 415/921-9784), is Bob and Marily Kavanaugh's noteworthy addition to the Bay Area's hostelries. It's located on a charming courtyard just off Union. Like the Mansion a turn-of-the-century Victorian dwelling, the B&B Inn offers exquisite accommodations with every luxury and personal service. Guests are greeted by name and introduced to each other. Sherry is available at all times, and breakfast (fresh-baked croissants, orange juice, and coffee, fancy teas, or cocoa) is brought to your room on a flower-bedecked tray with the daily paper, or else served in a sunny Victorian breakfast room. The table is set with antique china, including a cow creamer, plus a big vase of fresh flowers. There are ten rooms in the hotel, located in two side-by-side houses that predate the 1906 earthquake by several decades. Each is uniquely and charmingly decorated—perhaps in a Casablanca motif with a peacock chair and a ceiling fan, perhaps with a Victorian or brass bed. All are wonderfully cozy and contain some of the Kavanaughs' cherished family antiques, original art, plants and fresh flowers, fruit, a Thermos of ice water, clocks, beds with down pillows, a selection of quality books and magazines—even a fortune cookie on your pillow when you check in. Some rooms share a bath and some have sinks; all of the suites have private baths and color TVs, and four also have phones. Rooms without baths have doors leading to the lovely enclosed garden out back. There's a library for guests, furnished with a backgammon table, writing desk, TV, and pay phone.

Rooms with shared bath are priced at $73 to $90 a night, single or double, the higher prices levied for larger, more luxurious lodgings. With bath they're priced at $123 to $194. The Mayfair, formerly the Kavanaughs' flat, with a latticed terrace, private kitchen, a bedroom up a spiral staircase, and a double-tub bath, rents for $194 a night. All rates include breakfast.

Another of the Victorian-era renovations is Helen Stewart's **Union Street Inn,** 2229 Union St. (between Fillmore and Steiner), San Francisco, CA 94123 (tel. 415/346-0424), its six rooms furnished in perfect taste with carefully selected antiques. Downstairs is a beautiful homey parlor with apricot velvet walls, a velvet sofa, and a fireplace.

You can have breakfast (fresh-baked croissants, with Helen's homemade kiwi or plum jam, fresh-squeezed orange juice, and coffee) in the parlor, in your room, or on an outdoor terrace overlooking a rustic garden with its own lemon tree.

The rooms are fancifully named (Wildrose, Holly, Golden Gate, English Garden, New Yorker) and charmingly decorated. They have canopied or brass beds with polished cotton spreads, well-chosen art on the walls, a table and chairs, live plants and beautifully arranged flowers, and magazines to read. All are equipped with sinks, and two have private baths. Most have multipaned bay windows and overlook the garden. Phones are available upon request.

The newest addition, the Carriage House, is similarly decorated. It nestles in the garden and has its own private bathroom complete with Jacuzzi. Rooms rent for $85 to $185 a night, single or double. Breakfast is included in all rates.

The **Queen Anne Hotel,** just a mile from Union Square at 1590 Sutter (at Octavia), San Francisco, CA 94109 (tel. 415/441-2828, or toll free 800/227-3970, 800/262-2663 in California), looks exactly like what it is—a handsomely restored Victorian mansion. At the turn of the century, in its first life, the building was Miss Mary Lake's School for Girls; later it became a private gentlemen's club, then returned to its original gender as the Girl's Friendly Society Lodge. After a complete renovation and restoration it opened as the Queen Anne in 1981.

The English-oak-paneled lobby is furnished in antiques; inside, 49 unique rooms manage to preserve a turn-of-the-century atmosphere while providing all modern conveniences. Each room has been individually decorated: some have corner turret bay windows that look out on tree-lined streets, as well as separate parlor areas and wet bars; others have cozy reading nooks and fireplaces. All rooms have telephones with extensions in the bathroom and remote-control color TV. The Queen Anne provides complimentary continental breakfast, brought to your room along with the morning's newspaper. Complimentary afternoon tea and sherry are served in the parlor from 4 to 6 p.m.

Rates range from $95 to $150, and weekly rates are available.

Another inn-style hostelry is the **Stanyan Park Hotel,** 750 Stanyan St. (at Waller), San Francisco, CA 94117 (tel. 415/751-1000), located directly across the street from Golden Gate Park. It was built as a hotel in 1904–1905, and has operated as such since that time, under a variety of ownerships and names. In its current incarnation, it's a charming, three-story establishment with 36 rooms (including six suites) decorated with antique-style furnishings, Victorian flocked wallpaper, and pastel quilts, curtains, and carpets. Modern amenities include color TVs, direct-dial phones, and tub/shower baths complete with massaging shower head and shampoos, fancy soaps, etc. The suites each have two bedrooms, with one queen-size and two twin beds, plus a full kitchen, formal dining room, and living room with fold-out queen-size couch. Each suite can sleep six comfortably; they're ideal for families. A complimentary continental breakfast is included.

Rooms at the Stanyan Park cost $62 to $92 single or double; suites cost $110 to $150.

You don't have to be a former flower child to feel at home in the **Red Victorian Bed and Breakfast Inn,** 1665 Haight St. (near Belvedere), San Francisco, CA 94117 (tel. 415/864-1978). Owner Sami Sunchild, a former flower child herself, has been instrumental in the renaissance of the Haight-Ashbury; Haight Street is now the center of a pleasant, up-and-coming neighborhood.

The Red Victorian occupies the second and third floors of a red Victorian building. Each of 15 guest rooms is inspired by themes of San Francisco. Four rooms have private baths, and four baths in the hall serve the remaining rooms. The "Redwood Forest" has a photomural of redwoods on one wall as well as over the canopied bed; the "Rose Garden," the "Japanese Teagarden," and the "Flower Child" rooms all have décors reflecting their names. The exotic "Peacock Suite" is large enough to accommodate four people and has its own bath. Rooms and baths are clean, and furnishings are pleasant if eclectic.

A continental breakfast of croissants, muffins, fresh fruit, and coffee is served every morning in the inn's Pink Parlor. It's fun to browse through Sami's scrapbooks of the hotel's and neighborhood's history, or to study her artwork on the walls. Upstairs there's a meditation room for quiet moments.

The Red Victorian's bathless rooms rent for $45 to $68 single, $48 to $73 for double occupancy; and $75 to $85 with a bath. The

Peacock Suite is $120. Breakfast is included in all prices, as is evening wine and cheese. The inn has discount rates for students and seniors (over 60).

MODERATELY PRICED HOTELS

If the ambience of an English country inn, or breakfast with scones and crumpets, is your style, the small (62-room) **Abigail Hotel**, at 246 McAllister St. (near Larkin), San Francisco, CA 94102 (tel. 415/861-9728, or toll free 800/243-6510, 800/553-5575 in California), British-owned, may be your pot of tea. What the Abigail lacks in luxury it more than makes up for in charm. The hotel's handsome white exterior, with its canopy and polished brass, might have been picked up in London and set down two blocks from the San Francisco Opera. In the lobby you'll find a small desk, Oriental rugs, polished woods, ceiling-to-floor white drapes, and wicker straight-back chairs at red-clothed tables in the breakfast area, all reflecting typical English taste. The hunting trophies in the lobby are not relics of the Empire, just finds at an auction.

The guest rooms carry out the English tone with blue floral drapes, white curtains, old prints, and an occasional antique table or lamp. Most rooms are quite light and quiet, though you might inquire when making your reservations. All have the usual amenities —pushbutton telephone, color television, and private bath. Valet service is available. J. A. Melon's Restaurant and Bar adjoins the hotel.

Single rooms are $57 to $62, doubles run $68 to $73, and suites cost $160. An additional $8 is charged for an extra person.

The **Hotel Vintage Court,** 650 Bush St. (between Powell and Stockton), San Francisco, CA 94108 (tel. 415/392-4666, or toll free 800/654-1100, 800/654-7266 in California), is a handsome European-style hotel conveniently situated one block from Union Square and the cable car. Its relatively small size (106 rooms) allows for personal service. Classically comfortable armchairs, a fireplace, flowers, and the warm brown tones of the furnishings create an intimate, cozy feeling. The décor of the rooms has the same character. Floral-print bedspreads and drapes are complemented by white furnishings and framed floral prints. Each room has a private refrigerator and mini-bar stocked daily, as well as the usual color television and pushbutton phones. Complimentary tea and coffee are served in the morning, and wine in the evening. For a day in the country to write home about, the hotel can arrange an outing to the nearby wine country in a custom Rolls-Royce or a horse-drawn carriage. The charm and popularity of this hotel require that reservations be made at least two to three weeks in advance.

Guest rates are $94 for all rooms—single, double, and twin.

The famous Masa's restaurant, adjoining the hotel, is under separate ownership.

The **Bedford Hotel,** 761 Post St. (between Leavenworth and Jones), San Francisco, CA 94109 (tel. 415/673-6040, or toll free 800/227-5642, 800/652-1889 in California), is a charming, 17-story European-style hotel in a quiet but convenient location three blocks from Union Square, on the southwest slope of Nob Hill. Each of its 143 redecorated rooms is well furnished with king-size, queen-size, or double-double beds, color TV, video-tape players, a fully stocked refrigerator honor bar, AM/FM clock-radio, direct-dial phone, writing desk, and armchair. Color schemes are cheerful, in navy and white, dusty rose, forest green and white, or beige and green. Many of the rooms have remarkable views of the city. Bathrooms are well kept up; all have tub/shower combinations.

The Bedford's staff is friendly, enthusiastic, attentive, and very professional. There's a small bar (the Wedgwood Lounge) opposite the registration desk, and behind the lobby, under separate management, is the elegant, award-winning gourmet Café Bedford. Breakfast is served here daily, and California cuisine dinner is offered Tuesday through Saturday nights. Room service is available, as is valet parking for overnight guests.

Rooms at the Bedford cost $95 for a single or double; suites begin at $150.

Under the same management is the **Galleria Park Hotel,** 191 Sutter St. (at Kearny), San Francisco, CA 94104 (tel. 415/781-3060, or toll free 800/792-9639, 800/792-9855 in California). From its lobby, complete with fireplace, to its beautifully appointed 177 rooms and 15 suites, the Galleria Park has been totally restored in the art nouveau style of the time of its original construction. The hotel features a full-time concierge, room service, a bar, and a sundries shop. And the Galleria is the only hotel in San Francisco to have an outdoor running track and park. The hotel also features Bentley's Oyster Bar & Restaurant (under separate management), offering fresh seafood specialties, oysters at a grand-scale bar, and a variety of other dishes.

Rooms at the Galleria Park let for $99 to $115, single or double. Suites begin at $140.

The **Hotel Union Square,** 114 Powell St. (at Ellis), San Francisco, CA 94102 (tel. 415/397-3000, or toll free 800/553-1900), is another of the delightful hostelries in the Union Square area. And it proudly claims its place in American literary history: in the 1920s, as the Golden West Hotel, it was occasionally a stopping place for then-Pinkerton detective Dashiell Hammett, creator of Sam Spade.

The hotel has been renamed and considerably modernized since those days, but it retains its early charm. Its 131 newly refurbished guest rooms feature art deco décor and soft floral-print bed-spreads and curtains. Shampoos, conditioners, and soaps are sup-plied in the bathrooms. There is turndown service every evening. Complimentary coffee and croissants are served each morning in a small lounge area on each floor; weekdays, newspapers are available.

The Union Square has no restaurant of its own, but there are dozens of eating establishments within a block or two of the front door. Two of them, Tad's and Les Joulins, offer room service from 7 a.m. to 11 p.m. daily (you'll find menus in your room). Guests with cars can park for $12 a day in a guarded lot at the hotel's back door. All in all, the Union Square is a pleasant and friendly establishment.

Rates are $75 to $105 single or double. Penthouse suites with redwood decks and garden patios begin at $175.

The majority of the following hotels are located downtown close to the airline bus terminal and Union Square. Several are in the more charming residential areas of the city—specifically chosen for those who prefer to share neighborhood life with the natives. Most are excellent choices for families as they offer either money-saving family plans, large family rooms, or two-room/one-bath suites.

A green-fronted six-story building, built in 1920 and illuminated by iron lanterns, the **Commodore International,** 825 Sutter St. (at Jones), San Francisco, CA 94109 (tel. 415/923-6800, or toll free 800/327-9157), welcomes guests in a warmly old-fashioned lobby adorned by a ticking grandfather clock and lots of plaster curl-icues on the walls.

The 113 rooms have all been redecorated and provided with full baths and large wardrobes, as well as direct-dial phones and col-or TVs.

Just off the lobby is a pleasant coffeeshop/restaurant/cocktail lounge, open daily for breakfast and lunch. Some of the city's most famous restaurants are less than two blocks away.

The hotel is centrally located, four blocks from Union Square and five blocks from Chinatown.

Rates are $45 to $65 single; doubles and twins run $50 to $90.

The **Handlery Union Square Hotel,** 351 Geary St. (between Mason and Powell), San Francisco, CA 94102 (tel. 415/781-7800, or toll free 800/223-0888, 800/522-5455 in New York), is the at-tractive offspring of a formal union of the Handlery Motor Inn and the Hotel Stewart, following a $3-million renovation completed in 1988. All the guest rooms at the Hotel Stewart, now simply called the hotel section, were totally renovated and refurbished.

What had been the Handlery Motor Inn is now the Handlery Club—the concierge section of the new hotel which has managed to maintain reasonable rates although it now offers services one usually expects only from a larger hotel. Rooms in the club are truly large and luxurious. They include such frills as bedside remote-control color TV (with movies available), electric shoe polishers, coffee makers, in-room safes, dressing rooms with makeup mirrors, and balconies. The merged facilities still include a large, heated outdoor swimming pool and sauna. The shopping, theater, and financial districts are easily accessible from this location, half a block from Union Square. The hotel offers overnight valet parking, truly a bargain at $8.

Rates in the hotel section are $75 to $90 single, $84 to $99 double. Rates in the Handlery Club are $120 single, $135 double.

The **Hotel Californian**, 405 Taylor St. (at O'Farrell), San Francisco, CA 94102 (tel. 415/885-2500, or toll free 800/227-3346, 800/622-0961 in California), is ideally located, two blocks from Union Square, a block from the airline bus terminal, and within walking distance of all the downtown attractions. Built in 1924, this 17-story, 242-room hotel is carefully maintained and has several times been refurnished and redecorated.

The most outstanding feature of the spacious lobby is its ceiling, beamed and colorfully stenciled with carved gilt trim.

All the attractive accommodations are outside rooms, and have color TVs, direct-dial phones, and combination shower-tub baths.

Located on the premises is Dudley's Bar and Grill, serving continental cuisine, and open for three meals a day; home-cooked meals are also served at Mrs. Edward's Coffee Shop. A car-rental office, tour desk, and barbershop are on the premises.

Rates are $66 to $75 single, $75 to $85 double or twin. Mention *Frommer's San Francisco* and you'll receive a complimentary bottle of wine.

A popular hotel for families and business people alike, the 250-room, seven-story **Bellevue Hotel**, 505 Geary St. (at Taylor), San Francisco, CA 94102 (tel. 415/474-3600, or toll free 800/421-8851, 800/532-8800 in California), is well located in the heart of the theater district just 1½ blocks from the airline bus terminal. It is exceptionally well maintained, and all the rooms are fresh and attractive.

The lobby is elegant, with a carpet of blues and browns, crystal-and-gold chandeliers, and, especially magnificent, the staircase that leads up to the second floor.

Off the lobby you'll find the Yum Yum restaurant, which is open from 6 a.m. to 10 p.m. daily and serves relatively inexpensive dishes. Also, there's the Belle Tavern for cocktails.

Rooms are moderate in size and differ in décor, offering king-size, double, or twin beds. All are attractively furnished and have shag carpeting, color TV, radio, and direct-dial phone. The tile baths all come with combination shower-tubs.

The Bellevue has a barbershop and a beauty shop, plus a car-rental service.

Rates are $59 to $98 single, $68 to $104 for doubles and twins, and $95 to $165 for suites.

The red-carpeted lobby of the seven-story **Hotel Cecil,** 545 Post St., San Francisco, CA 94102 (tel. 415/673-3733, or toll free 800/227-3818, 800/652-1535 in California), opens onto Post Street next door to the Press Club, between Mason and Taylor. As lobbies go, this one is not large, but it is decidedly pleasant with three-quarter wood paneling, a grandfather clock, comfortable chairs, and writing tables.

With 150 rooms, this is a relatively small hotel with larger rooms than you'd expect, all decorated in French provincial or modern motif. The predominant colors in these light, airy, newly decorated rooms are green and gold with white walls. The housekeeping is excellent, the bathrooms well equipped, the closet space ample, and the service friendly. All rooms have color TV, in-room movies, direct-dial phone, tub and/or shower bath.

If you feel like a little sun, there's a sundeck and cabaña with patio furniture on the seventh floor. And for refreshments, there's a comfortable cocktail lounge on the premises.

Singles pay $58 to $75; doubles and twins, $70 to $80; triples, $90 to $100. Parking in a nearby garage is $13, with in-and-out privileges.

As of this writing, there are plans for renowned chef and entrepreneur Wolfgang Puck to open a restaurant (as yet unnamed) at the hotel. Puck will own a one-third interest in the restaurant and will be supervising the kitchen and doing the menu. Noted restaurant designer Pat Kuleto (of Kuleto's in the Villa Florence, the Fog City Diner, Corona Bar & Grill, to name a few) will be responsible for the interior. Puck's intent is to create a contemporary San Franciscan style based on the city's culinary heritage. Look for it (though if prior experience is any indication, the crowds will lead you there).

The **Beresford Hotel,** 635 Sutter St. (at Mason), San Francisco, CA 94102 (tel. 415/673-9900), is a small, lively, and delightfully friendly hostelry that bends over backward to cater to specialized tourist needs. An overflowing notice board bristles with announcements, ranging from church services to jazz sessions. Guests come in all age brackets and are as amiable as the management.

The hotel serves breakfast and lunch in its attractive, flower-bedecked White Horse Tavern, which it claims is an authentic replica of an old English pub. The restaurant serves fresh fish daily. Drinks are available throughout the day.

The 114 rooms vary in size, but all have either private bath or shower, bright white-walled décor, wall-to-wall carpeting, direct-dial phone, and color TV. Selected pets are welcome. (Call ahead to make sure yours fits the bill.)

Rates are $60 single, $65 double (with queen-twin), $70 for a family double (three people) or $75 (four people). A rollaway bed for an extra person costs $11.

Under the same management is the **Beresford Arms,** conveniently located at 701 Post St. (at Jones), San Francisco, CA 94109 (tel. 415/673-2600), with a friendly, helpful staff. The 87 units are all equipped with color TV, direct-dial phone, and complete bath. A recent renovation reduced the number of guest rooms and added Jacuzzis to some of the suites. Coffee and pastries are available for guests each morning. Rates are the same as at the Beresford, except for the Jacuzzi suites which also have kitchen units or wet bars and rent for $80. Parlor suites are $105.

A charming and distinctly cozy establishment, the **Cartwright Hotel,** 524 Sutter St. (at Powell), San Francisco, CA 94102 (tel. 415/421-2865, or toll free 800/227-3844), is remarkably quiet despite its very convenient location near one of the busiest corners downtown. The management takes great pride in its reputation for comfort, cleanliness, and efficiency, and this pride is reflected in every nook and cranny of the place, from the small, well-groomed lobby, to the 114 rooms furnished with antiques and brightened with fresh flowers. Each room, though different, is decorated in a charming style. All have bath with shower massage and thick fluffy towels, direct-dial telephone, and color TV.

The hotel is a very special place in many respects—it is family owned and operated, and special attention is paid to the guests' comfort. It shows in the little extras: a third sheet to insulate guests from the rougher texture of the blanket, turndown service, and the availability of extras like irons, hairdryers, and large reading pillows. Complimentary tea and cakes are served in the lobby from 4 to 6 p.m.

There's a little restaurant behind the lobby. Teddy's is spacious and charming; you can get a delicious continental breakfast here or one of a heartier variety, or enjoy a light lunch such as quiche, salad, or a gourmet sandwich.

Reserve far in advance at this very popular hostelry.

Singles pay $75 to $80, doubles and twins run $81 to $90, and family suites accommodating up to four are $135 to $155. The hotel has rooms with air conditioning and rooms with refrigerators, both on request at no additional charge.

The **Hotel Savoy,** 580 Geary St. (between Taylor and Jones), San Francisco, CA 94102 (tel. 415/441-2700, or toll free 800/ 227-4223, 800/622-0553 in California), is a pleasant seven-story structure just three blocks from Union Square. The rooms are medium size and decorated with antique furnishings and a variety of pastel color schemes. The little extras are here too: triple sheets, turndown service, full-length mirrors. There are also color TVs, direct-dial phones (though there is a charge for local calls), and modern bathrooms. A complimentary continental breakfast is served in your room or, if you wish, in the Savoy Lounge. Other extra touches include free weekly newspapers and complimentary late-afternoon sherry and tea.

Rooms rent for $67 to $80 single, $77 to $90 double or twin. Suites are available from $120.

The **El Cortez Hotel,** 550 Geary St. (near Taylor), San Francisco, CA 94102 (tel. 415/775-5000, or toll free 800/821-0493, 800/228-8830 in California), has, as its name indicates, a distinctly Spanish flavor—arched entrance, tile lobby with white stucco walls, and graceful pillars. Adjoining the lobby is a lovely French restaurant, La Mère Duquesne, serving lunch weekdays and dinner nightly. Designed to look like an elegant French hunting lodge, it is furnished in antiques and has quaint wallpaper adorned with hunting trophies.

The 17-story Cortez is an elderly building, but excellently maintained and quite unusually comfortable. The 170 rooms—all with outside exposure—are actually apartments, with separate dressing rooms and completely equipped all-electric kitchens, plus bathrooms, color TVs, and phones. The furniture is not overly modern, but the walk-in closets are huge, and those kitchenettes are a great way of saving on your restaurant bills. There's an initial fee of $2 for kitchen utensils (if requested).

Rates are $55 to $57 single, $63 to $70 double or twin, $160 for suites.

I was attracted to the **Lombard Hotel,** 1015 Geary St. (at Polk), San Francisco, CA 94109 (tel. 415/673-5232). From the outside it resembles the kind of hostelry you might expect to find on a fashionable London street. The lobby houses a small restaurant, the Gray Derby, where delectable continental meals (daily breakfast and lunch; dinner on Thursday, Friday, and Saturday; and weekend champagne brunch) are served by waiters in formal attire. The other part of the marble-floored lobby, boasting a grand piano and fireplace, is the perfect setting for an afternoon drink.

The 100 rooms are all newly decorated in terracotta or brown shades, and most feature king- or queen-size beds. All have color TVs, phones, and private baths with tubs and/or showers. The hotel is located about six blocks from Union Square and three blocks from the Civic Center.

The Lombard's rates are $76 to $80 single or double.

Right in the center of everything, just one block from Union Square, cable cars, and shops, the **King George Hotel,** 334 Mason St. (near Geary), San Francisco, CA 94102 (tel. 415/781-5050, or toll free 800/227-4240, 800/556-4545 in California), is another European-style renovation. Across from the stage door of the Geary Theater, the hotel is entered via a pleasant lobby with an air of country charm with its green-and-white décor and collection of European period prints.

On the mezzanine above the lobby, the Bread & Honey Tearoom offers a bountiful light breakfast. Every afternoon (except Sunday) a piano recital accompanies a proper high tea complete with scones, trifle, tea sandwiches, and assorted pastries. In addition, remarkable as it may seem, there's a Japanese restaurant, Ichirin, on the premises; you'll find a detailed discussion of this excellent establishment in Chapter VI. The hotel also has a most comfortable cocktail lounge and nightly piano bar.

The 143 rooms have all been redone in cheery colors, and equipped with color TVs, direct-dial phones, and private baths. Laundry, valet, and room service are available. Parking is conveniently located directly across the street.

Rooms range from $79 to $85.

The **Andrews Hotel,** 624 Post St. (near Taylor), San Francisco, CA 94109 (tel. 415/563-6877, or toll free 800/227-4742, 800/622-0557 in California), has 48 charming rooms and evokes the casual atmosphere of a country inn yet is just two blocks west of Union Square. Rooms are furnished with California gypsy willow chairs and tables and oak-framed mirrors, beds are covered with European spreads, and lace curtains grace the bay windows. Amenities include fresh flowers, private baths with tubs and/or showers, phones, and color TVs. Kimberly Higgins is a warm and friendly host and the rest of the staff emulates her courtesy. One of the nicest things about the Andrews is the adjoining Post St. Bar and Café (see Chapter VI for details).

Rates at the Andrews are $71 to $81 for a single or double, and $97 to $101 for the petite suites. All include complimentary continental breakfast and a glass of wine in the evening.

An attractive establishment on the "motel strip" that stretches from the Golden Gate Bridge to Van Ness Avenue is the **Chelsea Motor Inn,** 2095 Lombard St. (at Fillmore), San Francisco, CA 94123 (tel. 415/563-5600). Opened in 1982, this 60-room motor inn is perfectly located for a stroll along Union Street, and there are restaurants at almost every turn.

Rooms are very comfortable and pleasantly decorated in shades of rust, blue, or brown. Each is equipped with a color TV, tub and shower combination bath, and phone. Parking is free, and buses run regularly to every part of the city.

Rates are $70 to $75 single, $74 to $84 double.

Under the same ownership are the **Cow Hollow Motor Inn,** 2190 Lombard St. (at Steiner), San Francisco, CA 94123 (tel. 415/921-5800), and the **Coventry Motor Inn,** 1901 Lombard St. (at Buchanan), San Francisco, CA 94123 (tel. 415/567-1200). Accommodations and prices are similar to those at the Chelsea.

BUDGET HOTELS

The following represent some of the older hotels in the city. All are well maintained and offer good value for surprisingly little money. Many have rooms without private bath, in older hotel tradition. Consider these if you are watching pennies carefully. All these hotels have been inspected and their bath facilities found clean and adequate to the number of guests sharing them.

The **Adelaide Inn,** 5 Adelaide Pl. (off Taylor), San Francisco, CA 94102 (tel. 415/441-2261), evokes memories of a European pension and runs like one. The inn is on a tiny dead-end street and its 18 rooms on two floors above ground level enjoy peace and quiet.

Furnishings are simple, but the travel and art prints make you feel as though you are on holiday in France. You may have to walk up two flights to your room, but rest assured that all rooms are clean, bright, and comfortable. There are no private baths; all rooms have washing facilities and shared baths are well kept. Sorry, TV is black-and-white, and while there are no phones in the rooms, the inn will take messages.

The Adelaide Inn is a relaxed, pleasant place where guests quickly become friends. The hosts, Serge and Mary, are gracious fonts of information on almost any topic relating to your stay in San Francisco.

If hotel services are what you must have, this is not the place for you. However, if you'll accept simple, clean, and comfortable accommodations, it's hard to beat the price. Singles are $30 to $34 and doubles run $40 to $44, including continental breakfast.

Edward II Inn & Carriage House, 3155 Scott St. (at Lombard), San Francisco, CA 94123 (tel. 415/922-3000), among the newest and least expensive of San Francisco's inns, has recently been transformed into a handsome forest-green and white bed-and-breakfast. Even the fire hydrant out front is a sparkling white.

The décor of the 32 rooms and suites is simple and charming with quilted bedspreads, antique dressers, and white plantation shutters. There are black-and-white TVs in the rooms (color TVs for those with a private bath), and all rooms have phones. The inn also has two luxuriously appointed suites and two Carriage House suites complete with Jacuzzis and wet bars.

Upstairs, a skylight with a beautiful stained-glass panel offers an aesthetic experience; downstairs, a stained-glass door leads to more down-to-earth delights, connecting the lobby with the Cuneo Italian-French Bakery where guests can enjoy a complimentary continental breakfast. The bakery also sells an impressive collection of calorie-rich pastries, but if you can't survive on pastry alone, you might try the Marina Café and Restaurant next door. The Marina offers a good selection of Italian and seafood specialties. A complimentary glass of wine is offered the inn's guests with dinner at the Marina Café.

Rooms, either single or double occupancy, are $47 to $52 with shared bath, $65 to $75 with private bath. Light sleepers should request rooms to the rear of the building. Suites with Jacuzzis (no longer in the "budget" category) are $135; Carriage House suites are $160 or $210. Limited overnight parking close by is available for $8.

The **Pacific Bay Inn,** 520 Jones St. (between Geary and O'Farrell), San Francisco, CA 94102 (tel. 415/673-0234, or toll free 800/445-2631), is a pleasant recently renovated little hotel offering what it refers to as "no-nonsense service." As you approach the inn, it's easily identified by its blue-and-gold canopy resting on well-polished brass poles. The lobby is a cheery place with maroon-and-cream upholstered chairs and a small collection of palms, ficus trees, and other greenery.

Singles are $42.50; doubles, $47.50. Rates include a continental breakfast. The rooms are cozy, light (no view, but did you expect one at these prices), done in an airy peach color with maroon floral-print spreads, and maroon-and-gray carpeting throughout. The rooms have showers only, no tubs. The inn has a 24-hour desk which can arrange services from a tour to a late-night pizza or a limousine. They also provide reduced-rate tickets for parking in the Taylor Street Garage, around the corner.

The Pacific Bay Inn is just three blocks west of the Powell Street cable car and Union Square. What was once a rather frumpy neighborhood is rapidly improving by virtue of the expansion of some of its neighbors, the new San Francisco Hilton Square and the very elegant Nikko Hotel.

If you want a really inexpensive, hearty meal, it's hard to best the Family Inn across the street, open from 6:30 a.m. to 6 p.m. The menu varies daily, but homemade soups are part of the fare at lunch, and how can you beat pot roast, mashed potatoes, a vegetable,

bread, and dessert—all for $3.75? Need I add that it's nothing in
the least fancy—just counter seats, crowded, a hard-working kitch-
en in front of you—but the food is wholesome, good, and the price
is right.

The **YMCA Hotel**, 166 Embarcadero St. (near Mission), San
Francisco, CA 94105 (tel. 415/392-2191, or toll free 800/622-
9622), here is not limited to groups of Boy Scouts and sailors on
leave. It is a proper hotel for men, women, and families, with eight
residential floors.

Most of the 260 rooms are modestly furnished, but the top
floor offers carpeted, color-coordinated rooms with solid-oak furniture. Baths are shared; that for women is on a separate floor.

Guests have access to the laundromat, TV recreational lounge,
the Y's pool, and extensive gym facilities including a sauna, weight
rooms, and racquetball court. Tourist information is also available.

Rates for singles start at $26; doubles begin at $37.

Unfortunately for those who always look for the economy and
convenience of a **Motel 6,** there is not one to be found in town.
However, don't despair: two are about a 35-minute drive from San
Francisco—one in Palo Alto and the other in Oakland. For the extra
$1 in the basic room rate, I'd pick Palo Alto ($30). The Motel 6 in
Oakland is located in an industrial warehouse district adjacent to a
neighborhood not exactly suited to evening strolls, nor is the accommodation near a comfortable restaurant. Motel 6 in Palo Alto is
at 4301 El Camino Real, Palo Alto, CA 94306 (tel. 415/949-
0833), just off U.S. 101, and four miles from Stanford University.
The Motel 6 in Oakland is at 4919 Coliseum Way, Oakland, CA
94601 (tel. 415/261-7414), located near the Interstate 880 freeway.

If you don't mind a dormitory, of all the budget accommodations in San Francisco, none can beat the **San Francisco International Hostel,** Building 240, Fort Mason (tel. 415/771-7277), at
$9 a night. From Bay and Van Ness Streets, follow the hostel signs
to the grounds of Fort Mason. Call for space from 7 a.m. until midnight. Anyone can use the dormitory, regardless of age. The only
limitation to your stay is one of time—at the end of three nights you
must move to new lodgings. For families or compatible couples,
there are three rooms with four bunks, obviously in great demand.
Kitchen facilities are available, as are lockers, laundry facilities, snack
vending machines, and several community rooms with fireplaces,
stereo, piano, and a wide selection of books. You'll also find several
bulletin boards with information on tours and places to go during
your stay.

CHAPTER VI

WHERE TO EAT

□ □ □

According to columnist Herb Caen, "A city has to be a place where you can get blinis and caviar, fisherman's spaghetti, white figs and prosciutto, a '45 Mouton Rothschild, or a movie in any one of six languages. . . . San Francisco is such a city." Not only is all of that readily available—you can also get bao ngu xao ga nam (a Vietnamese abalone, chicken, and vegetable dish), Moroccan couscous, Szechuan shrimp, Indonesian rijsttafel, and most essential, a decent pastrami on rye.

San Francisco is possibly the most cuisine-conscious city in the United States. Her people take food seriously. Not quite as seriously, perhaps, as the French or residents of Manhattan, but immeasurably more so than most of their fellow Americans, who are frequently suspected of having had their tastebuds lobotomized.

Although nobody can say just how Bay Area citizens developed their discriminating palates, they are one reason for the quite exceptional standard of local gastronomy.

Another is the pronounced international influence. Spanish and Mexican cuisine was established before the arrival of the Anglos. During the Gold Rush, scores of Chinese, Frenchmen, and Germans came to dig, but remained to cook. They were followed by Russians, Italians, Basques, Filipinos, Japanese, Greeks, and Scandinavians, most of whom started by catering to their own compatriots, then found their eateries overrun by the Anglo-Saxon natives. Most recently, Vietnamese and Thai immigrants have added new culinary options.

The third reason, in my opinion, is the wine. The vast majority of San Francisco restaurants offer a good selection of California wines—some of them French-rural-style in unlabeled house bottles—and they make a tremendous difference to any meal. And California wines are often cheaper than the imported brands, which puts them within the range of a moderately priced meal. They account, to a great extent, for the special savor of dining out in San Francisco. Also, keep your eyes peeled for bar notices offering "steam beer." This is a western specialty, unavailable anywhere else, and one of the most potent brews ever tapped.

San Francisco has well over 2,500 restaurants, among them an astonishing number of internationally famous establishments, several of which will be included in the "Luxury Restaurants" section. Following that is a group of moderately priced restaurants, and finally, a list of budget spots.

Since San Francisco offers such a large number of eating places, the accent had to be on variety and quality rather than comprehensiveness. And I must caution that the list below amounts to merely a small fraction of the food dispensaries in each range.

As we go to press, I would be remiss in not mentioning the advent of a new restaurant (as yet unnamed) to be located at the Hotel Cecil (see Chapter V). If prior experience is any indication, the creations of the famous chef Wolfgang Puck will provide a new look to San Francisco's already famous cuisine.

A final word about prices. They're in a permanent state of one-way flux—upward. Here as elsewhere. So while you will find most of the quoted rates models of accuracy, you may discover unannounced increases by the time you get here. Don't blame me, please. With or without high inflation, prices do rise.

LUXURY RESTAURANTS

For a touch of gastronomic luxury during your visit, you couldn't do better than to choose one of the following restaurants. Several are world-famed for their cuisine and their prices reflect that fact. If your budget doesn't stretch to dinner, try lunch—at one of those places that serves lunch—same chef, same dishes, lower prices. Also notice that in some spots you can go early and get a full set dinner for the price that one entree might cost on the à la carte menu served later. Not listed here, by the way, but certainly among the best in the luxury category are the **Squire Room** at the Fairmont, and **Ristorante Donatello** at the Donatello (formerly the Pacific Plaza).

FRENCH AND CONTINENTAL: At 648 Bush St., between Powell and Stockton, **Masa's** (tel. 989-7154) is open for dinner only, Tuesday through Saturday from 6 to 9 p.m. (last seating). Masa's was started by Masaraha Kobayashi, who left New York City for the Auberge du Soleil in the Napa Valley, and ultimately opened Masa's in San Francisco. After his death in 1984, there was some question about the restaurant's survival. There is none now. The cuisine has been polished to a brilliance surpassing even the talents of Masa by chef Julian Serrano. Masa's is now regarded as one of the country's great French restaurants.

As you enter Masa's, note its elegant simplicity. The chairs and carpeting are a quiet plum, the walls buff, and small chandeliers sparkle at useful and attractive intervals. You expect this to be the setting for great performances to come.

The prix-fixe dinner at $70 is a memorable experience from the first to the final taste. Generally you choose from four appetizers, five entrees, and three or four desserts. The menu changes daily. You might begin the evening with the fresh foie gras sautéed and beatified with a sauce created from the pan juices, cognac, and black truffles. The entree of medallions of venison, marinated for several days in zinfandel, sautéed, and served with a superb rich brown sauce, is a glory and unlike any other you've ever tasted. Should any one of several game birds be available as entrees, take advantage of the occasion to order it. I don't know how to extoll the beauties of a salade mélange au fromage other than to say don't pass it by. The dessert, whether sorbet, frozen soufflé, or a special combination of sorbets and mousse, will be among the best endings to any meal you've ever had. As you might expect, Masa's selective wine list includes some excellent older French wines as well as an impressive group of California wines. You'll also be pleased to discover that the quality of the service happily matches that of the dinner.

Reservations are taken up to 21 days in advance. Although it may be an inconvenience to call or write ahead, I recommend that you do—it's well worth the time and money.

Ernie's, 847 Montgomery St., at Pacific Avenue (tel. 397-5969). Dinner is served from 6:30 to 10:30 p.m. daily.

Two blocks from Broadway, Ernie's is an experience in elegance and exquisite French cuisine. The "Bonanza Era" décor is rich, and the suave service comes close to being an art. The dining areas are pleasantly intimate and plush, with satin-covered walls, gilt-framed mirrors, crystal wall sconces, and mahogany-beamed ceilings. An elaborate Victorian foyer supplements the dining area, along with a cocktail lounge containing a massive mahogany and stained-glass bar—an authentic relic of the Barbary Coast. Many of the handsome furnishings at Ernie's were salvaged from early San Francisco's splendid mansions.

The luxe décor is matched by the award-winning five-star quality of the cuisine. The menu is all á la carte and every dish is an Ernie's specialty. I'd suggest a dinner starting with caviar of eggplant, followed by scallops ragoût in cilantro fumet, and then roasted squab and braised cabbage, with raspberry flan for dessert. If your taste is for fish, the turbot filets sautéed and presented with spinach lasagne are touched with brilliance. Or one of Ernie's truly exceptional creations is saddle of lamb en croûte (as with beef Wellington) with a green-mustard and honey sauce. Entrees average $22 to $45.

When you go, try to do it at someone else's expense (a practice carefully adhered to by all city corporation people). By the time you've ordered your soup, salad, main course, vegetables, dessert, and at least one of Ernie's vintage wines, you'll be lucky to get away for $150 for two. My only comment is—it's worth it. Reservations required, as are coats and ties for men.

Fleur de Lys, 777 Sutter St., between Taylor and Jones (tel. 673-7779). Open for dinner from 6 to 10 p.m. daily except Sunday.

This downtown restaurant is a visual and gastronomic delight. The Fleur de Lys is one of the city's most romantic dining spots; the lovely interior was designed by the late Michael Taylor, who created a feeling of an immense garden tent set in the French countryside. The deep-red fabric, locally hand-printed with an autumnal design, creates a rustic mood enhanced by strategically placed floor-to-ceiling mirrors.

One of the many joys of the Fleur de Lys is that co-owner and host Maurice Rouas has kept a watchful eye on service since 1970, assuring its continuing excellence for each guest. His new partner and executive chef, Hubert Keller, is a master of his trade, having served under such great French chefs as Roger Verge, Paul Haeberlin, and Paul Bocuse.

As for the fare, it's Provençal, with beautifully chosen appetizers such as a composition of American foie gras, sea scallop mousseline, and thinly sliced salmon; entrees (prices average $22 to $35) such as medallions of veal on a tomato and coriander coulis, green-onion compote and pasta crêpes; and perhaps a fresh berry sabayon soufflé for dessert. Besides the impressive à la carte menu, a four-and five-course tasting menu is offered ($47 and $52 respectively). The dishes are representative of what is freshest in the market and therefore change daily.

Even the coffee at Fleur de Lys is special; rather than the usual mass-produced brew, you are presented with your own pot of *café filtre* (regular or decaffeinated). To complement your meal there's an extensive wine list. Reservations are required. Fleur de Lys gets my highest recommendation.

L'Étoile, 1075 California St., between Mason and Taylor (tel. 771-1529). Open from 6 to 11 p.m. daily except Sunday.

Located in the posh Huntington Hotel, L'Étoile offers a romantic setting, with pink-clothed candlelit tables, lots of flower arrangements, copper-colored leather booths and banquettes, crystal chandeliers, oil paintings on the walls, and potted ferns on marble pedestals. As you dine in these elegant social-set surroundings, pianist Peter Mintun entertains with music from the '20s and '30s.

L'Étoile boasts not only a magnificent ambience but also a quality of cuisine that has motivated Julia Child, among others, to convey rapturous compliments to chef Claude Bougard. The dinner menu features entrees such as breast of duckling with pear, blueberries, and orange sauce, or Dover sole in Pinot Noir sauce, in the $27 to $35 range. For dessert you might choose one of the pâtisseries du chef. Reservations are required, as are jacket and tie.

EXPENSIVE TO HIGH MODERATE CHOICES

Falling into an indeterminate category somewhere between the luxury listings above and the moderately priced listings to follow, restaurants in this category tend to offer a variety of price options— perhaps inexpensive full dinners but pricey à la carte listings, or a wide range of entree prices. All offer good value for the money and are worth the extra cost; some are definitely moderate in price if you order carefully. They are listed alphabetically by nationality, as are all price categories that follow.

AMERICAN: Jack's, 615 Sacramento St., at Montgomery (tel. 986-9854). Open from 11:30 a.m. to 9:30 p.m. Monday through Friday, 5 to 9:30 p.m. on Saturday and Sunday.

This venerated San Francisco institution was founded in 1864 (when Lincoln was president) and proudly displays its "One Hundred Year Club" certificate awarded by the state. It has been run by the Redinger family (currently Jack Redinger, though the restaurant was not named for him) since 1902. Located deep in the financial district, it has a fanatically faithful following among the financial wizards.

The wooden Thonet chairs, the unpretentious gold-embossed walls adorned with brass coathooks, the old tile floors, and the dignified waiters all look as they might have a century ago. Jack's specializes in rex sole, calves' head, and fowl dishes, but entrees run the gamut from cheese blintzes to roast turkey with dressing and cranberry sauce to a rack of spring lamb with potatoes boulangère. Prices range from $8 to $20. Desserts also cater to a wide variety of moods —anything from apple pie à la mode to zabaglione. Complete dinners, served from 5 to 9 p.m. only, cost $18.50. Jack's accepts American Express. Reservations are advised, and jackets and ties are required for men.

CALIFORNIAN: Post Street Bar and Café, 632 Post St., next to the Andrews Hotel (tel. 928-2080). Open for lunch Monday through Friday from 11:30 a.m. to 2:30 p.m., and for dinner Tuesday through Saturday from 6 to 10 p.m.

This charming little restaurant is outstanding among a growing number in California beginning to take full advantage of the tremendous quality and variety of foodstuffs grown or raised in the state. The basic philosophy is to serve the best and the freshest ingredients available, in a style that is truly American, and chef Renée Gianettoni at the Post Street Café does it admirably.

Entering the café from the street, you'll pass a grand and quite handsome mahogany bar that leads into the main dining area. High ceilings and arched windows of hand-poured glass give the room a light, open, and airy feeling. In season, the brick fireplace contributes a cheery touch of warmth. White tablecloths, fresh flowers, and feathery ficus trees add charm and style. And completing the ambience is the jazz played softly in the background.

The Post Street Café's menu is seasonal, but at any time of the year you can expect delectable appetizers. The café also has daily pasta and fresh fish specials. Linguine with pancetta and squash and the sea bass with basil should not be ignored. Meat eaters will relish the home-cured pork loin medallions with hash-brown sweet potatoes, or the café's boneless chicken breast marinated with rosemary and served with pan gravy.

To accompany your meal, the café has a nice selection of California wines, several of which you can enjoy by the glass. Despite its relative low price, a fine choice is the Spencer California Chardonnay, one of the boutique wineries featured by the café. Be sure to save room for a grand finale, if you can; desserts are prepared specially every day. Dinner entrees average $15; an appetizer will add another $4 to $6.

The lunch menu at the Post Street Café offers a number of delicious and surprising combinations: for example, chicken salad with toasted pecans and pepper-cured bacon, or thinly sliced leg-of-lamb sandwich with sweet red onions and horseradish mayonnaise. For the more conservative there's a grilled rib-eye steak open-face sandwich with horseradish butter and grilled onions. Pasta and fresh fish are also available. Luncheon entrees range from $5.50 to $10.

Eating at the Post Street Café is an enjoyable experience you won't want to miss. Be sure to make reservations.

CHINESE: Harbor Village, 4 Embarcadero Center, on the center lobby (tel. 781-8833). Open daily: weekdays from 11 a.m. to 2:30 p.m. and 5:30 to 10 p.m., on Saturday and Sunday from 10:30 a.m.

The Harbor Village was opened in 1985 to introduce Imperial cuisine—the famous classical Cantonese cuisine of Hong Kong—to this country. It differs from most Chinese food served in American restaurants in its complexity and subtlety. Harbor Village has five chefs, each with a specialty, all of whom came from Hong Kong establishments. Executive chef Hui Pui Wing brings world-class stature to the cuisine. While most of the dishes are from the Canton region, spicy Szechuan items and "northern" specialties such as crackling Peking duck are part of the restaurant's repertoire.

Harbor Village is impressive: its atmosphere and décor represent a successful merger of nouveau California and Chinese influences. The look of the restaurant reflects the belief that only the best will do: crystal chandeliers, place settings of the finest Chinese porcelain, delicate gleaming glassware, engraved chopsticks. Four opulent private dining rooms with Chinese antiquities and teak furnishings serve 9- to 15-course miniature Imperial feasts, and one outdoor area can accommodate parties of 15 to 200.

The "only the best will do" philosophy applies also to the quality and freshness of the ingredients the Harbor Village uses in preparation of its dishes. Near the kitchen entrance are two large fish tanks filled with what may be your fresh dinner swimming about.

Lunch is an excellent dim sum affair, with an average cost of about $2.20 per dish. The extensive dinner menu offers a remarkable selection of appetizers, from pot stickers through a collection of elegant choices such as shredded spicy chicken, minced squab in lettuce cups, or roast duck. Soups, too, are unusual and exceptional— for example, the julienne duck with fish maw, Empress seafood, mushroom with eggflower soup, or the shark's fin in suprême broth. There are some 30 seafood dishes, including four featuring braised abalone—at least one to please most any palate.

A number of the entrees have a very delicate flavor, while others are more strongly seasoned—say, the fresh prawns stir-fried in garlic and butter, or the sizzling beef in black-bean sauce with vegetables. A very courteous professional staff can guide you through the menu or recommend dishes that do not appear there.

Dinner entrees average $7 to $14, with some obvious exceptions: abalone dishes are $22 to $24; crackling Peking duck, $26; shark's fin soup, $18. Prices vary for seasonal specialties such as the Dungeness crab or lobster. Appetizers will add another $7 to $12; soups, apart from the exceptional, are $6 to $10. Dinner for two can range from $30 to $85, without wine. The Harbor Village does have a respectable wine list, and the house chardonnay is quite good at $12 the bottle.

Harbor Village has free validated parking at 3 and 4 Embarcadero Center garages, at the foot of Clay Street, after 5 p.m. on weekdays and all day on weekends and holidays.

The Mandarin, 900 North Point, in Ghirardelli Square (tel. 673-8812). Open from noon to 11:30 p.m. daily.

STALKING SAM SPADE. For Dashiell Hammett and/or Sam Spade fans, **John's Grill**, 63 Ellis St., between Stockton and Powell (tel. 986-DASH), should be at the top of the "don't miss" list. Open Monday through Saturday (lunch is served from 11 a.m. to 4 p.m.; dinner, from 4 to 10 p.m.), the restaurant has been around since 1908; in the 1920s it was one of Hammett's hangouts. It's even one of the San Francisco landmarks Hammett used to make *The Maltese Falcon* come to life. (Before setting out on a wild goose chase after the mysterious Brigid O'Shaughnessy, Sam Spade stops by John's Grill for a dinner of chops, baked potato, and sliced tomatoes.)

The restaurant works hard to preserve the Hammett/Spade legend. The main dining room and bar on the ground floor are decorated in wood and leather, with glass chandeliers and white-clothed tables. It looks like it must have in Hammett's day. On the two upper floors are the Dashiell Hammett and Maltese Falcon rooms, used for spillover dining and banquets. John's Grill is headquarters for the Dashiell Hammett Society of San Francisco, which was founded in 1977 by William F. Nolan, who wrote a biographical study of Hammett, and Jack Kaplan, director of Pinkerton's. (Hammett was a Pinkerton detective during his early days in San Francisco.) Even a coincidence has added an extra touch: the restaurant is owned by Gus Konstantinides; Charilaos Konstantinides is named in *The Maltese Falcon* as a Greek dealer who found the bird "in an obscure shop in Paris."

You can begin your experience at John's Grill with a Bloody Brigid—named after Spade's Miss O'Shaughnessy—consisting of sweet-and-sour vodka, soda, fresh pineapple, lime, grenadine, and other ingredients. It comes in a souvenir glass, which you can take home with you. (Souvenir glasses, copies of the art deco menu cover, Maltese Falcon ties, and a Dash Hammett mural are also available for purchase.) For dinner, there's "Sam Spade's Chops," a re-creation of the detective's *Maltese Falcon* meal. You can also partake of several entrees recommended by *Gourmet* magazine: chicken à la Girard or chicken Jerusalem, with fresh artichokes and mushrooms and marsala or white wine; oysters Wellington; and filet of sole stuffed with crab and shrimp, baked in lemon-and-butter sauce. And then there's Jack LaLanne's favorite salad of crab, shrimp, avocado, mushrooms, chopped egg, tomato, and a special dressing for $14. Dinner entrees are mostly in the $12 to $20 range. At lunch many of the same dishes are available for $9 to $18. There are also salads, omelets, and sandwiches for $7 to $14.

Located in the Woolen Building on the western edge of the square facing onto North Point, the Mandarin offers excellent Peking-style cookery.

Madame Cecilia Chiang, who opened the restaurant in 1968, has attempted to re-create the remembered atmosphere of dining in a cultured northern China home, with Mandarin furnishings, silk-covered walls, and beamed twig ceilings. As you get off the elevator on the third floor, the ancient Chinese tapestry facing you sets the mood for the evening. Softly lit dining rooms, one of which offers matchless views of the bay and Ghirardelli Square, subtly blend the best of Chinese and San Francisco design. Rose brick walls frame priceless works of Chinese art. Natural-wood pillars and beams give the feeling of a home in the Forbidden City. Tables are set well apart to provide the luxury of conversational privacy.

Dinner for two could start with sizzling rice soup, a chicken broth with shrimp, mushrooms, and golden fried rice that actually sizzles as it goes into the bowl. For entrees you might share orders of walnut chicken, minced squab, tangerine beef, Szechuan string beans, or smoked tea duck, all for an average of $20 to $30. Or you could order a complete dinner that includes from three to ten dishes plus dessert for $25 to $40 per person. At lunch you can order a Mandarin chicken salad or sautéed shrimp with peas, complete with soup, rice, and tea for under $20. Reservations recommended for what may be the best Chinese restaurant in San Francisco.

FRENCH: Le Central, 453 Bush St., between Kearny Street and Grant Avenue (tel. 391-2233). Open from 11:30 a.m. to 3 p.m. and 5:30 to 10:30 p.m. Monday through Friday, on Saturday from 6 to 10:30 p.m.; closed Sunday.

Le Central is San Francisco's version of a classic Parisian bistro, with a truly elegant bar for waiting. Two long narrow rooms are lined with tables and mirrors, and ordering is done from chalked or printed menus; a sign announces that the cassoulet has been simmering on the stove since opening. It's a place to see and be seen, so go early or late to avoid long waits for a table. There is good roast chicken, and the pommes frites are excellent, as are the rack of lamb and steak béarnaise pommes frites for $11 to $17. The food is simple but very good. I suggest reservations.

If you can't get into this very popular restaurant, try **Le Candide,** 301 Kearny St., at Bush (tel. 981-2213). It's under the same ownership and has a similar menu. Its clientele includes the financial and advertising wizards of the town.

INDIAN: Gaylord's, Ghirardelli Square (tel. 771-8822). Open daily for lunch from noon to 2:30 p.m. and for dinner from 5 to 10:45 p.m.

With the notable exception of the excellent Gitanjali in Los Angeles, California is almost entirely bereft of decent Indian restaurants, which makes Gaylord's all the more special a treat. With branches in London, New York, Chicago, Palo Alto, Beverly Hills, and New Delhi, this far-flung chain has been offering the very best of North Indian haute cuisine to Bay Area residents since 1976.

Gaylord's has chosen a stunning setting in which to introduce Indian fare to the West Coast. A warm, candlelit interior is enhanced by superb bay views from almost every seat. Ragas played in the background complete the tranquil mood.

Although my favorite meal here is the chicken tikka masala accompanied by a side order of saffron-flavored rice with vegetables and nuts, the most sensible plan is to order a full dinner. Three of these "royal feasts" are offered, priced at $22 to $28 for everything from an immense vegetarian meal to the Maharaja, which gives you a choice of soup, tandoori chicken, two varieties of lamb kebab, chicken tikka, lamb in cream sauce with nuts, Indian bread, saffron rice with vegetables and nuts, Indian cheese with green peas, choice of dessert, and tea or coffee. At lunch Gaylord's offers complete meals only, priced from $14 to $18. Reservations are a good idea.

There's also a Gaylord's at One Embarcadero Center (tel. 397-7775).

ITALIAN: Kuleto's, 221 Powell St., at Geary (tel. 397-7720). Open daily from 7 a.m. to 10:30 a.m. for breakfast, from 11:30 a.m. to 11 p.m. for lunch and dinner. The same northern Italian menu with Tuscan specialties is offered for lunch and dinner.

Enter through the bar on Powell Street to get the full impact of this delightful and relaxing place: the years-gone-by high ceilings, black-and-white-marble tile floors, strings of dried peppers and garlic hanging over a magnificent long mahogany bar. Kuleto's has the familiar, friendly air of a restaurant you've known for years: small circular tables with tall bar chairs, dark-wood booths with gray-green cushions, a huge open kitchen with black hood and copper trim housing a group of hard-working chefs—all compose a homey picture.

Reviewing the menu from the top, the antipasti are sufficiently varied to satisfy most every taste, from the roasted garlic or the grilled prawns with sweet peppers to the calamari fritti or the steamed mussels. For the traditionalists, there's always the antipasto platter. As for the second course, there's nothing commonplace about the soup or such salads as the salad Caprice, with whole-milk mozzarella, tomato, basil, and extra-virgin olive oil.

Every entree I ordered was excellent, from the least expensive pasta dish on up the list. You can't go wrong with the risotto

Zafferano, with saffron risotto, prawns, scallops, and sun-dried to-matoes. The selection of fresh fish, grilled over hardwoods, changes daily. If you have a yen for chicken, consider the spit-roasted half chicken, lightly smoked and served with roasted garlic sauce, or the breast of chicken stuffed with ricotta and herbs, served with a roasted pepper-butter sauce. If veal is your fancy, the veal piccata consists of medallions served with lemon, capers, and artichokes. For beef eaters, there's a New York steak grilled with tarragon-shallot butter, or the Panini grilled sirloin sandwich with mozzarel-la, tomato, onion, and peppers. On this deliciously diverse menu, entree prices range from $7.50 for tasty capellini pomodoro to $16.50 for a grilled loin chop of veal with sautéed spinach. Desserts, from the peach tart to the chocolate gelato, are just as unforgettable as the rest of your meal.

The wine list does justice to this fine restaurant, ranging from a choice selection of California and imported wines to some fine champagnes. Kuleto's also offers a dozen first-quality beers, domestic and imported.

It's wise to make reservations for lunch or dinner at this deservedly popular place.

Corintia Ristorante, in the Ramada Renaissance Hotel, 55 Cyril Magnin St., at Market and North 5th (tel. 392-8000). Dinner is served nightly from 6 to 11:30 p.m.

One of San Francisco's finest restaurants, Corintia offers northern Italian cuisine prepared for the most discriminating palate. Changes have been made to lighten the interior of the Corintia, but the restaurant still maintains its magnificent deep- (almost midnight) blue setting with brass pedestals of light, handsome etched-glass panels and mirrors overhead, which give the room an aura of sumptuous elegance. Attentive and knowledgeable waiters in sparkling-white bistro aprons serve you to background music ranging from Sinatra to Pavarotti.

The Corintia menu features a delectable choice of distinctive entrees. You might begin with one of the excellent antipasti such as the baked brie and roasted garlic bulb, or the zucchini stuffed with prawns. Or go directly to one of several salad selections—say, the insalata Ilsa with arugula, spinach, and butter lettuce and wild mushrooms. Then on to the entrees: among the pasta dishes is a superb veal and wild-mushroom cannelloni in cream, parmigiano. If you yearn for beef, the Corintia has created exceptional tournedos of beef tenderloin with a sweet roasted garlic sauce. But don't overlook the sautéed veal filet with fresh tarragon sauce, or the baked jumbo prawns with shallots. Fresh fish is also available each day, and the specialty changes with market availability.

Some marvelous extra touches make dining at the Corintia

very pleasurable. Fresh-baked breads and grissini are presented with virgin olive oil and individual cheese graters. A well-stocked wine cart is brought to each table with a large selection of wines by the glass, and you're given complimentary samples to help you make your choice. The wine list features only Italian wines (ah, but what wines!) that have been carefully selected from the principal regions to complement the menu. For those who prefer California selections or wines from other European regions, the full hotel list is also available.

To conclude your evening, the cordial cart presents a full selection of Italian liqueurs and grappas, as well as the traditional cognacs. For those who prefer more solid finales, look for the pastry cart—you're sure to want one of everything. The dessert selection from the menu includes one of my favorites, the chocolate cassata Siciliana with ricotta and fruits.

Entrees range from $12 to $17. Most wines are reasonably priced below $20 the bottle. Reservations are necessary.

Caffè Sport, 574 Green St., between Grant and Columbus (tel. 981-1251). Open Tuesday through Saturday for lunch from noon to 2 p.m., and for dinner from 6:30 to 10:30 p.m.

This robust Sicilian eatery overflows with a clutter of hanging hams, sausages, fishnet, decorative plates, dolls, mirrors, peppers—you name it. The tables, chairs, and whatever else can be so treated are painted and collaged. It's all the creation of owner/chef/artiste Antonio Latona, who dispenses joviality or surliness depending on his mood, along with garlic-laden pasta dishes to an enthusiastic clientele (they're practically a cult), including the likes of former Mayor Diane Feinstein.

It's a good idea to come at lunch when things are a bit less hectic than in the evening. It's also cheaper. You might, for example, order pasta with meat and mushrooms for just $7. At dinner the Sport is mobbed and lively—a scene of Breughel-like revelry—and entrees are considerably pricier. There's a menu (*one*, that is) presented at each table in a frame. You're welcome to peruse it. But chances are that your waiter will override your choices and make "suggestions" of his own. Go along with him; whatever you get—a dish of calamari, mussels, and shrimp in tomato garlic sauce, or a pasta in pesto sauce—will be delicious. Entrees range from $13 to $29. Crusty Italian bread and butter come with all entrees. The Caffè Sport is an experience not to be missed, and the wait to get in (reservations for parties of four or more only) is worth it. Bring a huge appetite, but above all don't be late if you have a reservation.

Prego, 2000 Union St., at Buchanan (tel. 563-3305). Open daily from 11:30 a.m. to midnight.

A light and airy trattoria, Prego is pretty and pleasant with a veritable garden of seasonal flowers in the windows. Crisp, crusty pizza emerges from oak-fired brick ovens, and a variety of antipasti ($5 to $10) as well as marvelous pastas ($10 to $14) are available with a good selection of wines to accompany them. Desserts have always been my downfall, and the semifreddo al caffè—white-chocolate ice cream, espresso, and whipped cream—made me decide to eat now, diet later. Reservations are available at lunch, but be prepared to wait during evening hours, as this very popular eatery takes dinner reservations for parties of six or more only.

JAPANESE: Ichirin, 330 Mason St., adjacent to the King George Hotel near Geary (tel. 956-6085). Open daily from 7 to 10 a.m., 11:30 a.m. to 2 p.m., and 5 to 10 p.m. There is a cocktail lounge on the premises.

The advantages of dining at Ichirin ("single flower") are three-fold. First, it has a great location for the start of a night on the town —just around the corner from the Curran Theater and ACT at the Geary Theater, and strategically situated across from a large garage with all-night parking. Second, Ichirin has a menu with enough variety to please almost anyone. Third, the food and service are first-rate.

The simplicity of the main dining room, decorated in subtle green, mauve, and beige with relatively plain tables and booths, sets off the beautiful and colorful kimonos worn by the Japanese women who serve and prepare food at the table. Should the size of your party warrant it, or if you simply enjoy the privacy they afford, tatami rooms are available. And on each floor of the restaurant you can watch sushi chefs preparing delights.

Ichirin has some 28 special appetizers, ranging from such standards as pot stickers (gyoza) and deep-fried chicken wings (teba kara-age) to the exotic. Three excellent choices are the deep-fried eggplant served with a special teriyaki-type sauce (nasu shigi age), the fish cakes with Japanese horseradish (itawasa), and the marinated broiled beef wrapped with green onion (beef asatsuki maki).

The sushi bar offers various assortments, combination rolls, and chirashi—the chef's choice of fresh filets of fish served over sushi rice with seaweed. There's also a "beginners' sushi plate" for those who have never tried sushi before: the shrimp, egg cake, barbecued eel, and two pieces of futomaki roll will be certain to make sushi converts.

Then there are the delicious nabe dishes, cooked at the table for two or more: shabu shabu, thinly sliced beef, vegetables, and tofu, cooked in a tasty broth and served with two special sauces; a marvelous ishikari nabe with salmon and vegetables cooked in a soy-bean-based broth; and chanko nabe, with fresh seafood, tender chicken, and crisp vegetables in broth (said to be the most popular nabe among the Sumo wrestlers—and you know how large they grow to be). Other entrees include tempuras, teriyaki dishes, a Japanese-style beefsteak dinner, broiled lobster, and a multitude of udon (flour) and soba (buckwheat) noodle dishes. The adventurous can feast on the Ichirin Omakase dinner—for $35 per person, the chef selects a full-course dinner, from appetizer to dessert, in traditional Japanese fashion.

If you have the kiddies in tow, Ichirin serves a complete luncheon plate for them including broiled and deep-fried items, vegetables, plus fruit for dessert.

Dinner appetizers cost $2.50 to $8, though most are in the $4 range. Entrees are $10 to $14, and the ichirin dinner box with the chef's choices of the day is $19. At lunch, donburi dishes (served over a bowl of rice) are $6 to $10, and bento (combination lunch box) range from $7 to $14. Dinner plates for the kids are $6; lunch plates, $5.50.

MEXICAN: Corona Bar & Grill, 88 Cyril Magnin St., at the corner of Ellis (tel. 392-5500). Open daily for lunch and dinner from 11:30 a.m. to midnight; reservations suggested.

I didn't expect to find a really great Mexican restaurant as far north as San Francisco, but there it was, all new and shiny as of November 1987. Entrepreneur Bill Kimpton brought together the restaurant-designing talents of Pat Kuleto, the creative California-Mexican cuisine of chef Robert Helstrom, and the management skills of Sarah Graves. The light peach, delicate rose, and blue-green of the beautiful Corona Bar and Grill create the aura of a sunset over the Pacific.

The Corona is situated directly on the corner of Ellis and Cyril Magnin, with lots of windows for people-watching. Handcrafted Mexican masks, some as old as 100 years, and a large mural of a coastal sunset help make this a warm, comfortable place to relax and enjoy the superb margaritas and creative food. Part of the Corona's stunning effect lies in the way it incorporates the basic beauty of food and its preparation into the décor. A 90-foot-long cherrywood bar with an open cooking line stretches across much of the restaurant's length. At the end of the open kitchen, in a continuing state of creative activity, a large glass-front fridge contains an attractive display of oysters and clams on ice.

A variety of appetizers are available from the bar, and then a regular menu is divided into Starters, about appetizer size; Small Plates, for those with medium-size appetites or those who would like to try several dishes; and Large Plates, of entree size. My first order was a "Fresh Oyster Shooter," with peppered Cuervo 1800 from the bar appetizers: it came in a small, attractive square glass (about jigger size) with the sauce of Cuervo on top, and turned out to be a tantalizing introduction for the good things to come. Among the Starter highlights are the quesadilla with shiitake mushrooms and roquefort, once-fried oysters, twice-fried beans, and steamed clams with cilantro and lime. Some of the Small Plate treats are the black-bean cake and grilled prawns, the duck tamale with cilantro pesto and red-pepper butter (absolutely delicious), and the shrimp relleno with a mosaic of sweet peppers. As for the Large Plates, the exceptional choices include a superb roasted duck with tamarind glaze and shoestring yams, a fresh green-corn tamale with chicken breast or sirloin and black beans, and roast rack of lamb with a piñon-nut crust and light mole sauce. The food presentation is itself a work of art, and the servers are knowledgeable, friendly, and well-turned-out in white shirts, string ties, and black trousers.

The bar appetizer menu ranges from $1.75 for my "Fresh Oyster Shooter" to $8.50 for a grilled chicken salad; Starters are $4 to $7.75; Small Plates, $5.50 to $8.50; and Large Plates, $9 to $14.50, the top price being for a thin-pounded filet marinated with chiles, scallions, and black beans.

There is a good selection of domestic wines by the bottle and premium wines by the glass, as well as eight varieties of cerveza Mexicana, some gringo beers, magnificent margaritas, and even agua—Calistoga and Penafiel.

MOROCCAN: Marrakech, 419 O'Farrell St., between Taylor and Jones (tel. 776-6717). Open for dinner nightly, except Sunday, from 6 p.m. to 10 p.m.

As far as I'm concerned, dining at Marrakech is as much an essential to a San Francisco visit as riding the cable cars or visiting Fisherman's Wharf. It's worth the trip alone.

The exotic atmosphere envelops you as you enter the restaurant, which is decked out with Moroccan archways, colorful tilework, and a splashing fountain. There are several small dining areas, richly carpeted with Berber and Rabat rugs, and furnished with goatskin ottomans, low sofas strewn with silk and velvet pillows, and carved brass tables. Light filters through cut-brass lamps, reflecting on the intricately hand-painted and gold-leafed ceiling. The scene is completed with straw breadbaskets from Fez lying about.

The meal is a multicourse feast, served by waiters in traditional costume. It begins when a tea server washes your hands and gives you a large towel to use as a napkin. You'll need it. The entire meal is eaten with your hands and hunks of bread (no silverware allowed), everyone in your party partaking from the same dinner. All meals begin with soup followed by a piquant Moroccan salad scooped up with hunks of fresh bread. Keep in mind that many more courses are coming; it's easy to fill up on the first delectable ones. So linger over your food and enjoy the belly dancer, who moves from room to room performing sensuous dances of the Middle East. Next comes pastilla, a pastry of shredded chicken, almonds, and spices, topped with powdered sugar and cinnamon. This is followed by huge platters of delicious entrees, such as chicken and lemons, chicken and olives, lamb and onions, hare in paprika and cinnamon sauce, or—my favorite—lamb with honey and almonds. Next comes couscous with vegetables, which is easily a meal in itself. Fresh fruits and mint tea finish off the feast. The price: under $28 per person.

As you lounge over your tea, the tea server returns to wash your hands and spray you with refreshing rosewater.

This is more than just a meal—you can give over an entire evening to this relaxed and gracious dining experience. Reservations are advised.

NATURAL FOODS: Greens at Fort Mason, in Building A, Fort Mason Center—enter opposite the Safeway at Buchanan and Marina (tel. 771-6222). Open for lunch Tuesday through Saturday from 11:30 a.m. to 2:30 p.m. Dinner is served à la carte Tuesday through Thursday and prix fixe on Friday and Saturday; it's by reservation from 6 to 9:30 p.m. The bakery is open from 9:30 a.m. to 4:30 p.m. Tuesday to Saturday.

Operated by the Tassajara Zen Center, and located in an old warehouse, Greens has enormous windows overlooking the marina and the bay. There is a full-size sculptured redwood burl within, and on the right as you enter is the bakery purveying wonderful homemade breads and pastries. The fare is wholesome and natural, but any thought that this is a simple health-food restaurant is dispelled the minute you see the menu. Dinner is a prix-fixe feast of numerous courses, for about $30 per person. A sample meal: linguine with caramelized onions and walnuts in walnut oil; tomato and white-bean soup; cauliflower timbale in curry sauce with broccoli, carrots, mushrooms, and sun-dried tomatoes; and a salad of spinach, butter lettuce, and radicchio in orange vinaigrette. There's a choice of desserts, which might include lemon mousse, almond and raspberry tart, or chocolate and Grand Marnier custard. An extensive wine list is available.

Lunch, though simpler, is equally interesting, and entrees range from $6 to $10. Offerings include sandwiches, spinach salad, tofu and vegetable brochette, chili and soup, and specials like spinach fettuccine.

For brunch you can order a variety of three-egg omelets, french toast, or zucchini fritters with ancho chili sauce and crème fraîche for $7 to $10. There are also lots of fresh muffins and homemade desserts.

Reservations are recommended two weeks in advance.

MODERATELY PRICED RESTAURANTS

The following restaurants are in the more moderate price range, which most of us prefer when dining out.

AMERICAN/CONTINENTAL: MacArthur Park, 607 Front St., at Jackson (tel. 398-5700). The restaurant schedule seems more like train times. They are open for breakfast Monday through Friday from 7 to 10 a.m. and for Sunday brunch from 10 a.m. to 2 p.m.; for lunch Monday through Friday from 11:30 a.m. to 2:30 p.m.; for dinner Sunday through Thursday from 5 to 10:30 p.m., on Friday and Saturday to 11 p.m.

This is a good spot for dinner after the theater, or lunch after a morning of exploring Jackson Square.

MacArthur Park is in an atmospheric old brick building facing Sydney G. Walton Square. On a pleasant day, the glass doors that front the restaurant are opened, giving the feel of an outdoor café.

Inside, the restaurant again captures the outdoors in a garden enclosed by brick walls hung with framed *Paris Review* posters. The ceiling's skylights shed a soft daylight glow on the large, airy room green with hanging ferns and growing trees. The entire effect is chic and charming.

MacArthur Park prides itself on serving great American food. You can verify how exceptional a club sandwich or Cobb salad can be at lunchtime—order either one and you'll munch on chicken and bacon, smoked to perfection by the restaurant itself. Lunch will cost $7 to $12. At any time there are great baby back ribs and at least six kinds of mesquite-broiled fresh fish available. Dinner entrees will cost about $12 to $24. Dinner items can also be ordered at lunch. For dessert, Judy's mud pie—a rich blend of coffee and chocolate ice creams in a chocolate-cookie crust, smothered with hot-fudge sauce—is as luscious as it sounds. Or you can ask for baked-to-order chocolate-chip cookies, served warm from the oven. A very impressive wine list features many California wines available by the glass. Reservations are essential at this deservedly popular restaurant.

Hard Rock Café, 1699 Van Ness, at Sacramento (tel. 885-1699). Open weekdays and Sunday from 11:30 a.m. to midnight, on Friday and Saturday to 1 a.m. Like its fellow establishments in Los Angeles, New York City, Chicago, Houston, London, Stockholm, and Frankfurt, the Hard Rock Café attracts crowds of young people, especially at night. If standing in line is not your bag, go to the Hard Rock Café for lunch instead. But regardless of your age or the time of day, it's a fun, interesting, and noisy place filled with memorabilia of the '50s and '60s.

A former auto showroom, the café is decorated with a candy-apple Caddy hanging from the ceiling; gold records; front pages headlining the deaths of John Kennedy, Elvis Presley, and John Lennon; Elvis's cape in a frame; plus photos of Presley, Beatles memorabilia, a cow at the door (not live), and "Save the Planet" and "All Is One" signs. It's rather like a convention center with ceiling fans. The hub of activities is an oversize oblong oak bar. Surprisingly, the decibel level of the background music at midday doesn't inhibit conversation or eating, but it's period rock 'n roll.

If food is one of your objectives, there are booths, tables, and a counter with lots of elbow room to partake of the reasonably good and moderately priced fare. At the high end of the menu is steak for $13 and baby back ribs for $11. Then you go down to grilled burg-

---

HOTTEST IN THE WEST. At 853 Kearny St., off Columbus, **Hunan Restaurant** (tel. 788-2234) is open daily from 11:30 a.m. to 9:30 p.m.

It's not much to look at even by Chinese-restaurant standards —an insignificant-looking place, in fact—but even Craig Claiborne of the *New York Times* and Tony Hiss of *The New Yorker* magazine have sung its praises in print. Claiborne called it the "hottest Hunan restaurant" in the West, and he's undoubtedly right. It's paradise for Hunan cuisine lovers—and free of MSG. Both the onion cakes and dumplings (often called pot stickers) are *de rigueur* as appetizers; the hot-and-sour soup is good too. If you want something cold, try the bean-sprout salad, made with cucumbers and a special spicy dressing. There are a number of hot-and-spicy entrees on the menu, like hot-and-sour beef or chicken, and chef Henry Chung's special chicken, shrimps, and scallops with hot black-bean sauce (Henry's Special). Smoked specialties can be made spicy-hot or not; there are also vegetable dishes like bean curd (tofu) with pickled vegetables, and a selection of dishes that are touted as "spicy but not hot," like diced boneless chicken with fresh garlic sauce and sliced beef with green onions. Entrees cost $6 to $10.

The lunch menu is much more limited and even less expensive; most items cost under $6.

There's a second, larger, and fancier Hunan Restaurant at 924 Sansome St., near Broadway (tel. 956-7727). It's open daily from 11:30 a.m. to 9:30 p.m.

ers for $5 or a bowl of homemade chili for $4.50. Salads and sandwiches include the usual assortment, and liquid refreshments are soft or hard, as you wish. Desserts range from homemade apple pie and strawberry shortcake to thick shakes or your choice of floats from $2.50 to $3.25.

The **Stagecoach Restaurant,** 44 Montgomery St., at Sutter (tel. 956-4650). Open Monday through Friday from 11 a.m. to 8 p.m. for meals; the bar serves till 11 p.m.

Aptly located in the Wells Fargo Building, its décor evocative of Fargo's 19th-century heyday, the Stagecoach is richly appointed, comfortable, and prosperous-looking. Seating is in plush tufted-leather booths and banquettes, complemented by white linen tablecloths. Candles, lamps, wall sconces, and wrought-iron chandeliers provide a soft amber light. The walls are adorned with stained-glass panels, framed mirrors, and oil paintings, the most notable of which is the original nude, *Stella,* from the 1893 World's Fair in Chicago.

The menu offers a wide variety of choices, from light foods like sandwiches, salads, and omelets (for $5 to $10) to pastas, fish dishes like scallops or prawns sautéed with white wine and mushrooms, to filet mignon or New York steak (for $11 to $24). Reservations are essential at lunch when affluent business people arrive in droves.

BASQUE: Des Alpes, 732 Broadway, between Stockton and Powell (tel. 391-4249 or 788-9900). Open Tuesday through Saturday from 5:30 to 10 p.m., on Sunday from 5 to 9:30 p.m.

Entered via a bar adorned with jai alai baskets, Des Alpes has a homey Basque décor: brown-and-white-checked plastic cloths and wainscotted cream walls are hung with travel posters and paintings of French, Spanish, Alpine, and Basque countryside; note an early photo of the restaurant, which dates from 1908.

The cuisine is far from "haute"—it offers French family cooking of the kind you might have eaten once in some little "auberge" in the Midi and have been reminiscing about ever since. A single entree is offered each night—perhaps a choice of lamb stew, filet of sole, or roast beef. Your meal includes soup, stringbean salad, potatoes, green salad, coffee, and ice cream. The price: $9 to $12. A bottle of house wine with your dinner is easily affordable.

CHINESE: Pot Sticker, 150 Waverly Pl., just east of Grant Avenue between Clay and Washington (tel. 397-9985). Open seven days a week from 11:30 a.m. to 4 p.m. for lunch, from 4:30 to 9:45 p.m. for dinner.

This restaurant, specializing in northern Chinese cooking, is in the heart of Chinatown. A simple, quiet oasis away from the hustle of the mainstream, it is patronized largely by locals—who know.

The name comes from its specialty: pot stickers. These are pan-fried, thin-skinned dumplings stuffed with seasoned meat or vegetables that are a staple of Mandarin cooking and do just what their name says—stick to the pot they're cooked in. An order of these makes an excellent shared beginning to your meal. From there you might proceed to moo shu pork, Mongolian beef, or General Tsao's chicken—a spicy dish with prawn and red-pepper sauce, all in the $6 to $9 range. In addition, you can order a family dinner, including soup, appetizers, selected entrees, rice, fortune cookies, ice cream, and tea for $8 to $11. Lunch specials with soup, rice, and tea are an even bigger bargain for $6 to $7.

This is a plain restaurant with pleasantly modern décor. The street wall consists of glass doors hung with bamboo curtains, another is plain brick, and the other two are covered in textured gray paper, one with a peaceful Chinese scroll painting. But the waiters are friendly, delighted when you ask them what's in a dish, and never hurry you.

There's another Pot Sticker a bit below Haight-Ashbury at 335 Noe St., near 16th Street (tel. 861-6868). It's open daily from 11:30 a.m. to 10:30 p.m.

Hunan Shaolin on Polk, 1150 Polk St., between Sutter and Post (tel. 771-6888). Open Monday through Saturday from 11:30 a.m. to 10 p.m., on Sunday from 4 to 10 p.m.

Even in San Francisco, you don't have to go to Chinatown to get terrific Chinese food. Smack in the middle of "Polk Gulch," Hunan Shaolin has typical eclectic Chinese-restaurant décor, with pink plastic-covered tablecloths, bentwood chairs, an odd assortment of lighting fixtures, and Oriental art on the walls.

A meal at Hunan Shaolin gets off to a great start with orders of pot stickers (fried dumplings) and onion pancake (thin Chinese crêpes with egg and green onion sandwiched between them, fried to a delicate crispness). The hot-and-sour soup is one of the best in the city. There's a wide variety of entrees; I highly recommend the iron-platter specials (sizzling prawns, for one), and other dishes such as moo shu pork. Most dishes here are spicy, but they can be made milder at your request. Dinner entrees cost $6 to $8. Family dinners are available also: for $8 to $9 per person (and a minimum of two), you get soup, entrees, rice, tea, and cookies.

Lunch specials, offered weekdays from 11:30 a.m. to 2:30 p.m., are a special bargain at about $5, for which you get fruit salad, rice, soup, and a choice of nine entrees. And if you want just an entree for lunch, there's a choice of 20, including oyster-sauce beef with broccoli, shredded pork with brown sauce, and cashew chicken, for about $4.50.

The food at Hunan Shaolin is wonderful, and the service

friendly and efficient. In the evening there's valet parking, a bonus in an area where street spaces are limited. Reservations are accepted only on weekends for large parties.

Brandy Ho's Hunan Food, 217 Columbus, at Pacific (tel. 788-7527). Open daily from 11:30 a.m. to 11 p.m. (on Friday and Saturday till midnight).

This Chinese restaurant sits at the intersection of Italian North Beach, the financial district, and Chinatown. It has little décor to speak of—tables covered with plaid cloths and clear vinyl, a few Chinese lanterns for color. And when Brandy Ho's was originally remodeled, a simple counter was placed in front of an open cooking area so that patrons could watch their dishes being prepared. It's since become a popular area for seating. Who cares about the décor when the food is great? To start, don't miss the fried dumplings with sweet-and-sour sauce. And several uncommon soups are offered in addition to the traditional (and excellent) hot-and-sour: there's a moo shu soup with eggs, pork, vegetables, and tree-ear mushrooms, and fish-ball soup with spinach, bamboo shoots, noodles, and other goodies.

Entrees are varied and tasty. I recommend a dish called "Three Delicacies," a combination of scallops, shrimp, and chicken with onion, bell pepper, and bamboo shoots seasoned with ginger, garlic, and wine and served with black-bean sauce. The moo shu pork is also good. Most dishes here are quite hot and spicy; the kitchen will adjust the level to meet your specifications. Entrees average $8 to $11.

Brandy Ho's has a small selection of wines and beers to accompany your meal, including plum wine and sake. To cool your tongue after your meal, there's also the traditional lichees and ice cream.

Reds, 1475 Polk St., at California (tel. 441-7337). Open daily from 11:30 a.m. to 2 a.m.

For Chinese food in a hi-tech setting, you might try Reds. It's located on the top floor of a futuristic-looking building on the corner of Polk and California Streets. Reds' décor is minimalist and elegant in red, white, and black. The menu is extensive, with over 120 items offered. In addition to appetizers such as crabmeat puff and ginger eggplant, and such soups as bean curd with spinach and Dragon and Phoenix (chicken and shrimp), there are dozens of entrees—seafood, pork, beef, lamb, fowl, and vegetable. You might try the hot-and-sour clams or the steak kew with three kinds of mushrooms. There's even Peking duck. Most entrees cost $9 to $17. To accompany your meal there's a nice variety of wines available. Or you can enjoy one of Reds' exotic cocktails like a Chi Chi (vodka, coconut, and pineapple juice) or a Fogcutter (rum, gin, brandy, and fruit juices).

A lunch you can partake of specials for $7. There are combination platters like eggrolls, almond chicken, and fried rice, and rice plates of chicken with barbecue sauce or green-pepper beef with steamed rice. All special luncheons come with soup.

CZECHOSLOVAKIAN: Vlasta's Czechoslovakian Restaurant, 2420 Lombard St., between Scott and Divisadero (tel. 931-7533). Open Tuesday through Sunday from 5:30 to 11 p.m.

Run by Vlasta and Frank Kucera, and their son, John, this homey establishment is cozy and intimate. Wood-paneled walls are hung with framed oil paintings, tables are covered with starched white linen, a plant-lined divider creates two dining areas, and soft lighting is achieved by chandeliers overhead and wall sconces. The motherly Vlasta presides in the kitchen, and the entire family makes diners feel like welcome guests.

Dinners include soup of the day and salad. The house specialty is herbed roast duck with red cabbage and Bohemian dumplings. Viennese schnitzel is also on the menu, as are chicken paprika, and goulash topped with sour cream and served with dumplings or potatoes. Entrees, which range from $10 to $12.50, change daily; the above were among the choices on my last visit. Try some of Vlasta's homemade apple strudel for dessert. Reservations are essential.

ITALIAN: The North Beach Restaurant, 1512 Stockton St., between Union and Green (tel. 392-1587). Open daily from 11:30 a.m. to 11:45 p.m.

Highest praise goes to chef Bruno Orsi (who's also one of the owners) for the first-rate "cucina Toscana" served at the North Beach. Using only the finest meats and cheeses, the freshest fish and vegetables, homemade pasta, and his own cured prosciutto, Orsi creates great culinary masterpieces. The setting is unpretentious. A variety of paintings line the walls. Tables are covered with white cloths and lit at night by candles in red holders. Plants and strings of garlic are suspended overhead. But the ambience is flamboyantly Italian with much robust conversation going on and lots of charm in the service—especially to attractive women. Dining here is something of an occasion.

You might like to try the home-cured prosciutto with melon as an appetizer. Along with a side order of pasta, a light meal can be made of such an appetizer, or perhaps an antipasto. Of course, you'll want to order one of the wines from this restaurant's excellent cellar. Full dinners, costing $17 to $28, include an enormous antipasto, salad, soup, fresh vegetable, and pasta with prosciutto sauce. You can choose from entrees like cioppino, eggplant parmigiana, or veal scaloppine marsala. À la carte entrees are less expensive ($11 to $21), including a choice of 18 homemade pasta dishes. At lunch, in addition to many à la carte selections, there's a complete meal for under $18 that includes soup or salad, fresh vegetables, entree, and beverage. Desserts range from an excellent zabaglione to a tray of cheese, walnuts, and figs.

Dinner reservations are taken for parties of three or more only. At lunch any number can and should make reservations. *Note:* The North Beach is in the upper range of my moderately priced selections; order carefully or throw caution to the winds and splurge.

Little Joe's (Baby Joe's on Broadway), 523 Broadway, near Columbus (tel. 433-4343). Open Monday through Friday from 11 a.m. to 10 p.m., and on Saturday to 11 p.m.; closed Sunday.

SOUP'S ON! At 442 Geary St., between Taylor and Mason, **Salmagundi** (tel. 441-0894), is open daily from 11 a.m. to 11 p.m. (till 11:30 p.m. on Friday and Saturday).

Right in the heart of San Francisco's tiny theater district, Salmagundi (the word means a medley or potpourri) is a chic oasis in the heart of Jewish deli-land. Modern in décor, it is bright and pleasant with highly polished wood floors, rattan and bentwood furnishings upholstered in bright royal blue, and white Formica tables. Softening the modernistic décor are wall hangings, baskets, and framed woodcuts on the walls, lots of foliage, and a Spanish-tile fountain. Tables in the back look out on a tiny garden.

It's a very casual and comfortable place—as much a hangout as a restaurant. Many locals while away lazy afternoons here listening to the good recorded music—mostly classical and jazz— playing backgammon, writing letters, and reading. If you're hanging out you might want to order just beer or wine.

The main fare, though, is soup—28 varieties, of which three are served each day. Among the possibilities are English country cheddar, Hungarian goulash, North Beach minestrone, Barbary Coast bouillabaisse, and Ukrainian beef borscht. A bowl costs $3; a salad, $2.50; sandwiches, $3.15. Save room for some dessert— possibly homemade carrot or sour-cream chocolate cake.

Other Salmagundis are at 2 Embarcadero Center (tel. 982-5603) and 39 Grove St. (tel. 431-7337) at the Civic Center. For the day's soup selection, call 398-5032.

Little Joe's is a real San Francisco experience. No reservations are accepted, so people wait in line for as long as an hour and a half just to eat here. Even waiting in line is an experience; you can peruse the menu and sip a drink, and watch both the action in the kitchen (it's in full view of the restaurant) and the eating at the tables.

Specialties at Little Joe's are—not surprisingly—veal and pasta. You can get your veal in a variety of ways: a simple cutlet, or parmigiana, piccata, saltimbocca, scaloppine. And the pastas! There's spaghetti, ravioli, rigatoni, and cannelloni, to name a few. Italian entrees cost $8 to $13 at dinner, about $1 less at lunch. If you want to eat lighter, you might try an omelet or French bread sandwich for $5 to $8. Daily specials like beef stew, roast chicken and gnocchi, or roast lamb are offered for $8 to $10. And if you still have room for dessert, you can try some spumoni ice cream, flan, or cheesecake.

"Rain or shine, there's always a line" is Little Joe's motto, but you can avoid the wait by coming in during off-hours. But even if you have to queue up, you'll find Little Joe's a restaurant to remember. No credit cards.

Ciao, 230 Jackson St., near Front (tel. 982-9500). Open Monday through Saturday from 11 a.m. to midnight, on Sunday from 4 p.m. to midnight.

This is the best I've seen of the new wave of functionalist-industrial-Milano décor Italian restaurants. The ultramodern interior features white tile flooring, white enamel lamps and fans overhead, tables on a platform set off by a brass railing, and walls adorned by Jasper John prints and Wayne Thiebaud posters designed especially for Ciao. There's a long bar with a charcuterie at one end and an exhibition pasta kitchen and pantry where gorgeous antipasto salads are on tempting display in a glass case. All very *simpático*.

The same menu applies at lunch and dinner. You might begin a meal with carpaccio—paper-thin slices of raw steak with a light mustard sauce. Homemade fettuccine comes with a variety of sauces and accompaniments—Alfredo; al pesto with olive oil, garlic, basil, and cheese; tuttomare with shrimps, clams, squid, scallops, wine, tomatoes, and spices; and so on. You might order one of these pasta dishes alone or as a side order with charcoal-broiled chicken or lombata di vitello—a large grilled veal chop—which cost $10 to $19. All of the above come with fresh vegetables and toasted garlic bread spread with parmesan cheese. Reservations are essential and it's best to make them three to four days in advance.

JEWISH: David's, 474 Geary St., at Taylor (tel. 771-1600). Open from 8 a.m. to 1 a.m. daily.

David's is a second home to expatriate New Yorkers in quest of pastrami on rye. The convivial atmosphere is especially lively at night when the after-theater crowd packs in to discuss the latest play over chopped herring. The décor is typical Jewish deli, with Formica tables and white brick walls, and the food is like momma used to make. There's even a no-smoking section called the Celebrity Room, its walls plastered with photos of the famous who have dined at David's.

As soon as you sit down you're given a plate of David's fresh-baked hors d'oeuvres—a cross between French bread and rye—with whipped cream cheese. Don't eat too much or you won't have room for the $16 complete dinner—complete enough to put on about ten pounds. It begins with a choice of appetizers that includes chopped chicken livers, gefilte fish, pickled herring or kishka, and lox. This is followed by soup, anything from borscht with sour cream to chicken soup with matzoh balls, noodles, or kreplach. For an entree you might select stuffed sweet-and-sour cabbage, blintzes, roast chicken, Hungarian goulash, etc. Dessert is a choice of home-made pastries, and you get coffee or tea as well. Those with fainter appetites might want to order à la carte. Traditional deli sandwiches like pastrami on rye (made with half a pound of meat), dishes like gefilte fish with matzoh or challah, and soups with David's original bagel chips are all available for $8 or less.

SEAFOOD: Pacific Heights Bar & Grill, at the corner of Fillmore and Pine Streets (tel. 567-3337). Open Sunday from 10:30 a.m. to 10 p.m., Monday through Thursday from 11:30 a.m. to 10 p.m., on Friday to 11 p.m., and on Saturday from 3 to 11 p.m.

This setting for some of the best seafood in the city is hand-some and spacious, and has a warmth typical of the neighborhood. The long oak bar and the comfortable lounge chairs that are ar-ranged around cocktail tables create an appealing place to relax, visit a while, and listen to the soft jazz in the background. The high ceil-ings and cream-colored walls add to the room's airiness. Tables in the dining area and the banquettes are a rich plum color, as is the carpeting. A huge frosted-glass seascape framed in oak separates the entryway from the inner dining area. A broad expanse of window dominates the room—great for people-watching and viewing neighborhood activity. Sea-gray prints decorate one wall. Opposite this, a handsome collection of gray frames of assorted designs—but without pictures inside—add an intriguing note. Fresh flowers and greenery provide pleasant touches of color.

For lunch or dinner, some 12 to 16 varieties of oysters daily—including Belon, jumbo Blue Point, and Portuguese—are available, and clams, mussels, and scallops can be had on the half-shell. Prices average 90¢ to $1.30 each, or $5.25 to $7 for six. The house special-ty, fresh fish, from amberjack to sturgeon, is prepared with tomatillo salsa, tapenade, or lemon dill butter, though the sauces do change daily. Lunch prices range from $8.50 to $14.25. But if fish is not your choice, never fear––you won't be disappointed in either the quality or quantity of their other fare. The mesquite-grilled burger is a meal in itself for $6.75, or you might opt for the delectable spinach pasta with spicy Italian sausage or fried zucchini and tomato sauce for $8.50. Dinner at Pacific Heights Bar & Grill will cost $12 to $17 without your favorite oysters. A good selection of California wines is available by the glass. Reservations are recommended for dinner.

Sam's Grill and Seafood Restaurant, 374 Bush St., near Kearny (tel. 421-0594). Open from 11 a.m. to 8:30 p.m. Monday through Friday.

A San Francisco institution since 1867, Sam's has been doing a brisk business in its present location for over 40 years. It's very popular for lunch with nearby financial and advertising folk, so try to arrive early. Dinner is less crowded.

The entry, encompassing a small mahogany bar, lovingly polished over the decades, opens onto a main dining room where most seating is in booths with shoulder-high partitions. The atmosphere is somewhat noisy at midday. The 13 individually curtained booths, lining a corridor to the left of the main dining room, are perfect for very private meals.

For lunch, consider the clam chowder, charcoal-broiled filet of petrale, and a dessert of French pancakes anisette. Luncheon specials, including boned rex sole à la Sam and fresh crab au gratin, are mostly in the $7 to $14 range. Dinner specials might include broiled sweetbreads with bacon and half a chicken sautéed with mushrooms for $9 to $13. Reservations are taken for parties of six or more only.

TUSCAN: La Felce, 1570 Stockton St., at the corner of Union (tel. 392-8321). Open for lunch weekdays except Tuesday from 11:30 a.m. to 2 p.m., and for dinner Monday and Wednesday through Saturday from 5:30 to 10 p.m., on Sunday from 5 to 9:30 p.m.

This is a good place to end a morning, or begin an evening, of exploring North Beach. Located on the southeast corner of Washington Square, La Felce is a popular spot for local residents. You'll hear a lot of Italian. It's small and unpretentious, but cheerful, with fresh flowers on white tables and a few ferns overhead (La Felce means "the fern"). At night candlelight adds to the atmosphere.

The Tuscans, who live in an area centering on Florence, consider their cooking the basic Italian cuisine upon which other areas have overlaid a variety of strong spices and heavy sauces. Tuscan cooking has mild seasoning and light sauces, and this restaurant's delightful specialties, saltimbocca and veal piccata, are typical of this culinary approach.

Full dinners include salad, antipasto, soup, pasta, and dessert. Such a feast would run $12 to $17 with an entree of chicken cacciatore, fried calamari, or veal scaloppine. You can also order à la carte for $8 to $13. Full lunches feature a choice of about five entrees each day, served with a choice of soup, pasta, or salad, and dessert. The price: about $9.

VIETNAMESE: Mai's, 1838 Union St., at Laguna (tel. 921-2861). Open Monday through Thursday from 11 a.m. to 10 p.m., on Friday and Saturday till 11 p.m., on Sunday to 5 p.m.

This Mai's is one of a growing family of authentic Vietnamese restaurants in the city. It's a smallish place with a pleasant, understated décor. The only Oriental touches are some attractive prints and the Vietnamese music that plays softly in the background. Out front there's a small veranda with tables looking out on the sidewalk.

The food at Mai's is terrific—it's usually crowded, but worth the wait. To start out, try the Imperial or Vietnamese rolls: the former are like traditional eggrolls; the latter are shredded pork and lettuce wrapped in rice paper with a fish sauce for dipping. Don't miss the hot-and-sour soup. It's quite different from the Chinese variety, with a clear-broth base, crisp, fresh vegetables like tomatoes, bean sprouts, celery, and chives, and lots of cilantro. It's spicy, but not overpoweringly hot.

For an entree, you have a choice of lots of seafood, chicken, beef, pork, and vegetarian dishes, ranging in price from $4 to $8. You can also order a full dinner of soup, appetizer, selected entree, and rice for about $10. Jasmine tea accompanies your meal, or you can order beer, wine, or liquor from the well-stocked bar. If you want to finish with a dessert, there's flan, tropical fruits, or lichees.

There is also (so far) another Mai's in town: the original at 316 Clement St., between 4th and 5th Streets (tel. 221-3046), open weekdays from 11 a.m. to 10 p.m. and weekends from 10 a.m. to 11 p.m.

BUDGET RESTAURANTS

In this group, you'll discover some fascinating little "finds," as well as sturdy, inexpensive, standby restaurants for students and others with limited travel budgets.

AMERICAN: Sears Fine Foods, 439 Powell St., between Sutter and Post (tel. 986-1160). Open from 7 a.m. to 2:30 p.m. Wednesday through Sunday.

A San Francisco tradition, a constant for good food, this time for breakfast on the way to work or lunch to sustain a downtown shopping foray, Sears is located across the street from the Sir Francis Drake Hotel. It's famous locally for its luscious dark-brown waffles, light sourdough French toast, and unbelievably delicious pancakes. Be prepared for a short wait before you get your seat.

The restaurant is a pleasant place, decorated in browns and golds with framed oil paintings on the walls and pillars, and a choice of counter or table seating.

Two specialties I enjoy are the 18 Swedish pancakes (count 'em!) served with whipped butter and warm maple syrup, also available with smoky Canadian bacon or crisp sausage patties or links; and the strawberry waffle with fresh berries and whipped cream. These and other breakfast entrees cost $4 to $8. At lunch you can't beat the turkey with dressing and cranberry sauce, fresh vegetables, potatoes, and roll and butter. Full lunches or lighter meals run $6 to $9.

Tommy's Joynt, at the corner of Van Ness Avenue and Geary Street (tel. 775-4216). Open from 11 a.m. to 2 a.m. daily; the bar is open from 10 a.m.

The outside looks like a gigantic Coney Island carnival entrance, with brightly painted walls depicting the food and signs proclaiming world-famous sandwiches, etc. The inside is equally wild. There are old hockey sticks suspended from the ceiling, bamboo poles with stuffed birds, a mounted buffalo head, an ancient piano, rusty firearms, fading prints, a lion guzzling Löwenbräu, Santa Claus masks, etc.

Tommy's serves cafeteria style. There's an immense mahogany bar on one side, a buffet counter on the other, chairs and tables in the middle.

The famous specialty here is buffalo stew—stronger and gamier than ordinary beef stew. You can also fill up on a platter of ham, pastrami, or barbecued beef served with potatoes and a roll and butter, or a massive turkey leg. Entrees will set you back $5 to $9.

You can't leave Tommy's without sampling the beer. Here it comes alphabetically according to nation of origin—from Australia to Switzerland—about 78 varieties, including Japanese, Mexican, and Norwegian.

CHINESE: Sam Wo, 813 Washington St., off Grant Avenue (tel. 982-0596). Open six days a week from 11 a.m. to 3 a.m.; closed Sunday.

This is a Chinatown institution and one of the handiest spots to know, since it's open for anything from midnight snacks to predawn repasts. Whatever you feel about appearances, don't be put off by the look downstairs. The establishment consists of two minute dining rooms piled on top of each other on the second and third floors—you have to walk past the kitchen on the first floor and up the stairs to reach the dining areas. The rooms are bare and usually packed, and you almost invariably have to share a table. The guest-matching is done by a legendary waiter named (I kid you not!) Edsel Ford Fong, one of the Bay Area's most famous and authentic characters. Edsel has been ruling over the place for about 40 years, issuing orders in the manner of a warlord, and has had poems as well as innumerable press clippings composed about him. Sometimes he orders guests to pass the dishes; frequently he tells them what to eat.

The specialty of the house is jook (known as congee in its native Hong Kong)—a thick, wonderfully tasty rice gruel flavored with fish, shrimp, chicken, beef, or pork, and costing $3 to $4. Equally famous is the marinated raw fish salad. I guarantee that you've never seen many of these great-tasting dishes on the menu of your local Chinese restaurant—steelhead fish with greens over rice, sweet-and-sour pork rice, wonton soup with duck, or roast pork rice noodle roll. Chinese doughnuts go for 40¢ per hole. Sam's is for mingling almost as much as for eating and some of Edsel's fame is based on his knack for mixing the right—that is, compatible—folks around one table. According to rumor, hundreds of romances have budded from his dining arrangements.

CHINESE TEA LUNCH:
The Chinese call it dim sum. Liberally translated, dim sum is "a delight of the heart." Gastronomically, it is a delight to the palate. Small, succulent dumplings with skins made of wheat flour or rice dough, dim sum are filled with tasty concoctions of pork, beef, fish, or vegetables. This cuisine is not limited to the dumpling format, however—it also includes dishes such as congees (porridges), stuffed lotus leaves, spareribs, stuffed crab claws, scallion pancakes, shrimp balls, pork buns, egg-custard tarts, etc. At a dim sum meal you either pick these tidbits from a menu or, more often, from a cart wheeled from the kitchen to the customers. It's not necessary to select all the dishes for your meal on the first pass of the cart—carts come by quite regularly. The bill depends on how many dishes you choose, and this, in turn, is usually calculated by the number of serving dishes that have piled up at your table by the end of the meal. The more people in your party, the more fun this ritual is; a large group can go on sharing dim sum for hours. What's more, it's very economical.

Traditionally, dim sum has been served in teahouses—large, good-natured restaurants where families and friends sit around circular tables talking, eating, and drinking pots and pots of steaming Chinese tea. About 15 or so Chinatown restaurants, and some not in Chinatown, serve dim sum from 11 a.m. to 3 p.m. Herewith, a sample restaurant of them:

Yank Sing, 427 Battery, in the financial district (tel. 362-1640). Open from 11 a.m. to 3 p.m. weekdays, 9:30 a.m. to 4 p.m. weekends.

Like most dim sum restaurants, this one is bustling and noisy —something like a Chinese version of a Brueghel feast—waitresses hurrying to and fro with large platters of goodies. There are 27 varieties of dim sum available every day (different ones, however, on different days). There's no menu; most plates cost around $2, and you get two or three of the same item per plate. The way to enjoy it most is to take only those that appeal to you. More are on the way.

The offerings on any given day might include water dumplings; bean-curd rolls; a mixture of rice, sausage, and mushroom wrapped in a bamboo leaf; fried taro-root dumplings; paperwrapped chicken; curried-chicken dumplings; eggrolls; stuffed green peppers; and big butterfly shrimp. Save room for some dessert dim sum—perhaps a Chinese doughnut or egg custard. The average bill comes to about $9. Soft drinks, beer, and wine are available.

JAPANESE: Sanppo, 1702 Post St., across the street from Japan Center (tel. 346-3486). Open Tuesday through Saturday from 11:45 a.m. to 10 p.m., on Sunday from 3 to 10 p.m.; closed Monday.

Simple and unpretentious though it is—with tables (you may be asked to share one) scattered around a square counter area in a small dining room—Sanppo serves some of the best Japanese food in the city.

All lunches and dinners here include miso soup, rice, and pickled vegetables. At lunch you might have an order of sashimi, teriyaki, tempura, beef donburi, or an order of gyoza (dumplings filled with savory meat and herbs) for $5 to $12. The same items are available at dinner for about $1 additional. Combination dishes like tempura, sashimi and gyozo, or tempura and teriyaki, are also available for $9 to $17. Beer, wine, and sake are served. No reservations.

MEXICAN: La Victoria, 2937 24th St., at the corner of Alabama (tel. 550-9309). Open daily from 10 a.m. to 10 p.m.

La Victoria is entered via an appetite-whetting bakery and grocery, where fresh pastries are being made, and exotic goods range from cactus leaves to plantains. Plan to browse before or after your meal.

In the back are two small rooms, sunny and pleasant, with hanging plants thriving in the sunlight. It's not fancy—the walls are cement block adorned with travel posters of Mexico, there's ginger linoleum on the floor, and the tables are brown Formica. Part of the fun is watching the action in the open kitchen.

The portions are big and inexpensive, and everyone is very friendly and willing to do their best to help translate the menu, which is in Spanish only. You can stick to the usual burritos, tacos, tostadas, and enchiladas with rice and beans (all under $7), or venture into unknown culinary realms with the likes of menudo grande—a large serving of hunks of tripe with fresh lemon, chopped onions, fresh oregano, and red chile.

SALVADOREAN: La Santaneca, 3781 Mission St., at Richland (tel. 648-1034). Open Tuesday through Sunday from 10:30 a.m. to midnight, on Friday and Saturday till 3 a.m.

There's probably no ethnic cuisine not represented in San Francisco if you look hard enough. To wit, this Central American eatery in the Mission district that offers new taste sensations to the adventurous diner.

La Santaneca is a small storefront place with simple décor— wood-grain paneling, Formica-topped tables, wooden chairs, hanging plants. It's run by a brother and sister, Oscar and Nena Carcamo, who've been at it for over a decade.

If you aren't familiar with Salvadorean food, Nena will graciously help you make your selections. There are soups, like beef tripe or prawn. For $2.50 to $5 you can order any of a number of typical dishes. A plate of papusas (corn tortillas with cheese or pork stuffing) and another of plantains and beans with sour cream make a wonderful light lunch or supper. They can also serve as prelude to an entree like chile relleno, Salvadorean-style chicken, or a combination platter of steak, prawns, rice, french fries, and salad. Such Mexican classics as tostadas, chorizo (sausage), tacos, or burritos are also available. Entrees, which cost $6 to $8, are served with rice, beans, and a spicy-hot Salvadorean "cole slaw" of cabbage, carrots, vinegar, and chilies.

No liquor is served at La Santaneca, but there's coffee and tea as well as tropical fruit juices and a delicious Salvadorean drink made of rice, milk, peanuts, sesame, cinnamon, and other spices, with the consistency and color of light chocolate milk, called horchata.

La Santaneca is a bit off the beaten track, but it's well worth seeking out. It's easy to get to by car, and can also be reached on the no. 14/Mission bus or by BART (it's a short walk from the Glen Park stop).

CHAPTER VII

STROLLING AROUND

□ □ □

The Bay City is a stroller's paradise to the same extent as Los Angeles is a motorist's metropolis. I've said this elsewhere, but my reason for repeating it here is that the areas described below can only be enjoyed *on foot*—but in very comfortable walking shoes and if you're in good shape.

This doesn't mean that you necessarily have to walk to get to them, although it wouldn't entail much hardship. But once you're there, use your legs. Amble around, drift along, savor their unique individualism which hasn't yet succumbed to Main Street uniformity. With progress, real-estate values, and urban renewal at work—who knows how much longer they'll exist in their present delightful form?

As long as we're on the topic of walking excursions, you should know that volunteers sponsored by the **Friends of the San Francisco Public Library** (tel. 558-3857) conduct free tours of historic areas within the city's neighborhoods, generally from May through October. Tours usually take about 1½ hours, and reservations are not required. There are tours of City Hall, Coit Tower, Gold Rush City, North Beach, Victorian Houses of Pacific Heights, and Cathedral Hill and Japantown.

CHINATOWN

Start on **Grant Avenue** at its downtown end and walk up to where it crosses **Bush Street.** You'll come to a two-level archway crowned by a symbolic dragon. Just a few steps farther and you'll find yourself in a curious hybrid world—a world that looks as if it had been hatched as a result of the archway dragon's mating with an American eagle.

Every building and structure in sight has a celestial pagoda sheen, including streetlights and telephone booths. Even the banks have their gold-ornamented portals guarded by fat, fierce little stone lions. The streets are strung with colored lanterns, the air is filled with the tang of spices, and the streams of bustling people around you chatter in Cantonese and half a dozen other Chinese dialects. Every second store displays joss sticks and benignly smiling Buddhas.

Yet the American foundation on which this exotica rests shows through unmistakably. In the electric pony rides for kids outside the five-and-ten stores. In the red Coke containers. In the jean-clad girls and guys. In the multihued blaze of neon lights that turn the quarter into a Hollywood movie set at night.

This is San Francisco's Chinatown, the largest Chinese settlement outside Asia, growing larger with the migration from Hong Kong, and home for an estimated one-third of the city's Chinese inhabitants.

The first Chinese immigrants reached San Francisco during the gold rush of 1849. They called the collection of huts around the bay somewhat optimistically Gum San Dai Foo—"Great City of the Golden Hill."

But their concentration in one particular area was not a deliberate choice. They were forced into it, segregated by anti-Oriental prejudice. Chinatown—until quite recently—was a cramped, hideously overcrowded ghetto, and it still contains some grim overtones of the past . . . tucked out of sight in side alleys where tourists rarely venture.

Within this restricted quarter flourished the two worst vices of the East—opium and child prostitution. They flourished to amazing levels when the local Chinese noticed how attractive they were to their white fellow citizens.

Until the earthquake of 1906, the street on which you're walking was known as Dupont Street, and famed for being "the wickedest thoroughfare in the States." Only after the great fire swept away the strings of bordellos, gambling dens, and opium parlors, was it given a new name—**Grant Avenue**—and a different image.

Together with the vice life vanished another Chinatown phenomenon—the Tong hatchet men who once characterized the quarter.

Today the term "hatchet man" denotes any kind of strong-arm boy. But originally it specified a Tong torpedo who actually dispatched his victims with an ax. The most notorious of them—known as "Li'l Pete"—supposedly accounted for 17 people in that fashion.

The Tongs, too, were an outcrop of ghetto life. They were originally formed as benevolent and protective societies, because "pigtail-baiting" was the favorite pastime of San Francisco's notorious hoodlums. Gradually, however, the Tongs turned into criminal associations rather like the Mafia families, and just as frequently at war with each other. When the great Tong feuds flared around the turn of the century, they left the pavements of Chinatown as scattered with corpses as the gang wars were to leave Chicago some 20 years later.

The police didn't seriously interfere with the Tongs, but the earthquake wiped them off the map. After the rebuilding of Chinatown as a respectable tourist attraction, the Tongs never found a footing again.

Today the seven-block-long, three-block-wide section of Chinatown, stretching roughly from Bush Street to Pacific Avenue, is one of the safest neighborhoods in America. Its crime rate, in fact, is lower than the general San Francisco average. Just about the only vice you're liable to discover there is overeating (practiced by tourists).

Yet Chinatown is packed with fascinating sights, both historical and current.

SPOTS OF HISTORY: Walk up Grant Avenue—the main drag —till you reach the corner of Clay Street. This was the location of the first house in Yerba Buena (later San Francisco). It was built in 1836, by a merchant named Jacob Leese, next to the tent then occupied by Captain Richardson, the settlement's first harbormaster.

Walk down Clay Street and you'll come to a quiet little square called **Portsmouth Plaza.** It's just a pleasant grassy slope covering an underground garage, and a daytime gathering place for many of the older local residents, but this was the birthplace of Yerba Buena, the central plaza around which grew the city of San Francisco. It was also a favorite contemplation spot for Robert Louis Stevenson (whose monument stands there), as well as Jack London and Rudyard Kipling (who described San Francisco as "A mad city— inhabited for the most part by perfectly insane people whose women have remarkable beauty"). And at the south end of Portsmouth Plaza, on Clay Street, is a business whose name is perhaps one of the most appropriate I've ever seen—the Hang On Realty and Insurance Co.

On the western edge of the plaza once stood the unique China Telephone Exchange, which never gave callers a wrong number for the simple reason that the operators knew every subscriber by name and would often correct a caller—"No, that's not Mrs. Wu's number; you're calling Mr. Chang."

At the corner of Grant Avenue and California Street, visit **Old St. Mary's Church,** built in 1854 of brick brought around Cape Horn and a granite cornerstone quarried in China and looking oddly Gothic against the Oriental skyline. It was a survivor of the 1906 earthquake. Across California and halfway down the block is another peaceful oasis, **St. Mary's Square.** The heart of Chinatown's raucous red-light district before its 1906 destruction, this is presently a placid, flower-filled park for local residents. The benign **statue of Sun Yat-sen,** founder of the Chinese Republic, beams down on the plaza in his stainless-steel cloak—another of the outstanding works of San Francisco's late and much-beloved sculptor, Beniamino Bufano.

For an unforgettable glimpse into the lives and experiences of Chinese immigrants to America, stop into the **Chinese Historical Society of America,** at 17 Adler Pl., off Grant Avenue just before you reach Broadway (tel. 391-1188). The society's small museum (open from 1 to 5 p.m. Tuesday through Saturday) traces the beginnings of the Chinese in America—at a time when miners sent their dirty laundry in sailing ships to China because it was cheaper than having it done in California—through the opening of the transcontinental railroad, whose western link was built largely by Chinese labor. The society was started in 1962 to record the history of the Chinese in America; in 1963 the first exhibit of historical artifacts was held at the local Chinese YMCA. The contents of the old, often battered trunks of Chinese pioneers left for safekeeping but never claimed formed the basis of the exhibit. Later a fire destroyed this priceless collection of Chinatown memorabilia. Currently you'll view scores of sepia-toned photographs of early arrivals, tiny slippers for the bound feet of aristocratic ladies, a Chinese religious altar built in 1880, a wedding headdress, herb store paraphernalia, a shrimp winnower, mining artifacts, and gadgets and pipes used in opium dens. And as in the original collection, there is a trunk full of personal effects that was checked but never claimed. What kept the owner from coming back for his trunk?

In 1969 the society's current home was provided by the Shoong Foundation. That same year the society conducted a seminar on the history of the Chinese in California. Subsequently a 90-page syllabus was produced (now in its sixth printing) covering the arrival of the Chinese, their culture and language, and their contributions to various industries in California. Admission to the museum is free, but a generous donation is very much in order.

CHINESE NEW YEAR: Should you get to San Francisco in winter, you might catch one of the most noisily joyous festivals celebrated anywhere in America. It's the Chinese New Year, which falls somewhere in February or March.

1988, which was 4686 according to the Chinese lunar calendar, was the Year of the Dragon, 1989 is the Year of the Serpent, and 1990 is the Year of the Horse. The merrymaking lasts a full week and builds up to an ear-splitting climax, regardless of the animal symbol in charge.

The public celebrations spill onto every street in Chinatown, transform the squares into fairgrounds, and melt every ounce of what Oriental reserve might have existed. The final high point comes with the "Miss Chinatown U.S.A." pageant parade, an incredible mixture of marching bands, rolling floats, barrages of fireworks, and a wonderful block-long dragon writhing in and out of the crowds. Not to be missed.

ALONG GRANT AVENUE: Chinatown's Main Street needs no additional pageantry to make it colorful. It's an East-West parade every day of the year. You see Chinese girls in the traditional sheath dresses, old men in smocks and cloaks, and teenagers studiedly dressed in whatever their peers are wearing at the moment.

The shops are crammed with goods, ranging from ordinary utility wares to exotic treasures and—of course—mountains of what pass as "souvenirs." Some of it is pure junk, not even of Chinese origin but manufactured in Japan. But here and there you'll come across some beautiful and genuine pieces—and half the fun consists in looking for them.

You can, for instance, get Chinese rayon gowns from Hong Kong, magnificent bronze dragon paperweights, genuine onyx chess sets, and immense hand-carved Buddha statues.

At the other end of the price scale there are pairs of plain chopsticks, tiny teacups, Chinese porcelain soup spoons, and an array of wooden, delightfully gaga-looking mice, cats, frogs, etc.

And then there are edibles. Chinatown, as already indicated, is a mass of restaurants, one beside the other. But along Grant Avenue and on the side streets leading off it, you'll see dozens of small and large grocery stores selling Oriental delicacies whose existence you may never have suspected—everything from Peking duck to vinegared pig's feet.

Oddly enough—considering its scarlet past—Chinatown now has comparatively little nightlife, and that is a rather demure kind. The glittering Chinese niteries are mostly located elsewhere, though you'll find a scattering of bars providing floorshows of sorts.

GUIDED TOURS: The **Gray Line** offers a **San Francisco by Night** tour, which takes you first on a bus ride to Ghirardelli Square, the Cannery, and Fisherman's Wharf. Then it's on to a walking tour of Chinatown with an Oriental guide to point out the Painted Balconies, the Dragon Lanterns, and Tongs. You are given time for shopping, and the price is $20.50, half price for kids 5 to 11. Somewhat more expensive is the **Chinatown Dinner Tour,** which includes a multicourse Oriental dinner with the walking tour and ride through the city at night. Charges are $35 for adults, half price for children. Phone 558-9400.

Somewhat more elaborate—and unusual—are the **Ding How Tours,** 753½ Clay St. (tel. 981-8399). This is a Chinese enterprise and a little more formal in tone. A taxi picks you up from—and delivers you back to—your hotel. On the 3½-hour nighttime tour, you may have dinner (optional) at a Chinese restaurant, explore narrow back alleys, hear about the old and new Chinese culture and developing events in Chinatown, see the sights and activities of Chinatown at night, and learn about the Chinese language, Chinese painting, and the art of Chinese tea drinking. Without dinner the tour is $19; with dinner, $32.

Whether you explore the area by day or night, following a guide, or this book, or your nose, you'll find the same slogan holds true: *Fun Ying Quong Lum Wah Few*—which, in our barbarian Occidental tongue, means: "Welcome to Chinatown!"

NORTH BEACH

Grant Avenue is a chameleon of a street. It changes its color, texture, and character three times on its barely 1½-mile length. At the start it's a typical downtown shopping street. After Bush Street, it becomes an Oriental main drag. Then, after crossing Pacific, it suddenly turns into a semi-bohemian row of art stores, coffeehouses, and offbeat bars.

Chances are that you'll lose Grant Avenue altogether at this point, only to find it again a bit farther on where it becomes Upper Grant Avenue. In between, it's bisected by **Broadway** and **Columbus Avenue,** and you're caught in a dazzling web of beckoning neon lights luring you off in other directions.

This is North Beach, San Francisco's equivalent of New York's Greenwich Village, Chicago's Old Town or New Town, London's Soho, Paris's Left Bank, and Hamburg's Reeperbahn. It's a little like all those places, but not *really* like any of them. For North Beach is several things at once, depending on which portion you see.

You can walk into North Beach from Chinatown, as we just did. Or you can take a no. 15 bus from downtown Kearny Street and get off at Columbus Avenue. In either case you'll find yourself smack in the throbbing, whirling, pulsating heart of San Francisco's Night Town, and may jump to the false conclusion that North Beach is nothing but a glittering ribbon of strip joints, jazz clubs, cabarets, and hot-dog palaces. But that just ain't so.

North Beach is, above all, home for about 50,000 hard-working, early-rising, family-loving Italians, who live, eat, play bocce, and pray there. A large proportion of them never set foot in any of the niteries or sex shows that have become synonymous with their quarter.

If you proceed along Upper Grant Avenue or get past the scarlet blocks of Columbus Avenue, you'll come to the little homes, family restaurants, groceries, bakeries, shops, and banks that mean North Beach to native Italians. You'll find little bare female skin here, but lots of friendliness and some of the world's finest delicatessens.

The Italians are San Francisco's largest ethnic minority group, and they have put their imprint on every aspect of the city's activities —from art and sport to finance and politics. They have produced several mayors; a string of painters, sculptors, and musicians; one of America's top banking tycoons, Amadeo Giannini; and a baseball wizard named Joe DiMaggio, who earned numerous frowns around his old neighborhood when he went and married "that actress."

San Francisco's "Little Italy" is Italian with a vengeance. **Washington Square,** opposite the Church of Saints Peter and Paul, could have been transplanted from, say, Genoa or Bologna. The signs above the shopfronts announce "Farmacia," "Panatteria," and "Fiorista"; the espresso dispensed in the cafés (*not* coffeehouses) has the correct Roman tang; the markets are crammed with ricotta, mozzarella, provolone, and prosciutto; and the salami and mortadella sausages sold in the butcher shops have that special glow of garlic fire that make our Americanized imitations taste pallid in comparison.

The Italian atmosphere holds good all the way downhill to **Fisherman's Wharf,** except that it now acquires a distinct Mediterranean flavor. There is the characteristic forest of spars and masts of the moored fishing and pleasure craft, the wooden piers, and the wonderfully appetite-arousing smell of salt water mixed with boiling crabs.

The Wharf's many attractions will be dealt with later and separately. Right now, we'll move east for a glance at the third contrasting face of North Beach:

Telegraph Hill is a region of narrow alleys and small frame houses perched on alpine inclines, huddling around the candle-like shaft of **Coit Tower.**

It's an entrancing, quiet area after all the hum and bustle we've been through. Originally this patch, too, was solidly Italian. But in the '20s and '30s a more diverse crowd of bohemians moved in, renting the incredibly cheap houses and painting, writing, and debating without disturbing the texture of the region.

Then, in the 1950s, came the influx of beatniks, and with them the national spotlight. They caught the public imagination and reaped a rich cash harvest for at least some originators. They also

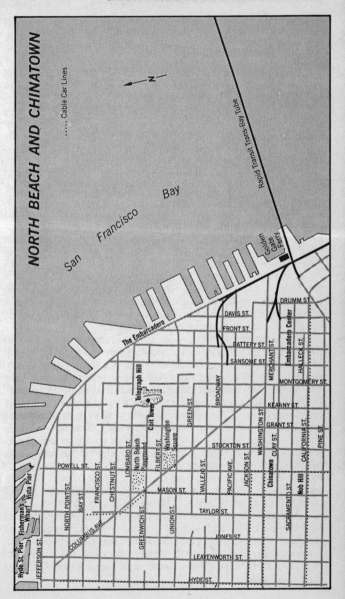

attracted newcomers of an altogether different ilk. The moneyed smart set moved in, transformed many of the old houses into ultra-chic apartments, and, incidentally, shot the rents up to dazzling heights.

Thus, when the hippies appeared in the '60s, Telegraph Hill was way beyond their ken. They had to crowd into what then was a far less attractive Haight-Ashbury instead.

Now, having shown you the other faces of North Beach, let's return to our starting point, the hedonistic night-owl portion. You'll find some of its attractions described individually in the nightlife chapter—where they belong. At this stage, we'll just drop in on a few spots that don't fit any particular category.

If you'll remember, we stopped at the intersection of Grant and Columbus Avenues. Turn sharp right and—at 255 Columbus Ave. —you'll find **Vesuvio** (tel. 362-3370).

Strictly speaking, this is a tavern, but it's also a local rendezvous place and information exchange that almost behaves like a club. Contrary to rumors, Vesuvio is not a very good "pickup joint"; the regulars tend to hang out together. But it's a marvelous spot to imbibe atmosphere along with your drink. It's reminiscent of a left-bank bistro and has been a hangout for writers, poets, and nonliterary Beats since it opened in 1948 as a bar. Not so curiously, it's also popular with cab drivers, seamen, and Europeans. Leo Riegler, the saloon keeper (otherwise known as the owner-manager) is a widely traveled ex-seaman who adds to the atmosphere.

Hanging above the bar is one of San Francisco's most famous paintings, perpetrated by Homer Ansley, reproduced on thousands of postcards, and titled *Double Exposure*. See it for yourself. Also above the bar is a screen on which—at irregular intervals—the management shows slides of picture postcards considered "risqué" in grandma's day. On the wall you'll find a bulletin board which features notices like "Wanted by uninhibited blonde, male traveling companion to hitchhike to Washington Square, New York." Another wall is hung with a changing exhibit of paintings and photographs. On the mezzanine, with one side open to the shifting scenes of the main bar below, is a private curtained booth, rather like a box in a theater. An inspired patron christened it the John Wilkes Memorial Booth, the name it bears today. A second booth has been added "for lady psychiatrists." IDs are checked at the door.

Vesuvio is regarded as one of the ten best drinking places in San Francisco. In addition to the usual brews, vintages, and standard mixed drinks, Vesuvio has Anchor Steam beer—a San Francisco specialty—on draft. Vesuvio does not serve food, but customers can bring their own lunch, or whatever. Open daily from 6 a.m. to 2 a.m.

A couple of doors down, at 261 Columbus Ave., at Broadway, is the **City Lights Bookstore** (tel. 362-8193). But you'd better forget all you know about bookstores if you want to visualize this one. It was founded by a poet, Lawrence Ferlinghetti, in 1953. And it has lost none of its originality and intimacy over the years. City Lights is not merely a shop, but a crusading publishing firm, an impromptu clubhouse for local poets, and possibly San Francisco's greatest gossip exchange.

The management doesn't just let you browse around—it invites you to sit down, make yourself at home, and even provides chairs and tables downstairs for that purpose. You can easily spend an entire evening here, leafing through the huge display of international magazines, catching up on the latest local publications in the literary, psychological, and philosophical fields, and getting an idea of the variety, scope, and intensity of the broadsides and pamphlets published in this country. Nobody will nudge you on or disturb whatever conversation you might have struck up with fellow browsers. It's the kind of bookshop that Paris used to boast, back in the days of *La Bohème*. Store hours are in keeping with its accommodating character: 10 a.m. to midnight daily, and often until 1 a.m. on Friday and Saturday.

Across the road, at 242 Columbus Ave., is the **Tosca** (tel. 986-9651), a personal favorite among San Francisco's cafés. Deep brown and unmistakably Old Italian, the Tosca features a wonderful collection of Grand Opera records on its jukebox, along with some equally wonderful potables.

Tucked into nearby Adler Place is **Specs'**, 12 Adler Museum Café (tel. 421-4112), possibly the liveliest pub in town, where many of City Light's avid readers turn up for after-browsing booze, and the cultural and social exchange continues. Read more about it in the nightlife chapter, where we'll return again to North Beach.

UNION STREET—COW HOLLOW

West of North Beach, but altogether different in atmosphere, the Cow Hollow stretch of Union Street (between Van Ness Avenue and Steiner Street) was once the milk jar of San Francisco, a green dale dotted with dairy herds that gave it its unofficial name. Later it turned into a rather drab shopping district which—until about 20 years ago—looked ready to curl up and die of boredom.

Then a group of businessmen, smitten in equal degrees by nostalgia and enterprise, got together and transformed the thoroughfare into what it is today—an almost brick-perfect replica of a Victorian shopping street, complete with wrought-iron fences and mellow sidewalk gaslights, the background music supplied partly by records, partly by tinkling cash registers. Victorian façades are trimmed with gingerbread decorations. Subtly painted mews are finished with ornate shingles. Half-hidden passages between the buildings lead into little courtyards filled with flowers, cooled by small fountains, and flanked by boutiques that conduct their business half outdoors in fair weather.

For, make no mistake about it—this is still very much a business section, except that browsing around here is like snooping into a gilded and slightly dreamy past.

The accent is on antiques, handcrafts, art, jewelry, and home furnishings. But you also find custom tailoring, feminine fripperies, flowers, garden ornaments, delicatessens, and—of course—the inevitable restaurants. The line-up continues with stamps, books, toys, art objects, cooking utensils, an auction gallery, a movie theater, beauty salons, an upholstery . . . and a plethora of pleasant, upbeat meeting and mingling bars for the city's unattached and seeking. Though these bars are kept in theme with Tiffany-style lamps and antique bar signs, the graceful forms that drape themselves over the leather-padded barstools are very much dedicated to today's mores. (The best of the shops, restaurants, and nightspots are covered in their appropriate chapters.)

In the noncommercial sphere, there's the **Octagon House,** at 2645 Gough St., corner of Union (tel. 441-7512). This is a local heirloom, a perfectly preserved, uniquely shaped building dating to 1861, now used as a small but superb museum of the decorative arts of the Colonial and Federal periods. Run by the National Society of Colonial Dames of America, it is open to the public the second Sunday and the second and fourth Thursdays of every month, except January, from noon to 2:45 p.m. Admission is by donation.

JACKSON SQUARE

This is another step into the past, just a few blocks away from San Francisco's skyscrapered financial district. The term "square" is a bit misleading. Actually, this is a three-block area bounded by Jackson, Montgomery, Gold, and Sansome Streets, but spilling over into the surrounding area and extending up Pacific Avenue.

The section has been restored—but luckily not to its original image. For this used to be the "Pit of Hell," the sulfuric core of the Barbary Coast, where every morning a body or two was carried off with the garbage and every "hostess" kept a knife in her garter. Until 1955 it was the oddly named "International Settlement"—neither international nor a settlement, but a pretty tawdry strip of honky-tonk dives sporting leather-lunged barkers and faded burlesque beauties.

But San Francisco's delightful restoration bug overcame all these handicaps. A group of inspired home-furnishings wholesalers took over the area in batches and proceeded to scrape, sandblast, paint, and refurbish the sturdy old buildings (some of them have weathered two earthquakes) back to their original charm.

The result is an astonishing enclave of hand-wrought iron shutters, Federal-style façades with colored awnings and graceful support pillars, combined with some of the most tastefully luxurious window displays in the country. The whole scene looks like an exceptionally sophisticated TV commercial, the kind that might form the background to an ad for either imported sports cars, top-notch furniture, or very expensive cognac.

The oldest structure in the complex is at 472 Jackson St., where the (later) general, William Tecumseh Sherman, opened the bank that bore his name in 1849. (Mr. Sherman also headed a streetcar company in St. Louis.) The bank's interior columns are genuine sailing ship's masts.

Most of the showrooms in the complex are not accessible to casual sightseers. But the area itself is worth several strolls.

EMBARCADERO CENTER

At the waterfront end of Market and California Streets, in an area once filled with sleazy bars and flophouses, lies the Embarcadero Center—8½ acres of innovative architecture, plazas, malls, fountains, sculptures, restaurants, galleries, and shops.

The best time to start exploring this area is about an hour before lunchtime. Begin at the foot of California Street, where the cable-car line ends. Across the mall to your left is the **Vaillancourt Fountain,** variously described by its critics as "Stonehenge unhinged, with plumbing troubles" and "dynamited debris." I happen to like it because it's the only fountain I can walk through without getting wet. Just follow the stepping-stones across the reflecting pool and scramble in and out of the fountain's huge, hollow oblong arms. It's fun to listen to water drumming on the outside and be startled by unexpected spouts of spray.

Now head back across the plaza toward the Hyatt Regency and its sidewalk café, the Market Place. Nearby is a continuing **street fair** where you can browse through or buy leather goods, macramé, handmade jewelry and musical instruments, pottery, paintings, and sculpture—all from the artists themselves. And all are geared up by noon to catch the lunchtime trade.

If you haven't already seen it, this is the time to take in the lobby of the Hyatt (described earlier in Chapter V) and rest your feet in one of the cushy conversation pits that dot the vast floor.

Sculptures are scattered throughout the Embarcadero Center, ranging in size from a three-foot Bufano bear to an eight-story steel abstract by Willi Gutmann. Louise Nevelson's *Sky Tree* is another notable work. And a whole herd of charming Bufano animals charges along the open deck of the Alcoa building, where you can take one of the pedestrian bridges to the courtyards and town houses of the **Golden Gateway** apartment/shopping/recreation complex, which replaced San Francisco's antiquated produce district.

GOLDEN GATE PROMENADE

An outdoor writer once stated that this 3½-mile stretch of shoreline between Fort Point, under the south portal of the Golden Gate Bridge, and Aquatic Park, three blocks west of Fisherman's Wharf, is the most spectacular walk in the United States.

The promenade starts at **Fort Point** (tel. 556-2857), originally built to protect San Francisco from the Confederate Army (well, they never took the city, did they?), now a handsome, thick-walled military museum with superb views from the gun ports. Guides in period uniforms are on hand. It's open daily from 10 a.m. to 5 p.m.

From there, you wander along a rocky beach past pole fishermen at the Fort Point dock, past the palm trees and white shingle buildings of the Coast Guard lifesaving station, over a broad sandy beach beside Crissy Field Landing Strip, where you can search for shells and driftwood, through a decorative waterfront plaza gracing (of all things) the municipal water-treatment plant, along the St. Francis Yacht Club and Marina breakwater, where elegant vessels bob in full view of their owners' equally elegant and high-priced bay windows above in Pacific Heights, through the militarily manicured turf of Fort Mason to the old Alcatraz dock at the edge of **Aquatic Park.**

Fascinating possibilities en route include exploring the **Presidio,** established as a Spanish garrison in 1776, now a 1,500-acre headquarters for the Sixth U.S. Army. Considered by army personnel the best post in the land, this lushly wooded base still harbors handsome white-walled structures with red-tile roofs. The **Presidio Army Museum** (tel. 921-1403) is open Tuesday through Saturday from 10 a.m. to 4 p.m. A second detour might be the **Palace of Fine Arts,** with its Exploratorium (see Chapter X) and swan-dotted lagoon, at the edge of the fresh, salt-scented sea air. Heady stuff!

The easiest way to start this walk (after donning comfortable shoes and grabbing a warm sweater, please) is to take a Golden Gate Transit bus from Market and 7th Streets or from one of its stops along Van Ness Avenue and get off at the bridge toll-gate plaza. Cross to the statue of the man who built the bridge, Joseph Strauss. Face north and you'll see a gate leading from the parking lot to the path down to Fort Point.

CHAPTER VIII

WHAT TO DO BY DAY

□ □ □

Please don't be misled by the chapter title above. Most of the attractions described here are also very much alive and kicking at night. My reason for bracketing them separately is twofold:

(1) Some of them are outdoors and therefore contingent on a certain amount of sunshine.

(2) San Francisco offers such a staggering array of genuine nightlife that I had to amputate the spots with a dual character in order to keep the night-owl chapter down to reasonable length. With this in mind, let's start with—

THE 49-MILE SCENIC DRIVE

If you want a self-guided tour of the scenic and historic spots of San Francisco and have access to a car, there is no better way to see the city than to follow the blue-and-white seagull signs of the beautiful 49-mile (actually more like 51-miles) Scenic Drive. Virtually all the best-known sights are on this tour, as well as some great views of the bay and ocean. The drive covers a majority of the sights listed in this chapter, and more.

In theory, this mini-excursion can be done in half a day, but if you stop to walk across the Golden Gate Bridge or have tea in the Japanese Tea Garden in Golden Gate Park, or enjoy many of the panoramic views, you'll spend the better part of a day. And of course you can break up the drive to extend this interesting trip to more than one day.

The Convention and Visitors Bureau Information Center at Powell and Market Streets can supply you with a map of the route. The blue-and-white seagull signs along the way will direct you counterclockwise, but since a few are missing, the map will be especially useful. It's also a good idea to take someone along to help navigate.

And for your sake, as well as the commuters', avoid the downtown area during the weekday rush hours from 7 to 9 a.m. and 4 to 6 p.m.

VICTORIAN HOUSES

San Francisco is a living museum of Victoriana. Thousands and thousands of Victorian houses line the streets; many even predate the fire and earthquake of 1906. Many are beautifully preserved and painted by residents who are proud of their city's heritage. A large area bordered by Baker Street on the west, Franklin on the east, Union on the north, and Post on the south is the best place to browse.

Some of the most famous buildings are the **Octagon House,** 2645 Gough St., at Union (tel. 441-7512); the **Haas-Lillienthal House,** 2007 Franklin St., at Washington (tel. 441-3004); and the **Whittier Mansion,** 2090 Jackson St., at Laguna (tel. 567-1848). All three are open a few times a month for tours; be sure to call ahead to find out the days and hours when visitors are allowed inside.

For the most famous view of the old and the new of San Francisco, you can travel up to **Alamo Square.** From the Hayes Street side of the park here, you can look northeast toward Steiner Street, where a row of pretty Victorians sits in front of a panoramic view of the skyscrapers of the financial district. It's a sight to behold. Even if you don't make the trek up yourself, you're bound to see the view on many a postcard.

LOMBARD STREET

Known as the "crookedest street in the world," if not one of the most hair-raising descents, the Hyde-Leavenworth block of Lombard Street amazes thousands of visitors a year. The block is so steep that the road curves back and forth, twisting like a snake. In the crook of each curve is a little garden; when the whole street's in bloom, it's gorgeous. If you drive the block (needless to say, it's one way—downhill), be sure to take it slowly and in low gear. And save your photographing for the bottom, where you can find a parking space and gaze to your heart's content. You can also walk the block, either up or down, via staircases (without curves) on both sides.

JAPAN CENTER

This is an immense multi-million-dollar showcase for some of the beauty, grace, ingenuity, efficiency, and versatility of Japan, set in—and completely overshadowing—San Francisco's revitalized **Nihonmachi** (Japantown).

The center—designed by one of America's outstanding architects, Minoru Yamasaki—occupies three blocks bounded by Laguna, Fillmore, Geary, and Post Streets. Opened with a terrific flourish of gongs in 1968, the complex is as modern as a jumbo jet.

Its hub is a serenely noble five-tiered **Peace Pagoda,** designed by the world-famous Japanese architect Yoshiro Taniguchi "to convey the friendship and goodwill of the Japanese to the people of the United States."

Spread around the pagoda, in a network of arcades, squares, and bridges, are shops and showrooms featuring everything we associate with Japan—from cameras and transistor radios to bonsai (dwarf trees) and daintily colored kimonos.

At the **Murata** pearl store, 1737 Post St. (tel. 922-0666), you can (for about $10) select your own pearl oyster from a water tank. These oysters are imported directly from the Murata Pearl Farms in Japan, and each one is guaranteed to contain at least one pearl. The store also sells lots of pearls that have already been removed from their shells—at much higher prices.

At the **Kabuki Hot Springs,** 1750 Geary Blvd. (tel. 922-6000), deep-tub bath, steambath, and shiatsu massage are available. The Kabuki is an authentic, traditional Japanese bathhouse, complete with deep ceramic tubs of steaming water and restful tatami rooms.

The center also houses a streamlined live theater used for special programs and the luxurious 14-story **Miyako Hotel,** reviewed in Chapter V, plus several restaurants, teahouses, and coffeehouses. Three times a year the center hosts a Japanese festival: a **Cherry Blossom** festival (Sakura Matsuri) in April, the Buddhist **Bon** festival in July, and the **Aki Matsuri** (autumn harvest) festival in September. Colorful occasions, these are beautifully costumed affairs with music and dance. Traditional Japanese entertainment can also be seen most Saturdays during the summer months.

Outside the center lies the **Nihonmachi,** the Post Street–Buchanan Street section of the so-called Western Addition that comprises Japantown.

Although less exotic and colorful than Chinatown, the Nihonmachi boasts some interesting gift stores, a movie theater showing Japanese films, and several good Japanese restaurants.

The most recent innovation here was the creation of a mall area on Buchanan Street between Post and Sutter. A cobblestone walkway, designed to resemble a meandering stream, is lined with flowering cherry and plum trees, and contains two origami-inspired fountains by Ruth Asawa.

COIT TOWER

A lot of native San Franciscans are just as puzzled as visitors at the strange sawed-off shaft on top of Telegraph Hill. Legend has it that the shape is meant to resemble the nozzle of a fire hose.

Coit Tower was named after the lady whose money built it. Lillie Hitchcock Coit was another in the long row of San Francisco's pet eccentrics, but with the distinction of being rich. Lillie had a thing about firemen, and wore a diamond-studded fire badge all her life, as an honorary member of the Fire Department. When she died in 1929, she left $100,000 for the construction of the white firehouse lookout topping the hill that once bore the city's semaphore signal.

The murals inside the tower are an astonishing mélange of art and politics—the art and politics of the radical, Depression-haunted 1930s. A mixture of magazine covers, newspaper headlines, faces, groups, and posters all reflect the struggle of America's unemployed and dispossessed.

Take the elevator to the top of the tower ($1.50 for adults, $1 for seniors, 50¢ for children) for a panoramic view of the Bay City. Coit Tower (tel. 362-8037) is open to the public daily from 10 a.m. to 4:30 p.m.

MISSION DOLORES

Back in 1776 Franciscan Father Junípero Serra sent Father Francisco Palou to found the sixth in the chain of missions dotting the howling wilderness of California. From this mission grew what was to become San Francisco. It's the oldest structure in the city (it survived the earthquake). You can see it today by simply taking the "J" MUNI metro up Market Street to the corner of Church and 16th Streets.

The adobe mission is surrounded by a four-foot-thick wall. There's a statue of Father Serra in the mission garden, though it looks rather more contemplative and less energetic than he must have been in real life. The small, simple chapel on the grounds was built by Indians whom the father converted to Christianity, and the interior is a curious mixture of native construction methods and the colonial style introduced by the Spaniards. Even today the mission is a cool and tranquil oasis, lovingly preserved by the Roman Catholic diocese. There is a museum area which is open daily from 9 a.m. to 4:30 p.m. May 1 to October 31, and to 4 p.m. November 1 to April 30; on New Year's Day and Easter Sunday, 10 a.m. to 1 p.m.; on Good Friday, to noon. It's closed Thanksgiving and Christmas. A voluntary donation of $1 per person is requested.

GOLDEN GATE PARK

Few cities take as much pride in their parklands as San Francisco does in the three-mile-long by half-mile-wide strip of green that reaches from the Pacific Ocean to Stanyan Street. And there's reason. For Golden Gate Park (tel. 558-4268) was not so much built as wrested from a wasteland of rolling dunes which the infant city purchased in 1868. Free guided walking tours of the park are offered every weekend from May through October by Friends of Recreation and Parks (tel. 221-1311).

The park is nothing less than a horticultural miracle. Year after year, park superintendent John McLaren planted trees and the driving sand smothered them faster than they could grow. McLaren planted more trees and shrubs—watched them die—and promptly planted still more. Little by little he won his fight against the dunes, finally taming the shifting sands by covering them with soil-holding plants. When he died in 1943—after a record 56 years in office— the park had become the thriving wonder of the West, providing grassy picnic areas, walking trails, a small chain of lakes, and space for bicycling, skating, golf, and tennis. The indomitable Scotsman had not only conquered the sands, but also the horde of local politicians whose idea of a "park" was a stone desert of monuments, parking lots, and driveways. Another piece of McLaren's legacy is something that *isn't* there—not a single "Keep Off the Grass" sign in the entire area.

Inside the park nestles the **Japanese Tea Garden** (tel. 387-6787), an enchanting patch of exotic artistry that looks like a quiet corner of Kyoto grafted bodily into the landscape. It owes its existence, strangely enough, to an expatriate Australian named George Turner Marsh. Mr. Marsh had become a connoisseur of landscape gardening while living in Japan. As one of the backers of the 1894 Exposition, he offered to create a replica of a Japanese garden as an added attraction. Built with imported Japanese labor and materials, the "Japanese Village" proved so captivating that the Park Commission retained it permanently.

You walk through a hand-carved gateway into a region of reflecting pools alive with goldfish, spanned by arched bridges, and flanked by dwarf trees as dainty as nursery decorations. The five-acre glen shines with deep-green and the gray tones of moss-covered rockeries. As you stroll along the bamboo-railed paths, you see traditional stone lanterns and the brooding *torii* statues that guard Shinto shrines. In one corner of this miniature park-within-a-park squats a bronze Buddha, cast in Japan in 1790. The garden is open daily from 8 a.m. to 6:30 p.m.; admission is 75¢.

And, of course, there is a Japanese teahouse with thatched roof, where kimono-clad waitresses serve blended teas and aromatic wafers. If you're fortunate enough to visit the place late in March or early in April, you'll see the cherry blossoms—a display rivaled only in Japan and in Washington, D.C. Always a magnificent sight, it is enhanced by a Bicentennial gift from Japan of 700 cherry trees which have been planted throughout the park.

Near the Tea Garden is **Stow Lake,** a square of water with a round island in the center, ideal for picnicking. You can rent a rowboat or peddleboat by the lakeside and cross over to the island without raising a single blister. On weekends there's usually a line of prospective rowers outside the boathouse (tel. 752-0347).

The whole park is packed with attractions, several of which will be described separately. Here I'll just deal with those that physically belong to the park.

The **Conservatory of Flowers,** Main Drive near Arguello Boulevard (tel. 558-3973), built in Ireland and shipped around Cape Horn to be assembled piece by piece in Golden Gate Park, has tropical plants and a continuous flower show in bloom. It's open daily from 10 a.m. to 5 p.m.; admission is 50¢. The **Strybing Arboretum,** South Drive at Ninth Avenue (tel. 558-3622), consists of about 70 acres displaying some 6,000 species of flowers and plants, open weekdays from 8 a.m. to 4:30 p.m., weekends and holidays from 10 a.m. to 5 p.m. The **Golf Course,** next to the Archery Field at 47th Avenue and Fulton Street (tel. 751-8987), is a nine-hole course with a short but tricky layout.

By far the best way of getting around the park is to rent a bicycle at one of the shops located along Stanyan Street. Some of these places also rent roller skates, as do vans on Fulton Street and Lincoln Way on Sunday.

One of the greatest thrills is to watch the roving herds of buffalo near John F. Kennedy Drive. They don't really "rove," but it looks that way because their paddock areas are so vast that you can hardly notice the fences.

And then there are bowling greens, boccie ball and tennis courts, a polo and a football field, checker pavilions, baseball diamonds, riding stables, a bandstand, and some 27 miles of footpaths. What's more, you can picnic any darned place you please.

FISHERMAN'S WHARF AND VICINITY

If you're planning to spend much time at Fisherman's Wharf or Pier 39, or are taking one of the tours offered by the Red and White Fleet or the Blue and Gold, consider coming to the area by cable car rather than driving. It's more fun, and certainly a lot cheaper, unless you've got a full carload. Parking in this area is about the same price as downtown—$1 per half hour, or per 20 minutes. If you can find a meter on the street, parking is 25¢ per hour, but one hour is the maximum parking time. Weekdays between mid-October and January you won't have too much of a problem finding a meter or space in a lot. Any other time, it's pot luck.

Reason no. 2 for taking the Powell-Mason cable car to get to Pier 41—it's a joy and it's fascinating. When you get on in the downtown area the car climbs to Nob Hill, swings around Chinatown, and heads up to the top of Russian Hill. That's where you see the vastness of the bay with Alcatraz in the foreground and Marin County spread out behind it. The cable car then goes down through North Beach and deposits you near the east end of Fisherman's Wharf.

Starting point for viewing this area is **Victorian Plaza,** a gaslit replica of a last-century park that is the center of an entire fun world stretching from the Maritime Museum at the western edge of Aquatic Park to Pier 43 at the eastern end of Fisherman's Wharf.

The entire area pulsates with "carny" festivity. Enormous kites dart and dance over the greens in the balmy bay breeze. People jam the sidewalks, especially on weekends, browsing through the street stalls selling art and handcrafts, stopping to buy from the artisans or to view such eccentric attractions as the Automatic Human Juke Box—deposit a coin, a flap lifts, and out pops a man's head, a trumpet, and the requested tune. There are also frozen mannequins, mimes, puppet shows, magicians, musicians, and more. San Franciscans are so fond of their street people that in 1974 they voted in a special proposition whereby permits are issued to artists playing or peddling their own work on the streets. And local merchants be damned!

Fisherman's Wharf proper occupies only a part of this eminently strollable area—the section along Jefferson Street on the waterfront—but we'll start there:

Originally called Meigg's Wharf, this bustling strip of waterfront got its present name through the generations of fishermen who sailed out from there into the Pacific. First there were the Chinese shrimp catchers in high-prowed, clumsy-looking, but astonishingly seaworthy junks. Then came the Genoese in lateen-rigged feluccas. And finally, the southern Italians and Sicilians, who still rule the fishing scene.

In the last decade fishing has been struggling to stay on the upswing—crab, herring, salmon, shrimp, abalone, perch, squid, sand dabs, sea bass, mackerel, and cod. There are scores of seafood restaurants and stalls. Jefferson Street is solid with them. The name *Alioto* might spark recognition among those who know San Francisco politics.

At about 3 a.m. the fishing fleet sails out through the Golden Gate—a picturesquely romantic sight, if you can bestir yourself that early. In the afternoon the boats are back again to sell their catch to the stalls and restaurants.

But eateries are only part of the Wharf's attractions. Fitting in with the carnival atmosphere are balloon vendors, and stores selling everything from elegant imported art and clothes to gag cans of "San Francisco Fog." You can buy a cartoon of yourself (drawn in three minutes). Or drop into the **Wax Museum** at 145 Jefferson St., featuring the usual congregation of famous and infamous personalities in lifelike replica plus a spine-chilling "Chamber of Horrors." Open from 9 a.m. to 11 p.m. Sunday through Thursday, to midnight on Friday and Saturday during the summer. The balance of the year hours are 10 a.m. to 10 p.m. (on Friday and Saturday till midnight). This and several other special kid pleasers in the area are featured in Chapter X; here are some that adults won't want to miss:

BAY CRUISES FROM THE WHARF: Perhaps the best way to get a total view of San Francisco is to take one of the cruises around the bay, starting from Fisherman's Wharf. This will, in effect, let you step back and look at the whole city. You have two to choose from:

The **Red and White Fleet** (tel. 546-2896) runs a 45-minute tour starting alternately from Pier 43½ next to the Franciscan Restaurant, and Pier 41. You can't miss the observation-tower ticket booth. The boats used are attractive two-toned double- and triple-deckers, capable of holding 150 to 500 passengers. You'll find a snackbar serving soft drinks, coffee, and sandwiches on board, a fair amount of deck space, and excellent all-around visibility. The round trip passes under the Golden Gate Bridge and steers close to Alcatraz for a good look at "the Rock."

There are frequent departures (about every 45 minutes) from 10 a.m. throughout the year. Tickets for adults are $11; ages 12 to 17 and 65 or over, $8; children 5 to 11, $6; under 5, free.

Additional service is offered by the **Blue and Gold Fleet** (tel. 781-7877), with frequent daily departures from Pier 39's west marina year round from 10 a.m. The Blue and Gold cruise, aboard a sleek 400-passenger sightseeing boat complete with food-and-beverage facilities, is a 1¼-hour, fully narrated affair. You'll cruise under both bridges and come within yards of Alcatraz. Other points of interest along the way are Sausalito, Tiburon, Angel Island, Treasure Island, and Yerba Buena Island. Tickets for adults are $11; ages 5 to 18 and seniors, $6; under 5, free.

ALCATRAZ ISLAND

The original inhabitants of this oblong chunk of rock rising out of the bay were pelicans—thousands of them. When the Spanish explorer de Ayala first sighted it in 1775, he christened the place "Isla de los Alcatraces" (Island of the Pelicans), but never set foot on it.

When the Americans took over, they drove off the birds and transformed the rock first into a fortress, then an army prison, finally into the most dreaded penitentiary in the United States. Alcatraz became America's own "Devil's Island."

The last transformation occurred in 1934, at the peak of America's gangster scare, when tough guys like John Dillinger and

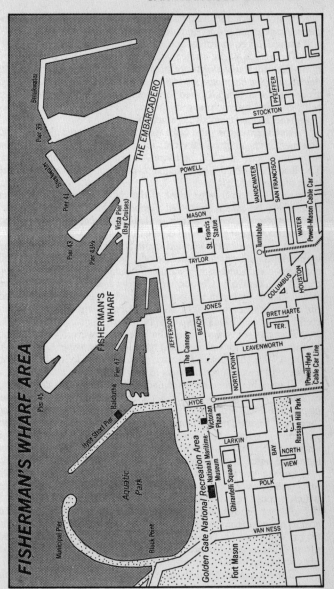

FISHERMAN'S WHARF AREA

Pier 45

Breakwater

Pier 39

Strada Vecchia

Pier 41

Pier 43

Pier 43½

Vista Pier (Bay Cruises)

THE EMBARCADERO

PFEFFER

STOCKTON

POWELL

VANDEWATER

SAN FRANCISCO

Powell-Mason Cable Car

MASON

St. Francis Statue

Turntable

WATER

TAYLOR

COLUMBUS

HOUSTON

JONES

BRET HARTE

TER.

FISHERMAN'S WHARF

Pier 47

JEFFERSON

BEACH

The Cannery

NORTH POINT

LEAVENWORTH

Municipal Pier

Hyde Street Pier

Balclutha

HYDE

Victorian Plaza

Powell-Hyde Cable Car Line

LARKIN

Aquatic Park

National Maritime Museum

Ghirardelli Square

BAY

NORTH VIEW

Russian Hill Park

Black Point

Golden Gate National Recreation Area

POLK

VAN NESS

Fort Mason

"Pretty Boy" Floyd seemed to bust out of ordinary jails with tooth-picks. An alarmed public demanded an escape-proof "tiger cage"—and the federal government chose Alcatraz for the part.

Theoretically, the choice was ideal. The Rock was ringed by bone-freezing water, swirling at from six to nine knots—enough to defeat even the strongest swimmers. At a cost of $260,000, the old army cages were transformed into tiers of tiny, toolproof one-man cells, guarded by machine-gun towers, walls, steel panels, and electronic metal detectors called "snitch boxes."

Even sterner than the walls were the prison rules. No talking, no newspapers, no privileged trusties, no canteen, no playing cards, no inducement to good behavior—merely punishment for bad. The Rock resembled a gigantic, absolutely spotless tomb with the hush of death upon it.

Into that tomb went most of the criminal big shots who let themselves be taken alive—Al Capone, "Machine Gun Kelly," "Doc" Barker, "Creepy" Karpis, and a dozen more. All were broken by Alcatraz, except those who died while trying to escape from it.

Yet while Alcatraz seemed a macabre success, it was a huge white elephant from the start. Its cells were intended to hold 300 convicts—and there simply wasn't anything like that number of top torpedos in captivity. Consequently, more and more small fry were added just to maintain the population, which eventually included ordinary car thieves, forgers, and burglars . . . tin-pot crooks who could just as well have been jailed elsewhere.

The cost of maintaining the prison, however, was colossal (drinking water, for instance, had to be ferried across in tank boats). By the 1950s the money required to keep a single inmate on the Rock could have housed him in a luxury hotel suite.

Thus, when three men seemed to have staged a successful escape from Alcatraz in June 1962, the federal government took the opportunity to order the prison "phased out"—closed. I say "seemed" because it's far from certain whether the trio actually did get away. They could have drowned while swimming for shore (like several others) and their bodies washed out to sea without anyone being the wiser. To this day, not a trace has been found of them.

For the next ten years Alcatraz was simply an eyesore, with various committees racking their brains trying to think of some use to which it could be put. In 1968 MGM rented the island for $200 a day to shoot a movie there, easing the load of the annual $24,000 it cost to maintain the Rock—empty. The only tenants were a caretaker, his wife, and an assistant. And for a while in 1969, a protest group of American Indians occupied the island with the intention of establishing a Native American cultural center. They left in 1971. Today great numbers of visitors explore the island's grim cells and fortification on tours conducted by the U.S. National Parks Service.

ALCATRAZ TOUR: The Red and White Fleet (tel. 546-2896) ferry leaves Pier 41 about every hour between 8:45 a.m. and 2:45 p.m. daily (to 5 p.m. in summer), bound for a 1½-hour guided walking tour into the history of this strange and somehow sinister island. (Time schedules change often, so check in advance.)

Three important notes: Order your tickets through Ticketron (tel. 392-7469) or purchase them at Pier 41 well in advance of your intended departure time.

Second, wear comfortable shoes and take a heavy sweater and/ or windbreaker. Even if the sun is shining when you embark, the bay can turn bitterly cold in minutes. Make sure the kids hit the rest rooms on the ferry going over. The only rest rooms on the island are at the landing, and once you start out on your 1½-hour hike, that's it.

Third, during your visit, there's a steep rise and some flights of stairs. The National Parks Service advises those with heart or respiratory conditions to reconsider taking the tour if climbing stairs leaves them short of breath. They can either stay at the ranger station and amble through the small museum or, as an alternative, take the trip around Alcatraz described below.

The ranger-guided outdoor walking tour on Alcatraz is free; however, it does not include a look into the cell house, so if you want details on how unpleasant confinement can be, pay $7.50 for the audio tour ($5.25 for children 5 to 11). Round-trip fare to the Rock is $5 for all over 12, $3 for those 5 to 11, and $4 for seniors; under 5, free.

Note: For those who want to see Alcatraz without all the hiking, the Red and White Fleet also offers a 45-minute boat trip (summer only) around the island leaving from Pier 41, Fisherman's Wharf. You don't experience the eeriness firsthand, but you don't exhaust yourself either. The tour is narrated by a former Alcatraz prison guard. There are five departures each Wednesday through Sunday between 11:15 a.m. and 3:45 p.m., from Memorial Day through Labor Day; the rest of the year there are only a few tours a week. Tickets cost $7 for adults, $6.50 for seniors, $4.50 for kids 5 to 11.

MARITIME MUSEUM

Walking west along the shore from Victorian Park, at the foot of Polk Street, you come to what was originally a very handsome and modernistic bathing casino, serving the sand beach of Aquatic Park. But San Francisco's climate and the temperature of the water being what they are, few people were willing to risk a dip in the briny. The casino stood practically unused until its conversion into the National Maritime Museum (tel. 556-2904).

Now it's a treasure trove of sailing, whaling, and fishing lore, with some of the most remarkable exhibits on the subject to be seen anywhere. There are wonderful model craft, including a huge one of the largest sailing ship ever built. Lining the walls are the wooden figureheads, favored by the old windjammers, mostly high-bosomed, gaily painted wenches with a permanent expression of astonishment carved on their faces. Also on display is the lovely scrimshaw work seamen did to while away their time and a terrific collection of shipwreck photographs and historic marine scenes—including one showing 500 ships lying abandoned in the bay in 1851, deserted by their crews as well as their passengers who had rushed off in a body to participate in the latest gold strike. Or so legend has it.

The *Balclutha* and other **Hyde Street Pier** historic ships are also part of the Maritime Museum. More about these attractions in Chapter X.

The museum is open daily from 10 a.m. to 5 p.m. (till 6 p.m. during Daylight Saving Time). Admission is free.

GHIRARDELLI SQUARE

The core of this ten-level complex was once a chocolate and spice factory and woolen mill (dating back to 1864), and today it retains lots of historic charm. Built under, over, and around these former factories, however, is a streamlined beehive of terraces, shops, theaters, cafés, restaurants, and exhibitions that has become one of the city's most popular rendezvous spots.

Access is easy: you can either climb the levels by the stairways or take the elevator from floor to floor.

The original chocolate factory was built by Domingo Ghirardelli, an Italian immigrant who made his money in tent stores during the gold rush. The Chocolate Manufactory factory has moved down to the East Bay and still turns out magnificent chocolate; you can see models of chocolate-making machines at the soda fountain of the same name and purchase the chocolate at its candy shop on the plaza level in the Clock Tower.

The rest of the $14-million center offers some tidbit for virtually every taste and purse capacity.

For openers, there are scheduled street performers in the West Plaza, all of them hand-picked for talent—mimes, a roller-skating accordionist, puppeteers, etc.

There are nine restaurants plus another ten spots for noshables, some of which I've already described in Chapter VI. It has, by the way, the better eating places of the Ghirardelli–Pier 39–Wharf–

Cannery complex of complexes, so plan to end up there at mealtime if you're exploring the area. And there are about 50 stores to browse through—many of them described in Chapter XII—retailing everything from the family's coat-of-arms to hand-cut lead crystal.

The whole complex is crowned by a quaint and charming clock tower, which is an exact replica of France's Château Blois.

During the summer, the square is open from 10 a.m. to 9 p.m. Monday through Saturday and 11 a.m. to 6 p.m. on Sunday. The rest of the year, hours are 10:30 a.m. to 6:30 p.m. Monday through Thursday, to 9 p.m. on Friday and Saturday, and 11 a.m. to 6 p.m. on Sunday.

Best way to see the complex is to pick up a very complete free map and guide called *Shop; Dine; Enjoy . . . Ghirardelli Square*. You can pick one up at the information center booth, located in the center courtyard of the complex. The tour starts at the Ruth Asawa *Mermaid Sculpture* fountain near the booth; the guide is illustrated with photographs to help you stay oriented. It also contains a history of the square and gives details of all its shops, restaurants, and other attractions.

Two blocks east of Ghirardelli Square lies an even more fashionable version of the same formula, known as—

THE CANNERY

Here the industrial base was provided by the old Del Monte Fruit Cannery (circa 1894), but the fairy godfather who wrought the transformation was a remarkable White Russian exile named Leonard V. Martin. Mr. Martin, who hails from Harbin, Manchuria, has been described as "a cross between Lorenzo di Medici and Mike Todd."

Obviously inspired by what could be done with a chocolate factory, Mr. Martin purchased the red-brick cannery, left its exterior intact, but built around it a vaguely Florentine three-story shopping, eating, and entertainment complex that has to be seen to be altogether believed.

You'll find some dozen or so eateries (I suggest sticking to the Ghirardelli recommendations when in the area, however), and over 50 shops, many of them described in Chapter XII. Then there are markets, amusement spots, a grove of century-old olive trees, and a former railway siding converted into a tree-shaded concourse with vendors' stalls and sidewalk cafés. Get the picture?

The three-story factory structure has been divided by a zigzagging alley, lined with arcades, spanned by bridges, and fitted with elevators as well as escalators.

On summer weekends the Cannery Courtyard presents some of the finer street talents in the city. The Powell-Hyde cable car will get you to Aquatic Park. The Cannery is at 2801 Leavenworth (at Beach).

Cannery hours are 10 a.m. to 6 p.m. Monday through Saturday, on Sunday from 11 a.m. to 6 p.m., holidays and in summer until 9 p.m.

PIER 39

This $54-million, 4.5-acre waterfront complex, a few blocks east of Fisherman's Wharf, is the latest demonstration of San Francisco's genius for converting workaday settings into pleasure grounds. Constructed on an abandoned cargo pier, it's an ostensible re-creation of a turn-of-the-century San Francisco street scene; however, if you expect to experience maritime life, you might do better with one of the ferry trips. Pier 39 has walkways built of aged, weathered wood salvaged from demolished piers. Two marinas—which combined accommodate over 350 boats—flank the sides of the park and house the Blue and Gold bay sightseeing fleet. Ongoing nautical events—boat races, etc.—add a special excitement to the Pier, as do the availability of sailing and sportfishing.

Pier 39 outdoes the competition in the sheer volume of its offerings. The free entertainment alone can keep you busy for hours (do tip, however, because this is the only money performers make). The continuing flow of free street entertainment alone can keep you busy for hours—jugglers, mimes, musicians, etc.

Then there's the **San Francisco Experience** (tel. 982-7394; call 982-7550 for showtimes). It's a 27-minute multimedia event that lets you see, hear, and even feel the city, past and present. You can relive San Francisco's history, from its founding, to the gold rush, to the earthquake, to the hippie days in the Haight-Ashbury. In addition to the fast-paced movement of three movie projectors and 2,000 slides in 32 slide projectors on the 70- by 35-foot screen, there are many three-dimensional surprises; at one point the famous San Francisco fog really "rolls in."

The San Francisco Experience can be viewed every half hour from 10 a.m. to 9:30 p.m. daily. Tickets are $5.50 for adults, $4 for those 5 to 18, and free for those under 5.

The San Francisco Experience is an event that should not be missed. It's a terrific introduction to the city and its heritage.

As for shops, Pier 39 has over 100 of them, selling everything from games, toys, and teddy bears to costume and gold jewelry, San Francisco mementos, Christmas decorations year round, everything for left-handers, and kites of the world. Details about Pier 39 shops are in Chapter XII. After all the to-ing and fro-ing, you'll probably be hungry. To please the palate, there are ten restaurants of varying ambience and price, some with great views of the bay, and

17 nosheries with everything from hot pretzels to Mexican pastry. Though I still maintain that many of the best waterfront-complex eateries are over at Ghirardelli, the ones at Pier 39 offer the best water views.

They include several seafood restaurants such as the art nouveau **Chic's Place**, a seafood bar and grill eatery with a menu of seafood, pasta, and good wines.

The two-level **Dante's Sea Catch** is also very art nouveau with a plush living room–style cocktail lounge upstairs, an exquisite food display up front, and incredible bay views. Char-broiled seafood and steaks, pasta, generous drinks, and sumptuous desserts are featured.

A bit of old San Francisco can be found at the **Eagle Café**. The cafeteria-style service is perfect as you share space at long tables. It's open for breakfast, lunch, and dinner.

A cascading waterfall is a unique aspect of the very rustic three-level **Nautilus**, where weathered-wood pilings serve as room dividers. Specialties include hearty bouillabaisse and cioppino, as well as numerous other seafood entrees.

Then there's **Vannelli's**, with its gorgeous mahogany bar and a large listing of seafood dishes and wines.

If you still have fish cravings there's Neptune's Palace, New England style in décor.

Nonseafood offerings include a branch of **Yet Wah**, a very popular San Francisco Chinese restaurant with first-rate Mandarin fare and terrific views.

Another Bay Area tradition, **Swiss Louis**, moved to the Pier from Broadway, where it was located for over 40 years. It's not Swiss, by the way—it's Italian.

If you do want Swiss fare (French Swiss, actually), you can have it in the homey and charming **Old Swiss House**, complete with alpine-style carved chairs, lace-curtained windows, and a blazing fireplace in the cocktail lounge.

Pepe's on the Pier provides the enchiladas and tostadas option in a south-of-the-border setting.

Wherever and whatever you eat at Pier 39, don't miss out on the chocolate-chip cookies from **Mrs. Field's Cookies,** a San Francisco addiction. Pier 39 held a chocolate-chip cookie contest to choose the owner of their chocolate-chip concession, and Mrs. Field's easily surpassed the competition.

The Pier has parking for 1,000 cars, and it's also easy to catch a cab out front. Its restaurants are open from 11:30 a.m. to 11:30 p.m.; cocktail lounges, until 2 a.m.; shops, from 10:30 a.m. to 8:30 p.m. To inquire about current Pier 39 events, restaurants, or marina activities, call 981-PIER.

CHAPTER IX

ACCENT ON CULTURE

□ □ □

San Francisco has frequently been accused of being a culture snob. Her citizens find this difficult to refute, because it happens to be true.

But then, let's face it, she has a good deal to be snobbish about. For an American city of almost 750,000 souls, her overall artistic enterprise is nothing short of phenomenal. In fact, the only U.S. city to better her is New York—more than ten times her size!

Take live theater, which has long been the weakest link in the American culture chain. San Francisco probably boasts more legitimate stages than any U.S. city other than New York.

She is only a little above average in the field of serious music (in which—believe it or not—America currently leads the world), but a strong runner in representational art. The Bay City has three art museums and literally strings of art galleries. I recently counted 12 in three blocks of Sutter Street alone, and they spring up as fast and nonchalantly as pizza parlors elsewhere. They range from the frankly trite to the breathlessly experimental, with every shade and variation in between.

Every September, part of the **Civic Center Plaza** is turned into a delightfully turbulent outdoor exhibition of local paintings, photographs, sculptures, and handcrafts, admired and criticized by throngs of people who wouldn't dream of stepping into an enclosed art gallery. Which, of course, is the purpose of the show.

THEATER

The best proof of the dynamism of San Francisco's live stage is the way it survived the loss of its most famous ingredient. The Actor's Workshop brought the Bay City international acclaim until it was lured to New York's Lincoln Center.

The role of the lamented Actor's Workshop was taken over by the **American Conservatory Theatre (ACT),** which made its debut in 1966 and has been compared to the superb British National Theater, the Berliner Ensemble, or the Comédie-Française. True to its wider role, ACT also performs special children's productions, tours schools throughout the Bay Area, holds pre- and post-performance discussions, and runs a professional training program for budding actors.

ACT offers solid, well-staged, and brilliantly acted theater, leaning slightly on the tried classics, but with enough new and experimental works to keep its repertoire exciting and contemporary. Recent productions, for instance, included *'Night, Mother, A Christmas Carol, Opéra Comique,* Shaw's *You Can Never Tell,* and Stephen Sondheim's *Sunday in the Park with George.*

ACT performs in repertory from October through May at the historic **Geary Theatre,** 415 Geary St.; telephone reservations can be made by calling 673-6440. Tickets range from $11 to $30.

The **Curran Theatre,** 445 Geary St. (tel. 673-4400), concentrates on Broadway musicals and comedies, usually with major stars, like Judd Hirsch in *I'm Not Rappaport,* James Earl Jones in *Fences,* and Lily Tomlin in *The Search for Signs of Intelligent Life in the Universe.* Tickets range from $17.50 to $40; Monday is dark.

Under the same ownership as the Curran, following an identical best-of-Broadway format, is the **Golden Gate Theatre,** 1 Taylor St., at Market Street and Golden Gate Avenue (tel. 474-3800). The lavish theater was built in 1922 and has hosted many a prestigious stage show and film screening over the years: everyone from the Marx Brothers to Carmen Miranda performed here. So plush was the original Golden Gate that there was even a lounge and library solely for orchestra members. And, of course, it had a Wurlitzer organ. It has been restored at tremendous expense to its original grandeur, with marble flooring, gilt trimmings, French carpeting, and rococo ceilings. It opened in 1979 with a ten-week run of *A Chorus Line,* followed by *The Music Man* starring Dick Van Dyke, *The Best Little Whorehouse in Texas* with Alexis Smith in the lead role, Rex Harrison in *My Fair Lady,* and Richard Burton in *Camelot.* Hard to beat for a first season's offerings! More recently they presented *La Cage aux Folles, My One and Only,* and *Me and My Girl.* They also stage expansive limited engagements, as with the Ukrainian State Dance Company. There are matinees Wednesday, Saturday, and Sunday, and evening performances Tuesday through Saturday nights; tickets are in the $20 to $45 range.

Club Fugazi, 678 Green St., near Columbus Avenue (tel. 421-4222), is not, strictly speaking, a theater. A 70-year-old North Beach landmark, it's more like a nightclub, with tiny candlelit tables, very high ceilings, and a rotating mirrored globe overhead. For several years they ran a fully orchestrated musical called *Beach Blan-*

ket Babylon Goes Bananas that was one of the most utterly delightful, funny, and original productions I've ever seen. It grew out of Steve Silver's Rent-a-Freak service—a group of party-givers extraordinaire who hired themselves out as a "cast of characters" to entertain, complete with fabulous costumes and sets, props and gags. They moved the first *Beach Blanket Babylon* (which had evolved from their party acts) to the Savoy-Tivoli in 1974, but the audience soon grew too large for the facility; hence the move to the Club Fugazi. Recent *Beach Blanket* sequels—*Beach Blanket Babylon Goes to the Prom, Beach Blanket Babylon's Makin' Whoopie,* and *Beach Blanket Babylon Goes Around the World*—have consistently sold out, as have all performances (over 5,000) for 15 years! It has a wide mass following, and I'm happy to report it's as wonderful as ever. Skip Fisherman's Wharf if you must, miss Chinatown if you're short on time—but don't miss *Beach Blanket Babylon.* Performances are at 8 p.m. on Wednesday and Thursday, 8 and 10:30 p.m. on Friday and Saturday, 3 and 7:30 p.m. on Sunday. Minors are welcome at Sunday matinees at 3 p.m. when no alcohol is served. Other times, two IDs may be required. Prices are $13.50 to $24. If you intend to be in town on a specific date, it's wise to write for tickets at least three weeks in advance, or obtain them through Ticketron or STBS (see below).

Note: The club now seats 393. When you purchase tickets they will be within a specific section depending upon price. However, seating is still first-come, first-seated within that section. Seats in the new balcony are $17 to $21. Royal Box seats are $20 to $24.

The **Orpheum,** 1192 Market St., at Hyde (tel. 474-3800), features, for the most part, Broadway musicals with name stars. Recent productions have included *Hair, Nine, Fiddler on the Roof,* and *Sweet Charity.* Tickets range from $20 to $45. There are performances Tuesday, Wednesday, and Thursday nights at 8 p.m., on Friday and Saturday at 8:30 p.m.; matinees are at 2:30 p.m. on Wednesday and Saturday, and 3 p.m. on Sunday.

The **Eureka Theater,** 2730 16th St., at Harrison south of Market (tel. 558-9898), a new 200-seat facility, offers contemporary and classical plays dealing with political and social issues. Eureka has produced a number of outstanding, award-winning plays such as *Top Girls, Cloud Nine,* and *A Bright Room Called Day.* Evening performances are at 8 p.m. Wednesday through Saturday, 7:30 p.m. on Sunday. Matinees are on Sunday at 2 p.m. Seats are $14 to $17.

The **Magic Theater,** Building D, Fort Mason, Laguna Street at Marina Boulevard (tel. 441-8822). While somewhat removed from the downtown area, this theater offers interesting and often controversial works of new and established playwrights. Sam Shepard's Pulitzer Prize–winning play *Buried Child* premiered here. More recent productions have included Samuel Beckett's *Happy Days*. Evening performances are at 8:30 p.m. Wednesday through Saturday, 7:30 p.m. on Sunday, with matinees on Sunday at 2 p.m. Seats are $14 to $18.

For programs and performance times of these theaters, consult a free handy little publication called **Key,** which appears weekly, covers most of the Bay City entertainment scene, and can be found in hotel lobbies and downtown newsstands. The daily papers and weekly city magazine are even more comprehensive. Best is the "Datebook Section" (known as the pink section) of the Sunday *San Francisco Examiner and Chronicle,* which will apprise you of every possible event and performance.

TICKETS

San Francisco Ticket Box Office Service (STBS), patterned after New York's TKTS, provides tickets at half price for day-of-performance sale to all types of performing arts—theaters, concerts, operas, and dance events—in the major theaters and concert halls. However, STBS does not know what tickets will be available at half price on a given day. In addition, STBS handles advance, full-price tickets for neighborhood and outlying performing companies, sporting events, concerts, and clubs, as a convenience to the public (tel. 433-STBS). Half-price ticket information is not available by phone.

Things to remember about STBS: Sales of half-price tickets are cash only, or traveler's checks; tickets are not available for every attraction, but there will always be something available; no telephone reservations accepted; only in-person sales. A service charge, ranging from $1 to $3, based on the full price of the ticket, is added to the STBS price of each ticket. VISA and MasterCard are accepted for full-price tickets.

STBS is located on Stockton Street between Geary and Post, on the east side of Union Square opposite Maiden Lane. Hours are Tuesday through Thursday from noon to 7:30 p.m., on Friday and Saturday to 8 p.m. (The hours are subject to change.) Half-price tickets for Sunday and Monday events, if available, are sold on Saturday.

OPERA, SYMPHONY, AND BALLET

San Francisco possesses the magnificent **War Memorial Opera House,** Van Ness Avenue at Grove Street, built along European lines and opened in 1932. This is the shrine and focal point for most of the city's opera and ballet and offers performances as great as you'd expect in London or New York.

The trouble, frequently, is getting into it. San Francisco's opera season is simply too short and tickets too difficult to get to make it an attraction for casual visitors. The entire season lasts only 14 weeks—starting in September—and the performances are considered social as well as artistic events.

The Bay City is extremely proud of having the first municipal opera inaugurated in the United States, but so ludicrous are the economics of grand opera that most of her citizens have never gained any benefit from this "first."

The **San Francisco Opera Company** presents a brilliantly balanced cast (under the direction of impresario Terence A. McEwen), which features celebrated stars like Joan Sutherland and Marilyn Horne, along with promising newcomers for whom this is often the first great break of their careers. Staging and direction are a wonderful blend of traditional effects and "avant-garde" innovations, which prevents the air of staleness to which grand opera is sometimes prone. Single (non-subscription) tickets go on sale the first week in August. Performances are each evening, except Monday, with matinees on Saturday and Sunday. Prices range from $15 to $65. Tickets usually are available up to the day of the performance. Standing-room tickets ($7) go on sale two hours prior to the performance. The box office (tel. 864-3330) is open from 10 a.m. to 6 p.m. Monday through Saturday. If you'd like to get on the opera's mailing list, simply write to San Francisco Opera, War Memorial Opera House, 301 Van Ness Ave., San Francisco, CA 94102.

Among the glories of San Francisco's theater and arts season is the unique **Pocket Opera,** 101 Embarcadero South (tel. 398-2220) —don't miss it if you're in town anytime from April through July. Confusing though it may seem at first, the Pocket Opera performs at the Waterfront Theatre, in Ghirardelli Square, 900 North Point (tel. 885-2929), but you'll need to call the administration office above for information. With just five to ten singers performing, you will be treated to a lively, entertaining operatic work in English. The setting is intimate and informal—there are no costumes or sets to impede your enjoyment or imagination. The operas are translated and rescored by Donald Pippin, music director and creator of Pocket Opera. If you've never enjoyed opera before, the Pocket Opera will surely convert you. Operas adapted in earlier seasons have included *Bluebeard* (1988 première), *Martha, Giulio Cesare, Norma,* and (can you believe it) *Yanked from the Harem or Abduction from the Seraglio* by Mozart, *Cosi Fan Tutte, Agrippina,* and *The Beggar's Opera* (1988 première). Performances are on Thursday and Saturday evenings at 8 p.m., and on Sunday at 3 p.m. Single-performance tickets are $18 and $21.

The **San Francisco Ballet** has won the highest possible praise abroad, even from London critics, who are notoriously spoiled by their own superlative Royal Ballet company and accept only the Russians and the Danes as equals. The S.F. troupe, founded in 1933, is the oldest permanent ballet in the United States, and is regarded by some as one of the best. Helgi Tomasson is the artistic director.

From January to May, occasionally with some gaps, they perform at the Opera House, offering a totally delightful mixture of classical and contemporary works. Performances are nightly, except Monday. Tickets range from $10 to $55. (In addition, *The Nutcracker Suite* is performed in December every year.) Call 621-3838 for ticket information.

SAN FRANCISCO SYMPHONY ORCHESTRA

A cornerstone of the Bay City's cultural life, the San Francisco Symphony Orchestra, led by music director Herbert Blomstedt, is currently in its 78th annual season. Headquartered in the **Louise M. Davies Symphony Hall,** the orchestra season lasts from September to May and features many internationally acclaimed guest artists and visiting orchestras. Known the world over by way of its touring and recordings, the orchestra has also built a widespread reputation for its "New and Unusual Music" series. Summer activities for the symphony include a Beethoven Festival, a Summer Pops series, and an annual presentation of the Joffrey Ballet. Tickets can be obtained at Louise M. Davies Symphony Hall, Van Ness and Grove Streets (tel. 431-5400).

SUMMER MUSIC

In summer, you can enjoy a series of concerts while sitting under the trees in Golden Gate Park on Sunday afternoons at 2 p.m. The first concert is traditionally offered by the San Francisco Symphony Orchestra; other performances include the ballet, jazz, and Gilbert and Sullivan. Bring some cold chicken and choose a shady spot. You'll find a cross section of San Franciscans, from toddlers to their grandparents, sharing the lawn with you. This **Music Festival** starts in mid-June and ends around mid-August. It's "for the people"—admission is free.

To round off the musical scene, there are nine **Municipal Pop Concerts,** led by famous conductors, at the Civic Auditorium, Civic Center, during July and August.

ART MUSEUMS

Apart from live theater, painting and sculpture are probably the Bay City's greatest cultural contribution. It will not necessarily be what you see in the museums (a museum's contents are entirely determined by its available funds), but more likely works that are being produced in a hundred nooks and crannies around town. So if you are an art lover, don't confine yourself to visiting the "name" galleries. Snoop around, drop into some of the obscure little side-street studios, watch the outdoor artists at work. You'll be amazed at the general quality level all around, even if some of the mass-produced, tourist-aimed stuff is pretty dismal.

San Francisco is the city of the part-time artist, like no other in America. Maybe the guy who sells you a necktie or the girl who gives you information about flight insurance gets busy molding clay or painting canvases when he or she gets home. And a year later you might see them on the cover of an art magazine.

As for sculpture, there is the work of the late Beniamino Bufano, one of the world's greatest contemporary sculptors. It's easy to miss, because so many of his pieces are placed quite casually outside museums or inside children's playgrounds. But chances are that if you happen to spot a particularly whimsical rabbit, contented cat, or luxuriating seal, it'll be one of his. You shouldn't miss his wonderfully serene and human statue of St. Francis, which offers outstretched arms to all passing birds at the edge of a parking lot at the corner of Taylor and Beach Streets.

The **San Francisco Museum of Modern Art,** 401 Van Ness Ave., at McAllister Street (tel. 863-8800), opened in 1935 and was a pioneer of abstract painting. It has established itself as a dynamic museum of contemporary art. It was the first museum on the West Coast devoted solely to 20th-century art. If modern art is your particular passion, this is one place to go. Half of the building is devoted to the museum's own permanent exhibits; the rest is for loaned works and traveling displays.

The permanent collection is strong on American abstract expressionism and other major schools of the 20th century, and includes works by Clyfford Still, Jackson Pollock, Mark Rothko, Willem de Kooning, Philip Guston, and Richard Diebenkorn. There is also a wide range of Mexican painters, including José de Rivera and José Orozco. The loan and traveling displays change frequently. Past shows here included a Philip Guston retrospective; a show of 200 works in the constructivist and geometric tradition; Wayne Thiebaud; and *Robert Hudson: A Survey.*

The museum was one of the first to recognize photography as an art form. Today its collection of 20th-century photography includes works by Alfred Stieglitz, Ansel Adams, Edward Weston, the German avant-garde artists of the '20s, and the European surrealists of the '30s.

The museum organizes special artistic events, lectures, concerts, dance performances, poetry readings, conceptual-art events, and many activities for children.

General admission is $3.50, $1.50 for seniors and children under 16. Children under 5 are admitted free. Hours are Tuesday (admission free), Wednesday, and Friday from 10 a.m. to 5 p.m., on Thursday till 9 p.m. (admission reduced from 5 to 9 p.m.: $2 for adults, $1 for seniors and under-16s), on Saturday and Sunday from 11 a.m. to 5 p.m.; closed Monday and holidays.

The 94-year-old **M. H. De Young Memorial Museum,** Golden Gate Park (tel. 221-4811), is the grandfather of San Francisco's museums. About as conservative as the previous institution is progressive, it has a good collection of old masters, including El Greco, Goya, Gainsborough, Van Dyck, Rembrandt, and Rubens. The recently renovated American gallery holds a fine collection of paintings dating from colonial times through the 19th century. It also has an imaginatively displayed gallery of the traditional arts of Africa, Oceania, and the Americas. There's a café on the premises with a garden for al fresco dining, and a bookshop that carries an excellent selection of art books.

Located on the Music Concourse of Golden Gate Park, the museum is open from 10 a.m. to 5 p.m. Wednesday through Sunday; admission is $4 for adults, $2 for senior citizens, free for those 18 and under. The same fee also admits you to the Asian Art Museum and the California Palace of the Legion of Honor. The first Wednesday of the month and every Saturday from 10 a.m. to noon are free.

The **Asian Art Museum** (tel. 668-8921), adjacent to the M. H. De Young Museum and the Japanese Tea Garden in Golden Gate Park, contains the Avery Brundage collection of Oriental art treasures. Among the largest collections of its kind in the world, it comprises over 10,000 pieces of sculpture, paintings, bronzes, ceramics, jades, and decorative objects of a wide range of historic periods from Iran, India, Tibet, China, Korea, Japan, and central and southeast Asia. From colorful Japanese paintings to the world's oldest-known dated Chinese Buddha, this is a fascinating museum.

Highly informative conducted tours are given several times each day. The museum is open Wednesday through Sunday from 10 a.m. to 5 p.m. Entrance is through the De Young Museum, and admission is collected when entering the De Young building (see above).

The **California Palace of the Legion of Honor** is in Lincoln Park (tel. 221-4811). To get to Lincoln Park, take a Clement bus from downtown Sutter Street. Walk through the park to the museum.

Rising classically white and pillared from a hilltop, this is San Francisco's most beautiful museum. Intended as a memorial for California's fallen of World War I, it is built as an exact replica of the Legion of Honor Palace in Paris, including the inscription "Honneur et Patrie" above the portal. The style is neoclassical

French—you walk in through rows of Ionic columns and a starkly massive archway. The inner courtyard—bare and green—forms a framework for one of the world's most famous bronze figures: *The Thinker* by Auguste Rodin (one of 13 casts made from the sculptor's original mold).

Most of the museum space is devoted to 18th- and 19th-century French art, but the museum also holds regular special showings, such as *The Vatican Collections, Venice: The American View, Leonardo da Vinci: Drawings of Horses, Maori Art from New Zealand,* and *The Prints of Edvard Münch.*

The museum runs a series of auxiliary attractions, such as concerts of classical music on Saturday and Sunday afternoons, a special shop for art books and prints, and the Café Chanticleer, a very pleasant lunch restaurant open during museum hours. From the museum grounds you get a magnificent view of the Golden Gate.

Admission is $4 for adults, $2 for senior citizens, and free for those 18 and under. Your ticket is also good for admission to the De Young Museum and the Asian Art Museum. The museum is open from 10 a.m. to 5 p.m. Wednesday through Sunday.

PROSE AND POETRY

San Francisco's role in the production of this country's prose and poetry has been so out of proportion to her size that the Bay City has been called the "Athens of America." Novelists and short-story writers like Bret Harte, Jack London, Mark Twain, Ambrose Bierce, Frank Norris, George Sterling, Herb Gold, and Jack Kerouac; poets and critics like Allen Ginsberg, Kenneth Rexroth, Kenneth Patchen, Lawrence Ferlinghetti, and Michael McClure—all have helped to shape the image of the city, even though few of them were actually born here, and some departed after fairly brief stays.

The trouble is that there are virtually no spots left where a tourist can listen to readings of their works or that of their younger successors. The literary scene has turned inward, become secluded and private, confined to irregular lectures—advertised in fine print—and exclusive group gatherings in which writers yawn or fume at the works of their colleagues. Readings are listed in the pink Datebook Section of the Sunday *Chronicle.* But for the most part, you'll have to sample the city's literature the same way it's done everywhere else—between book covers.

FILMS

At one time, so-called art movies were restricted to one or two specialized theaters, drawing audiences who didn't insist on either two-syllable dialogue or happy endings for their entertainment. But this situation has changed so drastically that it's almost impossible to distinguish "art houses" from the rest. One of the reasons was the loosening of censorship regulations and the subsequent toughening of sensibilities, which made it possible for ordinary theaters to run films that would have given most folks apoplexy a few years earlier.

However, you can still catch films unlikely to see general release at the **San Francisco International Film Festival** (tel. 931-3456 for a recorded schedule), held annually in the spring, usually March, at the **Kabuki 8 Theater,** 1881 Post St. (tel. 931-9800), the **Castro Theater,** 429 Castro St. (tel. 621-6120), and **Wheeler Hall** at the University of Berkeley (tel. 642-5550). You'll have to watch the newspapers for the exact dates, though, and most of the titles— imported from all over the world—are unlikely to mean anything to you. This annual festival, currently the 32nd, is recognized as one of the most important film events in the United States, and you'd better be prepared to line up at the box office for tickets at about $6 per. You can write in advance for information to San Francisco International Film Festival, 1560 Fillmore St. San Francisco, CA 94115 (tel. 567-4641).

The above-mentioned Castro Theater and Kabuki 8, as well as the **Lumière Theater,** 1572 California, at Polk Street (tel. 885-3200), feature select foreign films and American classics.

CHAPTER X

FOR THE KIDS

□ □ □

Let's face it—no matter how togetherness-dedicated you may be, traveling with kids requires some special planning.

The trouble is that children's tastes rarely coincide with those of their elders. Scenic splendors, architectural marvels, gourmet meals, historical sites, and art treasures are inclined to leave Junior cold. He may, on the other hand, spend two rapt hours watching the operations of a perfectly ordinary street-cleaning machine . . . while his sister gazes spellbound at a cable car turning on its platform, or into a shop window containing a particularly repulsive collection of guinea pigs.

This divergence of interests can turn a trip to, say, immortal Florence into a kind of miniature nightmare. But luckily, this can't happen in San Francisco.

The Bay City is—for all its vaunted sophistication—a kid's paradise. Children usually take one look at the cable cars and decide they want to wrap them up and take them home to play with. But that's merely a start.

The whole of the Fisherman's Wharf area is like one gigantic Coney Island–type playground. Large sections of Golden Gate Park are kid-heaven. I've never seen small fry who weren't enthralled by Chinatown. And there's an entire array of eateries—from Zim's to Ghirardelli's Soda Fountain—especially attuned to junior palates . . . as well as their elders' pocketbooks. Pier 39, by the way, has more kid-oriented attractions than any of the other waterfront complexes (details in Chapter VIII).

Here, then, I'll list some of the attractions guaranteed to capture your youngster's interest. A few of them, at least, are bound to capture yours as well.

On perusing this list, you will also notice what a delightful proportion of them are free of charge, depending on age. This doesn't exactly hurt either.

THE CABLE-CAR BARN

Here is another of those fun restoration pieces that only San Francisco seems to accomplish. Strictly speaking, it's the powerhouse and repair shop of the cable-car system, and in full workaday operation. But at a cost of $250,000, the city's Public Utilities Commission has restored its original 1878 gaslight look, installed a spectators' gallery, and added a museum of San Francisco transit history with emphasis on cable cars and cable-car relics that look like bits of Rube Goldberg machinery. Both Powell Street lines stop by the museum.

The quaint red-brick car barn stands at Washington and Mason Streets (tel. 474-1887). You can stand in the mezzanine gallery and watch the massive, groaning, and vibrating winders thread the cable on which the car runs through a huge figure-8 and back into the system via slack-absorbing tension wheels. Don't miss going through the room where you can see the cables operating underground.

On display here is the first cable car developed by Andrew S. Hallidie, and operated for the first time on August 2, 1873. After the earthquake, it strayed as far as Baltimore and was only discovered a couple of decades ago in a junkyard, and restored. At the Centennial celebration in 1973, it actually rolled down the tracks once more, tracing its original route, and bearing the mayor and other celebrities.

Among the other displays are three more antique cable cars and 57 exact scale models of all cars used on the various city lines. There's also a shop where you can buy a variety of cable-car gifts. The museum is open daily from 10 a.m. to 5 p.m. April through October; in other months, to 6 p.m. Admission is free.

WELLS FARGO HISTORY MUSEUM

Wells Fargo, as any junior TV or old flick addict knows, is synonymous with the Wild West. And at the bank's head office, 420 Montgomery St., at California (tel. 396-2619), the History Museum houses hundreds of genuine relics—pistols, photographs, early banking articles, posters, mining equipment, etc.—from the company's whip and six-shooter days.

On display is the handsome Henry rifle presented by the grateful company to one Stephen Venard, after he had killed three hold-up men who had robbed the North San Juan coach.

In the center of the room stands a genuine Concord stagecoach, probably the most celebrated vehicle in American history. This was the 2,500-pound buggy that opened the West as surely as the Winchester and the Iron Horse. The interior looks cramped even while empty, and it's hard to believe that it could hold nine passengers "passing comfortably"—with six more perched on the roof. That's not counting the "Knight of the Whip" who drove the six-horse team and the essential "shotgun rider" beside him.

On the mezzanine you can take an imaginary ride in the replica stagecoach or send off a telegraph message in code using a telegraph key and the codebooks, just the way the Wells Fargo agents did over a century ago.

Those visitors interested in mail of the early days can browse through the Wiltsee Collection of western stamps and postal franks.

There are samples of the treasure Wells Fargo carried—gold nuggets and coins from the fabulous Mother Lode mines—and mementos of the men who were after it. Chief of them was "Black Bart," a verse-writing humorist who robbed 28 stages single-handed. He was captured in 1883 by Wells Fargo's top detective, James B. Hume, through a laundry mark on his handkerchief.

The museum is open from 9 a.m. to 5 p.m. Monday through Friday. Admission is free.

HYDE STREET PIER

At the foot of Hyde Street, near Ghirardelli Square, Hyde Street Pier (tel. 556-6435), and its seven historic ships are part of the National Maritime Museum of San Francisco.

Here now lies the **Balclutha** (tel. 929-0202), one of the last surviving square-riggers and the handsomest vessel in San Francisco Bay. Built in Glasgow, Scotland, in 1886, she was then one of over 500 steel-hulled sailing ships carrying grain from California at a near-record speed of about 300 miles per day in a fair wind. The *Balclutha* was one of the legendary "Cape Horners" of the windjammer age, rounding the dreaded cape 17 times in her career. She survived shipwreck off the coast of Alaska, was refitted in 1906, and—renamed *Star of Alaska*—saw another quarter century of service.

She sailed under three flags: her original British colors, then the old Hawaiian flag (she was the last ship to fly it at sea), and finally the Stars and Stripes.

The *Balclutha* was purchased by the San Francisco Maritime Museum Association and restored to prime condition in a remarkable community effort that included volunteer labor from 18 Bay Area trade unions. Today she's completely fitted (except for her 25 sails) and just about the most perfect playground ever devised for nautical-minded youngsters.

They can spin the wheel, squint at the compass, and imagine they're weathering a Cape Horn blow. They can climb into the fo'c's'le and see the bunks for the 25-man crew she once carried. They can visit the "slop chest" (galley to you, matey) and read the sea chanties (clean ones only) that decorate the walls.

Currently adults pay $3 to explore the ship; children 12 to 18, $2; under-12s, just 50¢. Visiting hours are 10 a.m. to 5 p.m. daily.

The tiny two-masted *Alma* was built in 1891 and was one of the last scow schooners to bring hay to the horses in San Francisco. She also carried cargoes of bricks, sand, gravel, lumber, and grain, though her final career was as an oyster-shell dredge.

IS IT REAL, OR AM I SEEING THINGS? The **Exploratorium** is a mind-boggling place: You can't really call it a museum, an exhibit, or a display, because you participate with your senses and stretch them to new dimensions. Plan to spend at least an hour here with the kids.

You'll find this experience in San Francisco's rococo old Palace of Fine Arts, 3601 Lyon St., at Marina Boulevard (tel. 563-7337, or 563-3206 for recorded information); take the no. 30 bus on Stockton Street. This is the only building left standing from the Panama-Pacific Exposition of 1915, which celebrated the opening of the Panama Canal. Almost torn down to make way for real estate developments, it was restored in the mid-'60s because a local millionaire, Walter Johnson, shamed local government by putting up millions of his own money, which the voters supplemented.

There are over 600 exhibits dealing with everything from color theory to Einstein's Theory of Relativity.

Optics are demonstrated in booths where you can see a bust of a statue in three dimensions, but when you try to touch it, it isn't there. The same thing happens with an image of yourself where, as you stretch your hand forward, a hand comes out to touch you, and the hands pass in midair. Every exhibit is designed for participation; "do not touch" signs are nowhere to be seen.

You can talk into a telephone and see a light run a scale like the strength hammer at a carnival; or whisper into a concave reflector and have a friend hear you 60 feet away; or design your own animated abstract art, using sound.

Kids make up their own tours here and will spend as much time as you allow them without grumbling or asking "What's next?" And if they're surfeited with things scientific, you can take them out to the adjoining lagoon and let them feed the ducks, swans, and seagulls which mooch there.

Open July 1 through Labor Day, on Wednesday from 11 a.m. to 9:30 p.m., Thursday through Sunday to 5 p.m. After Labor Day to July 1, open on Wednesday from 1 to 9:30 p.m., on Thursday and Friday to 5 p.m., on weekends from 10 a.m. to 5 p.m. Admission is free after 6 p.m.; otherwise, adults pay $6 (good for six months), seniors pay $3 (a lifetime pass), those 6 to 17 pay $1.50 (good for six months), and under-6s are free.

The black-hulled, three-masted **C.A. Thayer,** built in 1895, was also a "pure" sailing ship, with no power other than the wind. She was built for the lumber trade, and for 17 years she carried logs felled in the Pacific Northwest to the carpentry shops of California. After steam pushed her out of the business, she continued in the salt salmon trade, making her last voyage (in codfishing) in 1950.

The **Wapama** was a vessel of the breed that did the pushing. Built in 1915, she was dubbed a "steam schooner" because originally schooners with her function were simply sailing ships into which steam engines had been fitted as an afterthought.

The **Eureka** still carries a cargo of nostalgia for San Franciscans. She was the last paddle-wheeled, walking-beam-engined ferry to operate on the bay, and made her final trip in 1957. At the height of the ferryboat era, some 50 of them crossed the bay, carrying an annual 50 million passengers to and from the Ferry Building at the foot of Market Street. In San Francisco, nostalgia almost invariably leads to action. So the *Eureka* was restored in all her 90-year-old splendor, loaded with deck cargo of antique cars and trucks, and permanently moored as a museum ship.

The **Hercules,** a huge ocean-going steam tug, designed and built in 1907, is one of the last of her kind still afloat in America. Until 1962 she put in many a working day moving ships and barges to and within West Coast ports.

A recent addition to the Hyde Street ships is **Eppleton Hall,** a side-wheeled tugboat built in England in 1914 to operate on the Thames.

At this writing, only the *Balclutha,* the *Eureka,* and the *Thayer* can be boarded. The other ships can be viewed from the pier. Admission is free; open from 10 a.m. to 5 p.m., to 6 p.m. in summer.

A new addition to the pier is the **small-boat shop** where visitors can see restoration in progress of historic boats from the collection. The boat shop also constructs replicas on the premises. The shop is located behind the Maritime bookstore on your right as you approach the ships. Shop hours are 10 a.m. to 4 p.m. daily: admission is free.

FISHERMAN'S WHARF

Just two blocks from Pier 43, at Pier 45, is the very popular Historic Landmark (even if it's more a Seamark), the **U.S.S. Pampanito.** She is a World War II fleet submarine which has been completely restored. An audio tour is available. Admission is $4 for adults, $3 for students 12 to 17, $2 for children and seniors; kids under 6, free.

Still at Fisherman's Wharf, 175 Jefferson St. (tel. 771-6188), is

Ripley's "Believe It or Not" Museum. This varied and very attractively displayed collection of oddities contains some 2,000 items from the famous Robert LeRoy Ripley arsenal. The range goes all the way from lifesize figures of chain-loaded Indian fakirs to the world's smallest violin, which fits into the palm of your hand and actually plays. Then there's Ripley's collection of humorous gravestone epitaphs, which include such gems as "I put my wife beneath this stone, for her repose and for my OWN." Open in summer from 9 a.m. to midnight; the rest of the year, Sunday to Thursday hours are 10 a.m. to 10 p.m., on Friday and Saturday to midnight. Admission is $7 for adults, $5.75 for children 13 to 17, $3.75 for kids 5 to 12; under 5, free.

The **Wax Museum,** at 145 Jefferson St. (tel. 885-4975), has over 270 wax figures, created to look as lifelike as possible. They have human hair (each strand is individually inserted), and males are all given complete beards; even the clean-shaven male figures have a faint stubble if you look closely. Eyes are medical glass eyes of the highest quality.

Most of the figures are arranged in tableaux. The *Royalty* grouping includes Prince Charles and Princess Diana, Prince Rainier and Princess Grace, Queen Elizabeth, H.R.H. Prince Philip, Duke of Edinburgh, and Emperor Hirohito. *Feared Leaders* brackets Fidel Castro and Nikita Khrushchev with such heavies as Mussolini and Hitler. Elizabeth Taylor is shown in a scene with Richard Burton from *The Taming of the Shrew.* Where entertainers are shown there's a musical soundtrack in the background—"You Ain't Nothin' But a Hound Dog" for Elvis and "Cabaret" for Liza. New arrivals include Boy George and Michael Jackson, as well as John Lennon seated in front of the Dakota gates. There are also tableaux depicting fairy tales; political figures from Napoleon to Mao Tse-Tung; *Great Humanitarians; Wickedest Ladies; World Religions;* and the inevitable *Chamber of Horrors,* where Dracula, Frankenstein, and a werewolf reside, along with the legendary Lizzie Borden.

The largest exhibit deals with King Tut. It includes wax replicas of all the treasures that were seen in the traveling King Tut exhibit— plus a considerable amount of additional material, with emphasis on his embalming and mummification, and on all of those involved who suffered the Curse of the Tomb. The newest exhibit is the *Palace of Living Art,* depicting famous masterpieces in three-dimensional wax sculpture.

Admission is $8 for adults, $4 for children 4 to 12, $5 for seniors; children under 4, free. Summer hours are 9 a.m. to 11 p.m. Sunday through Thursday, to midnight on Friday and Saturday; the rest of the year, 10 a.m. to 10 p.m. Sunday through Thursday, till midnight on Friday and Saturday.

Another wharf attraction under the same ownership as the Wax Museum is the **Haunted Gold Mine,** 113 Jefferson St., which is a fun-cum-haunted house complete with mazes, a hall of mirrors, spatial-disorientation tricks, wind tunnels, animated ghouls, etc. Even very young children will probably not find it too scary, but it is a lot of fun. The hours are the same as for the Wax Museum—admission is $4 for adults, $3 for seniors, $2.25 for ages 6 to 12; under 6, free.

To wind up, there's the **Guinness Museum of World Records,** at 235 Jefferson St. (tel. 771-9890). This fascinating collection of superlatives opened in 1980. Here you can put your arms around (if they reach) a replica of the world's fattest man; he tipped the scales at 1,069 pounds! You can march over to the participation area and try to break records of your own. You can watch movies and videotapes of record-breaking events—like the world's longest domino tumble. You can view artifacts such as the world's smallest camera or most expensive shoes. And usually there's a live record holder on the premises to gawk at or talk to.

The Guinness Museum is open from 10 a.m. to 10 p.m. Sunday through Thursday (till 11 p.m. in the summer), to midnight on Friday and Saturday. Admission for adults is $6.50, students, $5; children 5 to 12 pay $3; under 5, free.

CALIFORNIA ACADEMY OF SCIENCES

This is actually a group of widely differing museums and exhibitions (tel. 750-7145), all clustered in Golden Gate Park on the Music Concourse, including hundreds of exhibits about the natural world. Taking them one by one:

The **Steinhart Aquarium** houses one of the largest and most diverse collections of aquatic life in the nation. Some 14,000 specimens call Steinhart home, including amphibians, reptiles, marine mammals, and penguins. It contains a California tidepool and a "hands-on" area where children can handle starfish and sea urchins. The latest addition to the facilities is the Fish Roundabout, a unique 100,000-gallon circular tank where visitors are surrounded by the fast-swimming schooling fish of the open ocean. Seals and dolphins are fed every two hours beginning at 10:30 a.m.; the penguins are fed at 11:30 a.m. and 4 p.m.

The **Morrison Planetarium** is northern California's largest indoor theater of the outdoors. It offers sky shows that unravel the mysteries of the universe on a 65-foot dome ceiling. About four major shows, with names like *Star Death—the Birth of Black Holes* and *The Universe Unveiled,* are presented each year. The cosmos is further explored in exhibits in the Earth and Space Hall. The Planetarium show schedule is rather complicated, so it's best you call 750-7141 for information.

The **Wattis Hall of Human Cultures** features a unique presentation of ecological anthropology, utilizing lifesize habitat scenes to depict cultures the world over. You can step into the icy environs of the Arctic Eskimo during a midwinter seal hunt, then warm yourself in the parched desert campsite of Australian aborigines. A dozen such exhibits show how man has managed to adapt and thrive in our planet's most adverse climates.

Spacious halls and galleries are filled with birds and animals from North America and Africa, botanical specimens, brilliant gems and minerals, etc.

The Academy is open daily from 10 a.m. to 5 p.m.; from July 4 through Labor Day, till 7 p.m. Admission is $5 for adults, $2.50 for seniors and students ages 12 to 17. Children 6 to 11 pay $1.25, those under 6 are admitted free, and the first Wednesday of every month is free for all, when the museum is open till 9 p.m.

SAN FRANCISCO ZOOLOGICAL GARDENS AND CHILDREN'S ZOO

Take the L MUNI metro from downtown Market Street to the end of the line and you'll come to one of the great zoos in the United States. Entrances are located on Sloat Boulevard at 45th Avenue and on Herbst Road off Skyline Boulevard.

It all began with a grizzly bear named Monarch, donated in 1889 by the *San Francisco Examiner*. As it evolved at its present site, the San Francisco Zoo was patterned after the pioneering Hagenbeck Zoo near Hamburg, Germany. It now takes up 65 of 125 acres of land. The rest of the park is to be developed in the coming decade under the Zoo 2000 plan.

Most of the animals in the San Francisco Zoo are kept in wonderfully realistic landscaped enclosures guarded by cunningly concealed moats. Construction of Wolf Woods, Gorilla World, and Musk Ox Meadow (described below) began the renaissance of the zoo, replacing small enclosures with open naturalistic habitats. You can see 38 species currently classified as endangered or threatened.

With the record-breaking Giant Panda exhibition, and the opening of the Primate Discovery Center and Koala Crossing, the zoo's attendance has grown to over one million visitors per year. The zoo boasts close to 1,000 animals and birds, and 6,000 specimens of insects, including a hissing cockroach (those living in New York City haven't evolved to that stage yet) to be found in the remarkable Insect Zoo, which I'll get to in a minute.

The innovative Primate Discovery Center (we, too, are primates, though not yet rare) exhibits 16 rare and endangered species in naturalistic settings, from soaring outdoor atriums and meadows to a midnight world for exotic nocturnal primates. This is where you'll find a crab-eating macaque, one of the few primates that can swim; a Senegal bush baby that bounces as it walks, sometimes jumping four feet straight up though it's only six inches tall; and the Patas monkey, one of the fastest primates—it can run up to 35 miles per hour.

Other highlights include the Koala Crossing, patterned after an Australian outback station; Gorilla World, one of the world's largest naturalistic exhibits of these gentle giants; Wolf Woods, offering a chance to learn about the remarkably sophisticated social behavior of the North American timber wolf; Musk Ox Meadow, a 2.5-acre habitat for a herd of rare white-fronted musk oxen brought from Alaska; the Lion House, home to four species of cats, including Prince Charles, a rare white tiger (you can watch them being fed at 2 p.m. daily except Monday); and Penguin Island, with its colony of about 50 Magellanic penguins from Chile.

The Children's Zoo, adjacent to the main zoo, is a special place for everyone to get close to animals and watch zoo babies being tended in the Nursery. You'll have a tough time tearing the children away from the barnyard, alive with strokable, sniffing, cuddlesome baby animals. And then there's the fascinating Insect Zoo—the only one in the western U.S. and one of only three such exhibits in the country. You'll see velvet ants, honey bees, scorpions, and the marvelous hissing cockroaches I mentioned earlier. On weekends there are amazingly popular Tarantula Talks at 2:30 p.m. when visitors can get an intimate look at a live tarantula and learn more about its lifestyle. The Children's Zoo is open daily from 11 a.m. to 4 p.m. Admission is $1 for everyone (kids under 2 are free).

A free informal walking tour of the zoo leaves from Koala Crossing at 12:30 and 2:30 p.m. on weekends. The "Zebra Zephyr" tour train takes visitors on a 20-minute safari tour of the zoo, daily except in winter when it runs only on weekends. The tour is $2 for adults, $1 for children 15 and under.

The main zoo is open daily from 10 a.m. to 5 p.m. Admission is $5 for adults, $2 for a quarterly pass for seniors, free for children 15 and under if accompanied by an adult. For recorded information about the zoo, call 661-4844; otherwise, 661-2023.

CHAPTER XI

WHAT TO DO AFTER DARK

□ □ □

The Bay City's nightlife is the oddest and most intriguing bundle of contradictions I've encountered in a dozen or so years of dedicated globetrotting.

On the one hand, most of her niteries close at 2 a.m. sharp, slicing a good two hours off what a New Yorker, for instance, considers legitimate revelry time. On the other hand, she packs so much concentrated action into her allotted span that she seems to be celebrating a permanent New Year's Eve compared to the rest of the country.

On the one hand, she has very few really grandiose nightclubs on the New York or Los Angeles pattern (the Venetian Room of the Fairmont Hotel would be the closest thing to it) and only a sprinkling of truly lavish floorshows. On the other hand, she offers as much bare skin and exposed pulchritude in one North Beach block as you're likely to find in all of Las Vegas.

On the one hand, she's hopelessly entangled in a coil of municipal liquor regulations that would do justice to a near-dry county of Kansas. On the other hand, she has bars like some towns have cats, and you can stroll down Geary Street any night, trying to count them and dimly wonder what on earth *happened* to that myriad of decrees aimed at diminishing the local liquor deluge.

On the one hand . . . well, never mind. Let's proceed from the paradoxical to the practical.

An attractive feature of San Francisco's nightlife is the price tag. While it's not exactly cheap, it doesn't require making a loan at Wells Fargo or using up all your traveler's checks. There are a couple of big-name spots, like the Fairmont's Venetian Room, where prices are up to Manhattan levels (as are the floorshows), but these can be classified as exceptions. In the overwhelming majority of places you'll get by on about $25 per person, frequently less, excluding food.

San Francisco specializes in small, plush taverns, cabarets, and intimate neighborhood clubs, of which it has incredible numbers. Many of them feature piano bars, built around a pianist who may be superb or execrable, but is always versatile enough to switch from blues to Beethoven without dropping a note. After midnight, with the clustered drinkers singing along in skeleton key, their atmosphere gets pretty cozy.

The great thing about most (though not all) of these bars is that unescorted women can use them without creating any dubious impression. San Franciscans regard their bars very much like Parisians or Viennese view their cafés—as respectable social gathering spots for the equal enjoyment of both sexes. If a lady happens to walk in single and walk out with an escort—well, that's her whim, but needn't have been her original intention.

The above rule, however, does *not* apply to the places employing go-go girls, whose name—by now—is legion. Any single lady you'll find in those will almost invariably turn out to be either a "hostess" (that is, working for a percentage of the drinks she talks *you* into buying) or a straightforward hooker.

At this point, it might be a good idea to go into a few details on the subject of dancers (to use the term loosely), so there'll be no misunderstanding further on.

San Francisco, as most of us know, introduced "topless" entertainment to this country—or, rather, reintroduced it after the historic interval between the passing of the old Barbary Coast and the dawn of the New Freedom, circa 1964.

Then came the inevitable reaction—boredom: bar patrons hardly look up from their drinks. Business sagged distinctly. Clearly it was time for the next step.

The next step was—yes, you guessed it—"bottomless." This new development was confined to the North Beach; you seldom saw it anywhere else. But up there, it was exactly what it implied.

This form of entertainment—hitherto restricted to Copenhagen, Tokyo, Marseilles, and sections of Hamburg—has once again been returned to its points of origin. In a sudden rebirth of Puritanism among city leaders, "bottomless" dancers have been banned from all establishments serving liquor in San Francisco since 1973.

But, fortunately, the Bay City's nightlife has always had considerably more to offer than total exposure, as you'll notice by the length of this chapter. Most of it goes on in five quite distinct areas, where the entertainment spots are so closely packed that they frequently snatch each other's patrons.

□ First, there is the narrow **downtown** strip between Bush and O'Farrell Streets. This is the preserve of the piano bars, sociable and fairly sophisticated taverns, and a few rakish but respectable nightclubs. It's very touristy along Geary Street and below Union Square, but elegant along with it.

□ Below O'Farrell Street, wedged between Van Ness Avenue and Market Street, lies the vaguely defined quarter known as the **Tenderloin.** This the closest facsimile to a red-light district San Francisco has retained. There are no actual red lights, but all the activities connected with them, both in the street and in the innumerable sleazy bars, "breakfast clubs," and go-go joints growing everywhere like rampant fungi. This is definitely not a region for women minus escorts.

□ For the young seeking each other, the eight blocks of **Union Street** between Van Ness and Fillmore offer a score of pleasant, somewhat conservative bars and clubs that attract people in their 20s and 30s, most of them natives. It's a nice area for walking in the evening, so sample a few spots before settling on a favorite.

□ Then there's the gay community, an estimated population of about 100,000 or about one-sixth of the city's total. Lesbians and gay men are responsible for one of the most massive facelifts given to entire neighborhoods of valuable Victorian houses. The annual Gay Freedom Day Parade is usually held on the last Sunday of June, and the annual Castro Street Fair, day and night, takes place the first Sunday in October. And on November 27, a candlelight march from Castro Street to City Hall observes the day that San Francisco's first openly gay public official, the late Supervisor Harvey Milk, as well as Mayor George Moscone, were assassinated. While the tone of the celebration of gay liberation has recently become more subdued these days, the focal point of gay San Francisco remains Castro Street, primarily between 17th and 19th Streets, with its quaint Victorian storefronts and homes, boutiques, and pubs. Polk Street, which has been gentrified longer by the gay population, still has an assortment of gay bars and restaurants. Many lesbians gravitated to the East Bay, so you'll find the San Francisco gay scene to be primarily male.

□ Finally, there's **North Beach:** I outlined its geography in Chapter VII. There is a rather tawdry, concentrated mixture of the first two regions above, with a million lights, a hundred competing barkers, and an almost symphonic volume of noise thrown in. You'll find it absolutely packed with roistering humanity every summer weekend, just reasonably lively on work nights.

So take your pick, ladies and gentlemen, for here we go!

PANORAMIC COCKTAILS

I would suggest that you either start or conclude your night out with a visit to one of the city's famous skyline bars, all of which also serve food ranging from buffets to dinner, often prix fixe. The view from all of them is equally spectacular, but the plushest is definitely the **Crown Room** (tel. 772-5131) of the Fairmont Hotel. On the 24th floor, it is reached by a fabulous outside elevator extending, in a kind of bay-window glass tube, 3½ feet from the face of the building. It feels like riding inside a gargantuan thermometer, watching the city receding below. Once inside, the panoramic backdrop is breathtaking. Drinks average $6. Open for cocktails from 11 a.m. to 1 a.m. Sunday through Thursday, on Friday and Saturday till 2 a.m.

The Mark Hopkins Hotel, opposite on Nob Hill, has the more traditional **Top of the Mark** (tel. 392-3434), a nostalgia-loaded cocktail lounge with immense viewing windows on all sides, which should be enjoyed in turn. Nobody will mind if you wander around with your drink, sampling each direction. Drinks here cost about $5 to $6. More locals than tourists here, since this is a popular rendezvous spot for gilt-edged citizens. Open from 4 p.m. to 1:30 a.m.

The Sir Francis Drake Hotel, at Powell and Sutter Streets, features the **Starlite Roof** (tel. 392-7755), 21 stories skyward. Apart from the wine and excellent cocktails, you also get very smooth combo music and a dance floor to enjoy it. You can dance the night away—at least until 1 a.m. or thereabouts when the music stops. All drinks (even nonalcoholic ones) are $5. All tables offer a view.

Henri's (tel. 771-1400), at the top of the Hilton tower on the 46th floor, offers superb views of the bay to go with your sundowners. There's dancing Tuesday through Saturday from 8 p.m. under a glass roof which allows the illusion of dancing under the stars. It's all very posh, with rich gold-and-blue carpeting, mirrored columns, and floor-to-ceiling draperies. Drinks average $5 to $6.

One of the high spots in San Francisco is the **Carnelian Room** on the 52nd floor of the Bank of America Building, 555 California St., between Kearny and Montgomery (tel. 433-7500). The uninterrupted view is spectacular. Drinks average about $5.25.

The Union Square Holiday Inn offers an unusual ambience in the **S. Holmes, Esquire** (tel. 398-8900), on the 30th floor. A veritable Sherlock Holmes museum, it features a collection of Holmes memorabilia, including a replica of his Baker Street quarters with recorded London street sounds in the background. Furnishings are plush velvet, and the attractions include backgammon tables, a pianist or strolling violinist, and two wood-burning fireplaces. The average drink is $5.

DANCING AND FLOOR SHOWS

The most elegant club in the entire city is the Fairmont's **Venetian Room** (tel. 772-5163), a heavily draped and lavishly gilded supper club with scenes of gondoliers navigating around the arches at one end. The big names who drop into San Francisco can be found appearing here—people like Joel Grey, Mel Tormé, Tony Bennett, Judy Collins, Carol Channing, Eartha Kitt, or Ella Fitzgerald. You can dine, drink, and dance at the Venetian Room, but there is no way to make the evening inexpensive. The cover charge varies from about $25 to $35, depending on who's appearing. Weeknights are usually on the less expensive end. Drinks go for $6 to $7 apiece.

TANGO AT THE TONGA. For dinner, dancing, and a uniquely "camp" experience, try the **Tonga Room** (tel. 772-5278) in the Fairmont Hotel. This oldtime San Francisco restaurant is built around what used to be the hotel's swimming pool and is now a lagoon in a romantic South Seas village setting. Candlelight, Polynesian fabrics and sculptures, and thatched roofing all contribute to the ambience.

The band plays in the middle of the lagoon on a roofed barge, and you dance on what used to be the quarter deck of the three-masted schooner *Forester*, which plied the South Pacific trades in the early 1900s.

Don't be surprised if you hear thunder growling and see flashes of lightning. A full-fledged tropical storm bursts over the pool at random intervals, complete with pouring rain (only in the pool).

Dinner—Polynesian and Chinese specialties for the most part—is served from 5 p.m. Specialties include Szechuan beef, Mongolian lamb, and almond pressed duck in a sweet-and-sour sauce. In addition to regular drinks, there's a wide choice of exotic rum concoctions. The band tunes up for dancing at 8 p.m. weeknights and 9 p.m. weekends. The cover charge is $4 on Friday and Saturday, $3 other nights.

WHERE THE YOUNGER SET MINGLES

The reason why I'm bracketing the places below separately is that they are all predominately meeting spots for the under-30s. Those listed are merely a fraction of the total that fall into this category, but they'll do for a start.

Most of the action naturally goes on Friday and Saturday nights, with Monday and Thursday generally the quietest. Also—since all of these establishments serve liquor—you have to be over 21 to gain admission. ID cards are checked fairly rigorously.

Edinburgh Castle, 950 Geary St., near Polk (tel. 885-4074), is this wondrous Scottish pub such as you won't find anywhere in Scotland. For a start, it's huge; second, it's warm; and third, on Friday and Saturday nights there are bagpipers going full blast, marching bravely up and down. The walls are covered with Royal Air Force mementos, horse brasses, steel helmets, army rifles, and bugles, and the jukebox plays Scottish airs. Try Scotland's national liqueur, Drambuie, and an order of fish and chips. Open till 1 a.m. Sunday through Thursday, till 2 a.m. on Friday and Saturday.

Possibly the best wall-to-wall, action-packed singles bar in the city, **Perry's** stands at 1944 Union St., at Buchanan (tel. 922-9022). The clientele here often ranges above the 30 "age limit," and it includes a "yuppie" host of successful lawyers, doctors, and young business people, all of whom are pretty well dressed in the current mode. Everybody is friendly and all you have to do to start a conversation is to go over and say "Hi." There are several different areas within Perry's. Up front is one dining room, there's another to the rear, and in between stretches the long wooden bar where most of the socializing goes on. Following the brick walkway even farther back, you come to a glassed-in patio hung with planters and a secluded dining room where the tables are decked out in blue-and-white-checked tablecloths, and candlelit at night. Breakfast, lunch, dinner, and brunch are served. The menu is posted on wooden boards in each dining area and its offerings range from simple dishes like hamburgers (considered by many the best in town) to

---

ARTISTS AND MEMORABILIA: The liveliest—and most likable—pub in North Beach is **Specs** (the owner's nickname), at 12 Adler Pl. (tel. 421-4112), just a short walk down Columbus Avenue from the intersection of Columbus and Broadway. Here you find an honest re-creation of the North Beach that was before the topless: poets and acting types holding forth on important topics, a spontaneous flute and guitar group playing off in a corner, Irish musicians, old books and catalogs scattered around for the patrons. Maritime flags hang from the ceiling, and the exposed-brick walls are lined with posters, photos, and various and sundry oddities. Many of the patrons are in the arts in some way, even if their involvement is simply their knowledge of the subject: everybody talks acting, writing, and poetry at Specs. There's a long bar and an assortment of tables. You can sit over a single draft beer for the night if you please. One of the most interesting aspects here is Specs' collection—or "museum," as he calls it—with glass-fronted cupboards containing old San Francisco memorabilia and items brought back to Specs from the seamen who drop in between sailings. Specs himself is the man in the glasses behind the bar, doling out beer to his happy guests. Bar drinks range up from $2.50; beer and wine, $1.50 to $2.50; cheese and crackers, $2. Open weekdays from 4:30 p.m. to 2 a.m., weekends from 5 p.m.

fresh petrale sole meunière. Special dishes are featured daily. Along the walls are framed posters and clippings, such as pictures of the first moonwalk, the Mets winning the pennant, an advertisement for New York's *Village Voice*. Oldtime pub signs hang from the ceiling, proclaiming such sentiments as "Temperance." Nonetheless, drinks are priced from $3. Open nightly till 2 a.m.

Lord Jim's, 1500 Broadway, at the corner of Polk Street (tel. 928-3015), owner/hosted by Spiro, is designed for mingling. Seating facilities range from couches and settees to bar stools, and the décor includes enough antiquarian effects to provide any number of conversational openers. Tiffany-style lamps are overhead, stained glass all around, fresh-cut flowers, ferns and hanging plants in profusion. This is one of the decidedly plusher watering holes, although the bar prices don't reflect it. With the latest expansion, you can dance to live music or enjoy the continental cuisine available from the seafood bar-and-grill restaurant annex. The annex features a beautiful mahogany back bar and a great oyster depot. All this plus Cecil Wells and the Red Hots, in residence from 9 p.m. to 2 a.m., to sustain those who stay and play all night. Hot hors d'oeuvres are served from 4 to 8 p.m. when standard mixed drinks—premium booze all—are $3 to $4. Lord Jim's is open from 10 a.m. to 2 a.m. daily. Dinner is served until 1 a.m. Most important, there's free parking.

THE JAZZ JOINTS

Jazz has not only held its ground generally, but has staged a fair comeback in San Francisco. It's probably the only city in the U.S. listing more jazz joints today than, say, ten years ago. Chief reason for this is that jazz musicians have always loved the place and were prepared to stick to it during the lean years. Herewith some of the spots where they can be found and seen and heard and sometimes danced to.

The **New Orleans Room** is located in the Fairmont Hotel, 950 Mason St., at California (tel. 772-5259). It's the new home of Don Neely's Royal Society Six, playing some of the purest '30s and '40s swing to be heard on the West Coast. The group performs every Tuesday through Saturday from 9:30 p.m. to 1:30 a.m. Jimmy Price and Friends take the stage on Sunday and Monday. The New Orleans Room is open nightly from 6 p.m.

For campy surroundings it's hard to beat the **Great American Music Hall** at 859 O'Farrell St., between Polk and Larkin (tel. 885-0750). From the exterior, the 1907 building looks as though it could house anything from a restaurant to an insurance company, and probably has. Inside you're in a great open square under carved plaster cupids on the ceiling. Gilded mezzanine boxes supported by huge marble pillars protrude from three sides of the room. Nonetheless, the GAMH probably has the most eclectic bookings to be found anywhere. Sarah Vaughan, Wynton Marsalis, Joan Baez, B. B. King, Carmen McRae, Mose Allison, Herbie Mann, Maynard Ferguson, Betty Carter, and Taj Mahal are just a few of the big names who have played here. Other nights you may find new *a cappella* groups, satirical comedy, or a folk troubadour. There also are evenings of music for dancing, usually on weekends, with a wide range of music from the classic '20s and '30s jazz sounds to the '60s rhythm and blues. Occasionally comedy acts and lesser-known names also play here. The cover runs between $10 and $22, depending on the group playing. Light fare and drinks are available, and the hall is open from 7:30 p.m. to 2 a.m. five to seven nights a week (this varies, so call before starting out).

Right across the street from Davies Symphony Hall and the Opera House is **Kimball's,** 300 Grove St., at Franklin (tel. 861-5585 or 861-5555), a handsome old brick building converted to a good-looking, comfortable, two-level restaurant and jazz club. It's a fine stop for a nightcap. There's live music featuring some of the top world-class performers on the jazz scene. What's more, the food's good. Kimball's is open Tuesday through Saturday from 4 p.m. to 1 a.m.; however, closing time depends on whether or not there is a show. It's best to call.

Milestones, 376 5th St., at Harrison (tel. 777-9997), became part of San Francisco's jazz scene just four years ago. Since that time it has made a name as one of the top jazz clubs in town. It books headliners as well as the best of local talent into its elegant and award-winning listening scene. The tone here is intimate, in contrast to a few of the larger, cooler establishments. If you enjoy soft lights and warm jazz, you'll like Milestones. The club is open Monday through Friday from 4 p.m. to 2 a.m., on Saturday from 6 p.m. to 2 a.m., on Sunday to 1 a.m.

COMEDY

Holy City Zoo, 408 Clement St., between Fifth and Sixth Avenues (tel. 386-4242), is home to many a stand-up comic. Wednesday through Sunday they present a professional showcase with local and visiting headliners. Tuesday is "open-mike" night, which means that anybody—amateur or pro—can drop in and do a routine. Monday highlights the All-Pro Comedy Showcase. Showtime is 9 p.m., plus an 11 p.m. show on Friday and Saturday. There's a two-drink minimum with a cover charge of $4 to $10 (depending on the performers) Wednesday through Sunday.

Punch Line, 444 Battery St., between Washington and Clay (tel. 474-3801), is the largest comedy nightclub in the city. The club showcases top national and local talent plus up-and-coming comedians. Improv night is Tuesday, and there's an open mike on Sunday. Showtimes are 9 p.m. Tuesday through Sunday, plus 11 p.m. on Friday and Saturday. Depending on the night, the cover averages $5 to $9, with a two-drink minimum; drinks start at $2.50. It's advisable to buy tickets in advance if you don't want to wait on line.

Cobb's Comedy Club, The Cannery, 2801 Leavenworth, at Jefferson (tel. 928-4320), gathers an upscale family audience presenting national headliners such as Bob Goldthwait, Paula Poundestone, and Bobby Slayton. There is comedy every night, and a seven-comedian Monday Showcase, for $6 to $9. Showtimes are 9 p.m. Tuesday through Sunday; there are 11 p.m. shows on Friday and Saturday. Monday's show at 8 p.m. features talent auditioning for future appearances. Open to minors 18 through 20, and those 16 and 17 accompanied by legal guardian. The club also has an adjoining restaurant and bar, the Café Zero° C.

The **Other Café,** 100 Carl St., at Cole (tel. 681-7400 or 681-0748), is in the Haight-Ashbury section made famous in the '60s. The café is where Robin Williams is said to have gotten his start, and where he sometimes appears, as does Jay Leno, when in San Francisco. Tuesday-night shows feature 15 to 20 auditioning comics—amateur and pro—while Wednesday through Sunday shows present headliners, both national and local, like Elayne Boosler and Richard Lewis. There are shows nightly at 9 p.m., with an additional 11 p.m. show on Friday and Saturday. The cover varies from $4 to $12, depending on the performers, with a two-drink minimum. Most drinks are in the $2.50 to $3.50 range.

The Other Café also features a limited menu specializing in homemade soups, sandwiches, and salads. Reservations can be made for priority seating.

A MIXED BAG

It's hard to define **Harry's,** at 2020 Fillmore St., at California (tel. 921-1000). There's jazz piano nightly in this crowded, friendly saloon where Harry Denton holds sway and mingles with politicians, local hoi polloi—young and well beyond the legal drinking age. If for no other reason than to observe the local fauna, or the rich blue walls and huge antique mahogany bar, or just to sit and listen to the music after the ballet or the opera, Harry's is a fun place to be. There's also a small but satisfying menu. It's open nightly from 4 p.m. to 2 a.m.

The **Curtain Call Lounge,** 456 Geary St., near Taylor (tel. 474-5918), is just across from the American Conservatory Theatre (ACT). It's a comfortable, relaxed place where you expect theater people to walk in after a performance, and they do. There's a great long bar with bentwood chairs and simulated calfskin cushions, lit by overhead lamps with Tiffany-type shades. Reddish-brown walls remind you more of New Mexico than San Francisco, but never mind—they're just about covered with pictures of every movie star you've ever known and some you haven't. Jazz is in front on Saturday and Sunday, variety entertainment is in back, plus an "open mike." Stop by after the theater, or after a late dinner. The Curtain Call is open daily from 10 a.m. to 2 a.m. No cover and no minimum.

Sports events, concerts, exhibits, conventions, trade shows, you name it—all take place at the **Cow Palace,** at Geneva and Santos Streets, about ten miles from downtown in Daly City (tel. 469-6000), a multipurpose facility with a 14,500-seat showplace that presents top-name entertainment. Check the paper to see what's on; it could be anything from Walt Disney's *World on Ice,* the San Francisco Sports and Boat Show, to the Ringling Bros. and Barnum & Bailey Circus, which comes here annually. Among the stars who have entertained at the Cow Palace are John Denver, Neil Diamond, Kenny Rogers, and Prince. The Cow Palace has hosted two Republican National Conventions, presented Soviet gymnasts (with Olga Korbut), and is the home of the Grand National Rodeo, Horse Show, and Livestock Exposition each October.

Ticket prices vary by event and performer. Tickets are available through BASS/Ticketmaster, Ticketron, major ticket outlets, or at the Cow Palace box office.

PIANO LOUNGES

These are San Francisco's specialties, and the Bay City is chock full of numerous variations on this theme. Their décor ranges from the simple to the luxurious, but they invariably have two bars—one for general drinkers; the other, forming an intimate semicircle around a piano or organ, for patrons more interested in what's going on. Depending on the clients' mood, talent, or daring, the musician either plays solo for quiet listening, leads a sing-along, or accompanies impromptu vocalists.

These places keep normal bar hours and charge normal bar prices; they get people acquainted rapidly and frequently turn habitual shrinking violets into rampant exhibitionists. They can offer exceedingly jolly evenings providing (a) you like people and (b) you're not a musical aesthete.

At the **Ramada Renaissance Hotel,** 55 Cyril Magnin St., at Market and North 5th Streets (tel. 392-8000), you can relax in comfort in handsome plush-velvet chairs and listen to a mix of old and new melodies played on a magnificent grand piano in the Piazza.

The three-story atrium surrounding the room provides an elegant background for the music played from noon to 2 a.m.

One of the nicest places in town to listen to piano music is the conservatory-style **Fournou's Bar** at the Stanford Court, 905 California St., at Powell (tel. 989-3500). It's an extremely luxurious, not to say romantic, setting, with windows all around providing splendid views in every direction, including the bay.

The **Mark Hopkins**, just up the street at 1 Nob Hill (tel. 392-3434), also has a pianist entertaining nightly in a delightfully intimate room with hand-painted murals—the skylighted Lower Bar just off the lobby. It's another very simpático environment in which to enjoy drinks and music.

DISCOTHÈQUES AND DANCE BARS

San Francisco caught "Saturday Night Fever" with a vengeance a few years ago. As a result the entire Bay Area mushroomed an immense crop of disco spots, ranging from heavenly to hideous, catering to every financial bracket and to a much wider age group than is generally assumed.

All discos share a similar layout, and you'll find a bar, dance floor, sound system, and either a very visible or discreetly camouflaged DJ to spin the records. The platter person may be male or female, garrulous or silent, but the DJ represents an essential fixture —the American innovation that distinguishes these spots from their European forerunners, which relied on tapes minus the human touch.

The current disco lineup is not quite as long or as intense as it was a couple of years ago, but it's still around and in some cases still quaking the floors.

Alexis, 1001 California St., at Mason, across from the Mark Hopkins Hotel (tel. 771-1001). Super-elegant and extremely Nob Hill, Le Disque is the downstairs portion of a celebrated restaurant. It has a dress code which insists that gentlemen wear coats and ties. The ambience is plush, with mounted animal trophies, Russian tapestries on the walls, and a large fireplace to keep things cozy. The club caters to an older crowd, playing music skewed toward the sounds of a few years ago and the golden oldies. Open Thursday through Saturday from 10 p.m. to 2 a.m. No cover or minimum; drinks are about $5 to $6.

I-Beam, 1748 Haight St., at Cole (tel. 668-6006 for a recorded message only). Large and stylishly done, this is the spot for new rock. Lasers go, and go, and go. It's the home of the floor-quake with a different vibration each night. Monday brings on line local and national bands, Tuesday to Saturday the I-Beam moves with new rock dancing, video, and laser shows from 9 p.m. to 2 a.m.

Weekends attract the Bay Area crowd. Sunday is Gay's Night—there's a tea dance not like any other you may have attended, which begins at 5 p.m. and goes on to 2 a.m. Video screens feature the latest releases. Sunday nights there is Nifty '50s music. Admission is $2 to $12, depending on the night and the performers. Drinks are $2 to $4.

The most sophisticated dance club in the Bay Area is the posh **Oz,** on the 32nd floor of the St. Francis Hotel, Powell Street, between Post and Geary (tel. 397-7000). It's a private club, but non-members can enter by paying a $8 to $16 cover charge. However, it's rather formal: no one is allowed in wearing jeans, and men must wear jackets and button-down shirts. Oz's disc jockeys are supplied by Juliana's of London, a disco consulting firm with a chic worldwide clientele. They play disco, New Wave, Motown, and oldies—European as well as American. Reached via a glass elevator, Oz has a marble dance floor and a superb lighting system, including mirrored columns with Tivoli lights that move to the beat of the music. The setting evokes a forest glade, complete with birch trees, ferns, and rockery; you also get superb views of the city at night. Among the amenities are a marble bar, cushioned bamboo armchairs, and plush sofas, as well as backgammon and chess tables. Cocktails are served from 4:30 to 8:30 p.m. nightly, a good time to enjoy the setting sun. There's disco Sunday through Thursday from 9:30 p.m. to 2 a.m., on Friday and Saturday until 4 a.m. The average drink is $5.

Club DV8, 55 Natoma St., between Mission and Howard at 1st St. (tel. 957-1730), is the town's terribly stylish and posh disco. There's no question that the décor is spectacular—a mix of trompe l'oeil, pop art, candelabras, mirrors, and some extraordinary Dali-esque props. There are two huge dance floors on different levels which separate the members of Club Prive from the plebians. Several rooms have been set apart for just talking over a drink or an espresso. The club is open on Thursday from 10 p.m. to 2 a.m., on Friday and Saturday to 4 a.m. The average drink is $4.

The youth of the city gravitates, in part, to **City Nights,** 715 Harrison St., at 3rd (tel. 546-7774). The establishment has a DJ, a two-house-size dance floor, large-screen videos, a laser-light show, and mood music from the top 40s. During the day it's part of Little Joe's on Harrison. Life begins Thursday through Saturday at 9 p.m. and goes on through 2 a.m. on Thursday, other nights to 3 a.m. Those 18 to 20 are admitted on Thursday and Friday, but not on Saturday. Cover charge is $9 on Friday, $8 on Saturday; drinks average $3.50.

Then there's **Firehouse 7,** 3160 16th St., at Guerrero (tel. 621-1617), once (you guessed it) a firehouse, now a great disco. If you've always known that you were a friendly soul oriented toward the art, music, and film set, Firehouse 7 is your disco destiny. A good local rock or reggae band usually inhabits the premises every Friday, and there's DJ dance music nightly except Monday, which is Film Showcase night when experimental films are screened. And don't miss (as though you could) the display of oversize artworks. Firehouse 7 is open daily from noon to 2 a.m. There's a $6 cover charge on Friday, but drink prices are reasonable—about $2.50.

CONDUCTED TOURS

For those who prefer their nightlife in comfortably packaged doses, there are several outfits to choose from. The advantage of these tours is, of course, that they save you from worrying about transportation, table reservations, bills, and tipping. One lump amount takes care of the lot. You get picked up at your hotel and delivered back there, by either bus, taxi, or limousine, depending on the size of the party.

Remember that these are nightspot tours, so don't bring along minors who might be refused admission to some establishments. And don't dress *too* casually; gentlemen should wear coats and ties.

The **Gray Line** conducts a variety of nightclub tours on which you can book reservations by phoning 558-9400. There's a choice of tours, with dinner and without, and you can go to two or three nightclubs, including **Finocchio's,** a North Beach club featuring California's best female impersonators, or on a cruise with dinner. Tours are offered Tuesday through Sunday nights, and range in price from $27.50 to $65 per person. Reservations are required.

A somewhat more unusual view of a fascinating part of the city at night is the trip through Chinatown conducted by **Ding How Tours** (tel. 981-8399). This 3½-hour tour, with dinner at a Chinese restaurant (optional), explores the sights, back alleys, and activities of Chinatown at night. Without dinner, the tour is $19; with dinner, $32. Reservations are required.

CHAPTER XII

A SHOPPING SPREE

□ □ □

If New York and Chicago are department store cities, then San Francisco could be termed a boutique town. Although she has several reasonably large emporiums, her main attraction lies in the small, smart specialty shops, which boast a distinctive touch all their own.

They may sell fashions, books, jewelry, tobacco, shoes, lamps, antiques, or stationery, but they usually do so with an individualistic chic and flair, which you find overseas only in Paris, Vienna, and London.

The Bay City's other shopping forte is the Oriental bazaar type of establishment—the place where you get anything from an Arabian water pipe to a Chinese butter dish under one roof and frequently side by side. And whereas the first category invites lustful window-shopping, the second offers unlimited browsing.

However, by no stretch of the term could San Francisco be called a cheap shopping city. Her men's and women's clothing are among the most fashionable in America, but most of the items are marked "Slightly dearer West of the Rockies." It's lucky that the natives, because of the barely changing climate, need only one wardrobe all year round.

There are, of course, exceptions to this rule, but unfortunately not in the realm of general merchandise. You can pick up some very good import bargains and some low-priced Oriental knick-knacks in Chinatown. But while San Francisco offers high quality, it offers few opportunities for bargain-hunting.

It does, however, present some of the most distinguished and exciting shopping districts on earth.

The first is the **downtown** region, centered on Union Square, and enclosed by Bush, Taylor, Market, and Montgomery Streets. This area contains all of the city's department stores, most of her specialty shops, and the narrow enclave called **Maiden Lane** (east of

Union Square), lined with some of the most elegant showcases in town.

The second is **Chinatown,** along Grant Avenue, which becomes Oriental after you pass through the ceremonial gateway at Bush Street. With a few notable exceptions, the shops here are far from fashionable, but wildly colorful, fascinating, and frequently cheap. Normal shopping hours don't apply, though most of the stores are open until 10 p.m. every day.

It's best not to try driving down Grant or Stockton in this area, because traffic is slow, at best. My first word of advice for those browsing through Chinatown is, if you've come by car, don't frustrate yourself by searching for a parking spot—they rarely exist. The best (and cheapest) place to park is the Portsmouth Square Garage. The entrance is on Kearney Street between Clay and Washington. If you arrive before 10:30 a.m., you will probably be able to drive right in, but between 10:30 a.m. and 2:30 p.m. there's a line to enter that usually goes around the block. Since many Chinese do their shopping here, the rates for one or two hours are a bargain: 50¢ for the first hour, 75¢ for the second hour, $1.75 for the third hour and each hour thereafter—for a maximum of $12 for 24 hours. Therefore, if you're there for two hours the tab is $1.25 in total, or for three hours it's $3. By comparison, you'll find that other garages in this area charge as much as $3 per hour, on up to $1.75 for 20 minutes. Another advantage of parking at Portsmouth Square is that it's in the heart of Chinatown, where the first Chinese immigrants settled, and just one block from Grant Avenue.

The third shopping district is **Union Street** between Van Ness and Steiner, currently the "in" stretch for antique shops, of which it has more than 20. You will also find American, Far Eastern, and Scandinavian handcrafts, high fashions, and deluxe glassware. A very fancy array beckons, making it a delightful and relaxed shopping territory.

The fourth is the region around **Fisherman's Wharf** (see Chapter VIII), which contains the marvelous shopping centers of Ghirardelli Square, Pier 39, the Cannery, and The Anchorage, as well as two of the most intriguing bazaars in town, which we'll visit a bit further on.

It's quite impossible to give you even a faintly comprehensive rundown of San Francisco's shopping facilities in the space of this book. That would require a one-volume encyclopedia. My reason for outlining the above shopping areas is to let you stroll and browse around and make discoveries for yourself. Here, I'll merely give you a few random highlights and personal favorites. Though they cover but a minute corner of the Bay City's retail field, they all—as do the rest of San Francisco's shops—seem to share one pleasant characteristic: the unhurried courtesy of the service, the personalized welcome that has been known to startle hard-nosed Easterners.

Starting with the downtown region, then:

DOWNTOWN

Post Street is the chic shopping arena that trails from Kearny Street, where you'll find the Crocker Galleria (a lovely inducement to spend), on to Taylor, and perhaps a bit farther (heading in the direction of Union Square). Some of San Francisco's poshest establishments have their lairs here, and if you plan to do more than sightsee, you'll need deep pockets.

Polo/Ralph Lauren, 90 Post St., at Kearny (tel. 567-7656), features the entire collection of apparel for the family from casual and roughwear to couture clothing, footwear, and accessories. The multilevel store is beautifully assembled and is a tribute to the elegance and taste of the designer. Open Monday through Saturday from 10 a.m. to 6 p.m.

Farther up the block, between Kearny and Grant, **Mark Cross,** 170 Post St. (tel. 391-7770), offers the ultimate in leather goods. For over 100 years Mark Cross has been known for the quality and beauty of its workmanship. All leather goods are hand-constructed and classically styled of calfskin, pigskin, ostrich, and lizard. The store will even have your purchase gold-embossed with your initials, free of charge. Mark Cross is open Monday through Saturday from 10 a.m. to 6 p.m.

In the same block, at 180 Post St. is **F.A.O. Schwarz** (tel. 391-0100), the world's greatest toy store for children and adults. It's filled with every imaginable toy, from hand-carved, custom-painted carousel rocking horses, myriad dolls, and stuffed animals of every type and dimension, to gas-powered cars, train sets, information games, mind-twisters, and hobby supplies galore. Be forewarned: I have found that no one I know—of whatever age—has ever entered Schwarz's and come out without a purchase. Open Monday through Saturday from 9:30 a.m. to 5:30 p.m.

A bit farther up the block is **A. Sulka & Company,** at 188 Post St. (tel. 362-3450), famous for its sophisticated haberdashery. This is a gentleman's store, the place to review an exquisite collection of shirts, ties, dressing gowns, scarfs, pajamas, and sweaters, to list just some of the fine apparel for men. The Sulka label has always been synonymous with superb quality. Open Monday through Saturday from 10 a.m. to 5:30 p.m.

I assume that there are some city dwellers who have never heard of **Brooks Brothers,** but they must be rather scarce. In San Francisco, this bulwark of tradition is located at 201 Post St., near Grant (tel. 397-4500), along your stroll up Post. Brooks Brothers introduced the button-down collar, and with that, changed the look of

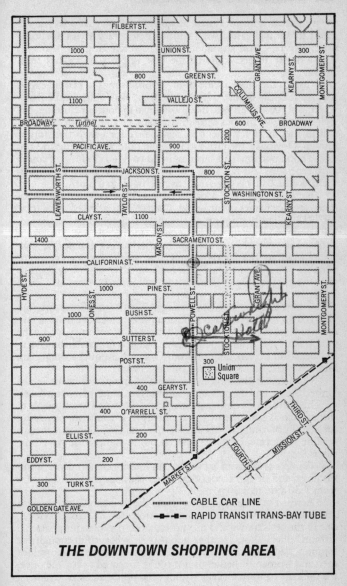

THE DOWNTOWN SHOPPING AREA

CABLE CAR LINE

RAPID TRANSIT TRANS-BAY TUBE

the well-dressed businessman, at work and at play. Brooks has updated traditional casual wear with contemporary styles in sportswear, sweaters, and shirts. It's also an interesting shop to visit if you'd like to see some of the best imports of apparel from Britain.

Just up the block is one of my favorite shops—I could spend the day at **Eddie Bauer,** 220 Post St. (tel. 986-7600). Eddie Bauer was one of the first firms to use goosedown in outdoor clothing. My well-worn down booties with leather soles, given to me in 1975 and still in use, are a testament to the quality for which the store is known. Obviously the firm specializes in outdoor clothing and still does a good portion of its business in down-filled clothing. If you're a fisherperson, you can spend hours in the store's fishing department. Eddie Bauer is open daily from 10 a.m. to 6 p.m.

Between Grant and Stockton you will find one of the most famous jewelry names in the world, **Cartier, Inc.,** at 231 Post St. (tel. 397-3180). The boutique is an elegant setting for some very beautifully designed jewelry, watches, crystal, and accessories. The firm is almost 150 years old and the famous interlocking double "C" continues to shine. Despite the store's fame, service is always gracious, whether you intend to buy diamonds or silver or simply want to view the goodies. Open Monday through Saturday from 10 a.m. to 5:30 p.m.

Gump's, 250 Post St., between Grant and Stockton (tel. 982-1616), is San Francisco's most impressive treasure trove, a museum and store all in one. Founded more than a century ago by the Gump family, this supremely elegant and tasteful establishment offers beautiful objects ranging from Oriental antiques to porcelain Steuben glass and Baccarat and Lalique crystal.

Gump's has the largest collection of freshwater pearls in the United States, and designs and manufactures much of its own jewelry. The firm also specializes in fine jade jewelry, and lovely pieces in stones such as aquamarine and tourmaline. If you're in the market for a family of hand-carved Chilean lapis lazuli penguins, a Venetian opaline glass vase, or a silver-plated monogrammed jewelry box, this is the place.

Gump's also has an art gallery, an interior-design salon of furnishings, and design accessories. Open Monday through Saturday from 9:30 a.m. to 5:30 p.m.

Across the street and a few doors down is the **Gucci** shop, at 253 Post St., between Grant and Stockton (tel. 772-2522). Gucci, one of the best-known and most prestigious names in international fashion, offers shoes, leather goods, scarfs beautiful enough for framing, slacks, blouses—in all, an elegant selection of apparel for men and women. Whether or not you're prepared to pay the price, it's difficult to leave Gucci's without the purchase of an enduring treasure. Open Monday through Saturday from 10 a.m. to 5:30 p.m.

Jaeger International, 272 Post St., near Stockton (tel. 421-3714) has an international reputation for superb fabrics, especially lightweight wools, in classic designs for women. You'll find jackets, sweaters, pants, and skirts, casual or formal, coordinated to your taste. Open Monday through Saturday from 10 a.m. to 6 p.m.

Alfred Dunhill of London, 290 Post St., at Stockton (tel. 781-3368), began as a tobacconist at the turn of the century. It still is, specializing in custom-blended tobacco and, more recently, smoking accessories—Dunhill lighters are among the most elegantly designed and consistently functional. Over the years, Dunhill has added an exquisite line of men's clothing, including sweaters, jackets, and shirts. Leather goods and luggage, which were added fairly recently, bear the trademark of Dunhill quality. Open Monday through Saturday from 10 a.m. to 5:30 p.m.

Right about now, at Stockton Street, you can make a left and walk one block to Geary Street. There you will find the **Pearl Empire,** 127 Geary, between Stockton and Grant (tel. 362-0606). The Pearl Empire has been importing all its fabulous jewelry directly from Hong Kong and Japan since 1957. From pearls to coral and jade, from tie tacks to necklaces, the Pearl Empire offers the finest available anywhere, and is well worth a visit. Open Monday through Saturday from 9:30 a.m. to 5:30 p.m.

S. Christian of Copenhagen, now south of Market at 201 Potrero Ave., at the corner of 15th Street (tel. 552-8540), is where people from all over the country come for Christmas and Mother's Day plates. These are collector's items because the molds are broken after the first run, and the plates are usually worth five times the purchase price in a few years. Everything in the store comes from Europe, including "seconds" of Rosenthal crystal which cost two-thirds less than the completely perfect pieces. You'll also find superb Scandinavian jewelry, as well as one of the country's largest selections of top-quality teak and rosewood Scandinavian furniture. Open Monday through Saturday from 9 a.m. to 5:30 p.m.

If you find yourself heading for Athens without the slightest idea of whether your hairdryer will work, go straight to the **Travel Market,** Golden Gateway Commons, 130 Pacific Avenue Mall (tel. 421-4080). This complete travel-goods store will outfit you with the proper plug for any destination—and while you're there, you can pick up street maps and guidebooks. Anne Brunsell started the store several years ago to provide all those indispensable odds and ends that make travel easier and more enjoyable.

She has stocked the store with all kinds of ingenious and useful items. There are water purifiers, currency converters, many styles of money belts, containers for protecting film, marvelous carry-on bags, pocket radios, and small, easy-to-pack games, just the thing for whiling away hours on a plane, unless you'd prefer to spend your flying time reading language books or listening to cassettes—both available here in every major language. Open Monday through Friday from 10 a.m. to 6 p.m., on Saturday from 11 a.m. to 5 p.m.

Walking around the downtown shopping area you'll find flower stands on almost every corner. Taking flowers home, or to your host or hostess, is an old San Francisco tradition. The ultimate in flower shops is **Podesta Baldocchi,** at One Embarcadero Center (tel. 397-7630). Just walking through the thousands of flowers and plants in this artful jungle is an exquisite experience. Open Monday through Friday from 7 a.m. to 6 p.m., on Saturday from 10 a.m. to 2 p.m. The main store is at 2525 California St., between Steiner and Pierce (tel. 346-1300).

There are lots of other shops and restaurants at the Embarcadero Center, where you can also inspect Ruth Asawa's fountain sculpture of San Francisco scenes and listen to live music.

Since clicking shutters are the predominant sound in the Bay City during tourist season, you might need a store supplying the wherewithals, plus maintenance of same. **Brooks Cameras,** 45 Kearny St., at Maiden Lane (tel. 392-1900), claims to have the most complete inventory of cameras and accessories on the West Coast. They also offer an authorized repair service and expert advice by factory-trained salesmen, as well as one-hour photofinishing, obviously a benefit to travelers. Open Monday through Friday from 9 a.m. to 6 p.m., on Saturday from 9:30 a.m. to 5:30 p.m.

Brooks also has stores at 998 Market St., at 6th (tel. 775-5100), and in the financial district at 243 Montgomery St. (tel. 392-5815).

Having friends who are hopeless pipe addicts, I know the woes of trying to locate decent pipe tobaccos in a strange city. The standard cigar-store brands just don't make it for them. I'll therefore include the **Jim Mate Pipe Shop,** 575 Geary St., between Taylor and Jones Streets (tel. 775-6634), for the benefit of fellow searchers. Apart from a huge selection of pipes and imported English tobaccos, Jim Mate sells premium imported cigars and their own special tobacco mixture, which is first-rate. Mail orders can be shipped to 43 countries and throughout the U.S. Open Monday through Saturday from 9 a.m. to 5:30 p.m.

CHINATOWN

The **Unique Company,** 444 Grant Ave., between Pine and Bush Streets (tel. 981-2036), is the shop to go to if one of your interests is calligraphy. The Unique Company specializes in calligraphy and watercolor supplies, and has a good assortment of books relating to these topics. The store also carries a wide selection of carved stones used as seals on letters and documents. They will carve seals to order should you want a special design or group of initials. Open Monday through Saturday from 10 a.m. to 6 p.m.

The **Canton Bazaar,** 616 Grant Ave., between California and Sacramento Streets (tel. 362-5750), features a variety of fancy handcrafts, including fine-quality ivory carvings from all over the Orient, including mainland China. This is the largest direct importer of ivory in the Bay Area. The Canton Bazaar displays an excellent selection of rattan and carved furniture, cloisonné enamelwork ranging in size from small oval boxes to cachepots and vases, rose Canton chinaware, glassware, carved jade, embroideries, jewelry, and antiques from mainland China. There are three floors that you can browse through in a leisurely fashion. Open seven days a week from 10 a.m. to 10:30 p.m.

The **Chinatown Kite Shop,** 717 Grant Ave., near Sacramento Street (tel. 391-8217, 989-5182), has an astonishing assortment of kites, kites, and more kites. You can find attractive fish kites and windsock kites in nylon or cotton, wood-and-paper biplanes, pentagonal kites—all of which make great souvenirs or decorations. The biplanes and pentagonal kites as well as some of the others are assemble-it-yourself projects, but they are beauties. Open daily from 10 a.m. to 10 p.m.

The **Wok Shop,** 804 Grant Ave., at Clay (tel. 989-3797), has every conceivable implement for Chinese cooking, including, of course, woks, a nine-piece, nonstick wok set, sake sets, wok brushes, cleavers, circular chopping blocks, dishes, oyster knives, bamboo steamers, strainers—you name it. The shop also sells a wide range of kitchen utensils, baskets, aprons, etc., and if you're worried about buying more than you can carry or pack, the Wok Shop will be glad to mail your purchases home for you. The people are very congenial and helpful. Open daily from 10 a.m. to 10 p.m.

Imperial Fashion, 838 Grant Ave., at Washington Street (tel. 362-0981, or 362-8174), has some of the most attractive merchandise in Chinatown, most of it from mainland China. You'll find silk blouses, jackets, and kimonos, and you can also buy silk fabrics and have them custom-tailored especially for you. Beautiful embroideries, handkerchiefs, and linens are for sale here too. Open daily from 10 a.m. to 10 p.m. Under the same ownership (and with the same hours) is **Far East Fashion** at 953 Grant Ave. (tel. 362-0986 or 362-8171). Check out both shops for top-quality wares.

Art of China, 839-843 Grant Ave., at Washington Street (tel. 981-1602 or 981-2593), has a wide variety of collectibles, but specializes in exquisite hand-carved Chinese figurines; they have dozens from which you can choose. You'll also find a lovely assortment of ivory beads, bracelets, necklaces, and earrings. And there are Chinese dogs, pink-quartz dogs, jade figurines, porcelain vases, cachepots, and blue-and-white barrels suitable for use as table bases.

But above all, you're bound to be enchanted by the beautiful ivory collectibles known as Netsukes (pronounced net-skis). These small decorative carvings were originally used in Japan to serve as counterweights on men's sashes, from which small belongings were hung. The shop's collection of animal Netsukes includes such enchanting small figures as rabbits, geese, horses, frogs, monkeys, turtles—a whole menagerie of ivory carvings.

And if you're a chess buff, or are looking for an exceptional gift for one, there's even a magnificent hand-carved ivory chess set for $15,000. Bear in mind that it's quite common for a shop in Chinatown to carry inexpensive items for $2 or less, as well as such expensive items. Open daily from 10 a.m. to 7 p.m.

By now you probably need a pick-me-up. So stop in at the **Ten Ren Tea Company,** 949 Grant Ave., between Jackson and Washington (tel. 362-0656), to partake of the free tea samples, and perhaps to buy some tea, ginseng, a variety of herbal teas, or tea paraphernalia like pots, cups, infusers, etc. If you can't make up your mind what kind of tea to buy, pick up a mail-order form and order once you get home. Open seven days from 9:30 a.m. to 10 p.m.

UNION STREET

A very pleasant afternoon indeed can be spent poking through the boutiques, antique shops, and highly original stores along the five blocks of Union Street between Gough and Fillmore. I'd recommend making this tour at a crawl, with stops for refreshments along the way.

If you happen to be in San Francisco during June, the **Union Street Spring Arts & Crafts Festival** is held the first weekend in that month—it's fun, and you can also enjoy the food, wine tasting, fashion shows, and entertainment. During the festival, Union Street is closed to traffic from Fillmore to Gough from 10 a.m. to 6 p.m. on Saturday and Sunday.

Now let's begin our tour. Facing west on Union at Gough, I'll start with the block—

FROM GOUGH TO OCTAVIA: l'herbier de provence, at 1728 Union St. (tel. 928-4483), is the Union Street specialist in herbs, herb teas, herbs as skin conditioners and in bath products; shampoos, soaps, and savonnettes of Marseilles; and aromatic plants and spices for cooking, as well as bath oils. The fragrance here is lovely, and the selection of products is large enough to satisfy anyone interested in natural and pure essential oils, as well as dried flowers, petals, and floral wreaths. Open Monday through Saturday from 10:30 a.m. to 7 p.m., on Sunday to 6 p.m.

To begin with a view of the Orient, stop in at **Futons by Akiko,** at no. 1747 (tel. 776-8884), where Akiko herself presides, making kimonos, exotic T-shirts, and of course, futons (Japanese cotton-stuffed mattresses). The shop is open Monday through Saturday from 10:30 a.m. to 7 p.m., on Sunday from noon to 6:30 p.m.

Exquisite custom-designed gold jewelry is sold at the **Union Street Goldsmith,** no. 1763 (tel. 776-8048). The goldsmith in residence is Glenda Queen, but the shop has also become a showcase for other Bay Area artists. Open Monday through Saturday from 11 a.m. to 5:45 p.m., on Sunday from noon to 4:45 p.m.

Across the street, check out **O'Plume,** at no. 1764 (tel. 771-6100), for European down comforters, throws, fancy French pillows, shams, and comforter covers. O'Plume also has fine linens of Egyptian cotton from Belgium and France. Open Monday through Saturday from 10 a.m. to 6 p.m.

If you've always wanted a crystal ball, **The Enchanted Crystal,** no. 1771 (tel. 885-1335), is the place to buy it. The shop has an extensive collection of fine crystal and one-of-a-kind decorative art, including one of the largest crystal balls in the world (from Madagascar). Open Monday through Saturday from 10 a.m. to 5:30 p.m. and on Sunday from noon to 5 p.m.

Images of the North, no. 1782 (tel. 673-1273), has one of the most extensive collections of Inuit art—Canadian and Alaskan—in the United States. It is San Francisco's only gallery specializing in native North American art. Each piece is personally chosen for Images of the North from Inuit cooperatives, and represents the finest work available, including museum-quality sculpture by foremost Inuit artists. Works in several media are featured (including superb miniatures) and younger artists of potential as well as established masters are on display. By all means, make a stop here for an education in the beauty and diversity of very collectible Inuit art. Open Monday through Saturday from 11 a.m. to 5:30 p.m., on Sunday from noon to 4 p.m.

More far-flung items can be found at **Kundus,** no. 1782 (tel. 441-8772), housing a large selection of Indian, Tibetan, and Nepalese paintings, bronzes, and statuary dating from the 1st to the 15th centuries A.D. Beautiful antique rugs are available from Afghanistan, Turkey, and Iran. Kundus sells mainly to museums and collectors, but it's a great place to browse, and the owners are friendly. Open Tuesday through Saturday from noon to 6 p.m.

OCTAVIA TO LAGUNA: H. P. Corwith Ltd., no. 1833 (tel. 567-7252), is a store full of really neat *chatchkes*. There are bronze puffins; designer foods (not edible); teeny Victorian houses; piggy banks; blueprints for cooking (yes, I do mean blueprints) hamburgers, lasagne, or tacos; prints of a teddy bear parade; tulip floor lamps —you get the idea. It's lots of fun and has terrific collectibles or gifts. Go. Open Monday through Saturday from 10 a.m. to 5 p.m.

Oggetti, Inc., no. 1846 (tel. 346-0631), is a fascinating shop specializing in the sale of objects decorated with papier à cuvé, or what has been known as marbelized paper. Oggetti has elegant boxes, frames, jewelry boxes, pencils, pencil boxes, and blank books, among other lovely objects. One of the most original techniques used to hand-decorate paper, papier à cuvé, according to tradition, was invented in the 17th century by Mace Ruette, the royal bookbinder of Louis XIII. Today this type of paper printing is rare, but still lovely in all its applications. Oggetti is open Monday through Thursday from 10 a.m. to 6 p.m., on Friday to 8 p.m., on Saturday to 6 p.m., and on Sunday from noon to 6 p.m.

There's fascinating exotica at **Far Corners,** no. 1854 (tel. 922-6086), in a courtyard off the street. The proprietor does all her own buying in such far corners as Indonesia, India, Nepal, China, etc., and stocks all sorts of fascinating clothing and unusual artifacts. Open Tuesday through Saturday from 10:30 a.m. to 5 p.m.

The **Dynasty Gallery,** no. 1854 (tel. 922-9105), specializes in rug basketry, the craft of creating vases, baskets, and a variety of what would ordinarily be pottery shapes out of braided rug. These lovely forms obviously are much lighter than pottery, are formed in delicate pastels, and—for those of you who are eminently practical —they are dirt repellent. The gallery also has beautifully decorated stone and porcelain plaques. Open Monday through Saturday from 10 a.m. to 7 p.m. and on Sunday from noon to 5 p.m.

Fumiki Fine Asian Arts, no. 1894 (tel. 922-0573), specializes in fine Oriental art and antiques, including Japanese baskets and Chinese silk paintings and embroidery. The shop also features antique and accent furniture. It has an exceptional collection of jade, coral, and lapis jewelry, as well as jade and ivory carvings. Open Monday through Saturday from 10 a.m. to 6 p.m., on Sunday from noon to 5 p.m.

LAGUNA TO BUCHANAN: If you need a little fortification at this point, stop by **La Petite Boulangerie,** at no. 1909 (tel. 567-4665), for delicious croissants in numerous varieties, including chocolate, berry, apple, and almond, as well as bagels and breads. The bakery is open from 7 a.m. to 9 p.m. Monday through Saturday, to 6 p.m. on Sunday.

If you love one-of-a-kind handmade items, you'll definitely want to visit **Anne,** at no. 1931 (tel. 921-6818). Most of the unusual items in the shop are carefully selected by owner Anne Hewitt, who, when not traveling in search of exotica, spends much of her time in the shop. The work of local artisans is also represented among the international folk art, jewelry, and ethnic garments. Open Monday through Saturday from noon to 6 p.m., on Sunday to 5 p.m.

Bepples Pie Shop and Restaurant, no. 1934 (tel. 931-6225), has mouthwatering noshables: soups, muffins, pies, breads—the important things to sustain life at almost any hour. Bepples is open Monday through Wednesday from 7 a.m. to 11:30 p.m., on Friday from 7 a.m. to 1 a.m., on Saturday from 9 a.m. to 1 a.m., and on Sunday from 9 a.m. to 10 p.m.

When you stop at **Fabulous Things Ltd.,** no. 1974 (tel. 346-0346 or 346-3337), be prepared to be there for at least half an hour. The gallery has our nation's largest collection of pre-1935 quilts. You'll find folk-art carvings from some of the country's leading artists, contemporary primitive paintings, and handmade collector teddy bears. Everything displayed in this country-style store is unique and either intriguing, beautiful, or cuddly. The store has been in operation since 1967 and in its extensive collection of arts and crafts you will also see magnificent handcrafted silver jewelry, and hand-beaded articles from the Creek, Seminole, and Cheyenne nations. Open Monday through Saturday from 10:30 a.m. to 5:30 p.m., on Sunday from noon to 5 p.m.

The Deli Bar and Restaurant, no. 1980 (tel. 563-7274), has an extensive menu of sandwiches, soup, salads, and light entrees ranging from $3 to $12. More important than the food is its location—it's a great place for people-watching and socializing. If you've been strolling up and down Union, stop at the Deli and relax. Their hours suit yours if you're a late riser: they're open daily from 11 a.m. to 2 a.m.

BUCHANAN TO WEBSTER: If you're looking for things to do for your body, you'll find plenty of ideas at the **Body Shop,** no. 2072 (tel. 922-4076). All the oils, unguents, lotions, and whatnot here are made to the Body Shop's specifications, and every product is biodegradable. For your bath there's cocoa butter oil or lilac bubble bath. Perhaps rosemary oil will bring back the sheen to lackluster hair. Soaps come in over 30 scents including blueberry, rain, pikaki, and black rose. And if you don't find the scent you want, the Body Shop people will mix and match to create a fragrance to your specifications. An endless variety of perfumes and lotions is available, and there's all sorts of stuff to put on your face—aloe vera fresheners, clay masks, cleansing grains, lemon-oat cleansers, etc. And to apply it all you can buy sponges and bath brushes. Stop in and smell things. Even if you don't want to buy, you might want to sign up for their mail-order catalog. Open Monday through Saturday from 11 a.m. to 6 p.m., on Sunday from noon to 5 p.m.

If croissants didn't strike your fancy, you may be more tempted by the offerings at **Mrs. Field's Cookies,** at no. 2070 (tel. 922-6583). In addition to a variety of cookies, you can buy coffee, sodas, and milk. Mrs. Field's is open from 11 a.m. to 8 p.m. Sunday through Thursday, to 10 p.m. on Friday and Saturday.

WEBSTER TO FILLMORE: Cross the street and it's almost like being in New York's Soho. The ex-Gothamite owner of **New York West,** 2100 Union St. (tel. 567-8130), brings East Coast high-fashion chic to San Francisco at this very fine women's clothing store. Open Monday through Saturday from 11 a.m. to 6:30 p.m., on Sunday from noon to 5:30 p.m.

Exquisite sweaters, many of them one-of-a-kind as well as the store's own design, handmade and imported, are among the wares for men and women at **Three Bags Full,** no. 2181 (tel. 567-5753). Open Monday through Saturday from 11 a.m. to 6 p.m., on Sunday from noon to 5 p.m.

Around the corner from Union Street is **Silkroute International,** 3119 Fillmore St. (tel. 563-4936). It's owned and operated by an Afghani who offers fascinating wares, old and new, from his native country. Here you can buy needlework, clothing, brass and copperware, jewelry, and even antique guns. There are lots and lots of Oriental carpets, tribal rugs, and tapestries for sale, including antiques, as well as Afghan dhurries—small, flat-woven cotton pieces. The shop is open Monday through Saturday from 10 a.m. to 6:30 p.m., on Sunday from noon to 5 p.m. The store will pack and ship anywhere.

FISHERMAN'S WHARF

The Fisherman's Wharf area—here including Ghirardelli Square, the Cannery, Pier 39, and the Anchorage—can be broken into streets of individual shops and complexes where you can spend a full day running the gamut of imaginative retailing.

The following complexes are well worth spending time exploring.

GHIRARDELLI SQUARE: Because there are about 80 international shops and restaurants at Ghirardelli, 900 North Point (tel. 775-5500), the first thing to do is to stop at the **Information Center,** in the open courtyard between the east and west plazas, and pick up a free guide map of the complex. I've poked into every store here and these are my favorites. Most of the Ghirardelli shops are open Sunday through Thursday from 10 a.m. to 6 p.m., on Friday and Saturday to 9 p.m.

L'Armoire (tel. 771-2488) has the exquisite lingerie and dainty underthings that are hard to find in major department stores, and potpourri to keep everything smelling nice. Silks, satins, cotton batistes, hosiery, and hair accessories are also featured.

If the kids are with you, stop at **Jeffrey's** (tel. 776-6780), stocked with a largish selection of toys, games, and hobby supplies.

AN OFFBEAT BAZAAR. At 2552 Taylor St., between Bay Street and North Point, at Fisherman's Wharf cable-car turntable, **Cost Plus Imports** (tel. 928-6200) consists of a vast warehouse crammed to the rafters with imports (plus a coffee, tea, etc., store). It defies any attempt to classify its goods. I'd have to recite them alphabetically by country of origin, startng with Algeria and ending with Zanzibar. The important thing is that these goods are purchased directly from the countries where they are made, thus avoiding the middleman's cut. The resultant saving is passed on to you.

The gamut runs from Japanese ceramics to kitchen tools from Europe. And just in passing you might pick up some Chinese baskets, Indian camel bells, batik scarves from Malaysia, or coffee beans from any of several coffee-gowing nations. Or perhaps you're in the market for a teak table from Hong Kong. Or . . .

They also have a nursery (trees, plants) at 2633 Taylor St. (tel. 885-5100), with all the accompanying pots, statuary, fountains, etc.

There are items that sell at a quarter of their downtown price and others costing exactly the same elsewhere. The quality and taste of the merchandise is consistently high, but finding the grand-slam bargain depends on your eyesight.

The place is open from 10 a.m. to 9 p.m. Monday through Saturday, from 11 a.m. to 7 p.m. on Sunday. And as a rule it's jammed. For your convenience, they now have free underground parking.

The **Kilkenny Shop** (tel. 771-8984) smells like sheep and specializes in wool suits and blankets, Aran knit sweaters, and other exclusive Irish imports, including Galway crystal.

Fur fantasies can be fulfilled at **Original Furs by Max** (tel. 474-4822), with a fabulous fur collection at all prices and for all tastes.

Originals by Nature (tel. 928-1592) has a vast and fascinating gathering of minerals, fossils, and jewelry. If you're looking for a unique present or perhaps something to add to a collection, stop by.

There's something about music boxes that I find enchanting and intriguing. **Richter's Music Boxes** (tel. 441-2663) has an interesting assortment, including some novelties.

THE CANNERY: In addition to its other attractions, the Cannery, 2801 Leavenworth, at Jefferson (tel. 771-3112) like

Ghirardelli Square, has a score or two of shops. Approximate hours are 10 a.m. to 6 p.m. Monday through Saturday, and 11 a.m. to 6 p.m. on Sunday. Here are some I especially like:

The **Cannery Wine Cellar** (tel. 673-0400) sells an amazing variety of fine domestic and imported wines; next door, the **Gourmet Market** sells international foods, coffee, and tea.

The **Print Store** (tel. 771-3576) has a well-chosen selection of fine art prints. There's absolutely no schlock here, and the classical/jazz background music is pleasant when you're browsing.

PIER 39: This waterfront complex (tel. 981-7437) offers almost as many shops as Ghirardelli and the Cannery put together. They're open daily from 10:30 a.m. to 8:30 p.m. A comprehensive tour revealed these highlights:

First stop (well, almost) should be **Mrs. Field's Chocolate Chippery** (tel. 398-3567). Buy an ample amount of cookies to sustain you while you check out the other stores. Come back for more if necessary.

And for art that can compete with TV for your attention, stop at **Designs in Motion** (tel. 397-5050). The shop has a fascinating collection of mobiles and wire sculpture—some whimsical, some a bit less so.

Another shop that intrigues me is that of **The Puzzle People** (tel. 421-5090), who sell not your usual type of mass-produced items, but rather some very interesting and attractive hand-carved wooden puzzles.

And can you resist puppets? I can't. There's a whole shop full of them at **Puppets on the Pier** (tel. 781-4435). Stop in and see if manipulation is a talent in your bag.

And **Ready Teddy** (tel. 781-1255) has bears, bears, and more bears.

You can watch woodcarvers at work at **Whittler's Mother,** and, of course, purchase what they make.

At **Kitemakers of San Francisco** (tel. 956-3181), you can buy a fanciful creation to fly in the breeze off the bay.

Southpaws can stock up on scissors, potholders, watches, corkscrews, and T-shirts that proclaim "Left Is Right" at **Left Hand World** (tel. 433-3547).

Finally, you can spend some time playing with the rubber chickens or fake blood and scars, trying on great masks, and attempting to figure out magic tricks at the **Palace of Magic** (tel. 434-3122).

THE ANCHORAGE: The newest of the waterfront complexes, the Anchorage has one-stop shopping, dining, and lodging. This center is located at Fisherman's Wharf, downstream a bit from the

Cannery and Ghirardelli Square, bounded by Leavenworth, Beach, Jones, and Jefferson Streets (tel. 775-6000). There's an impressive two-story anchor sculpture at the center of the Leavenworth Street Plaza. The Anchorage has a 128-room Howard Johnson's Motor Lodge, outdoor promenades and decks, and over 40 boutiques offering everything from music boxes to home furnishings, plus an assortment of restaurants and food specialty shops. In the courtyard, musicians, mimes, jugglers, and other street performers entertain frequently. The Anchorage is open daily from 10 a.m. to 6 p.m.; during the summer, to 9 p.m.

SOME SPECIALTY SHOPS

Apart from some of the specialty shops listed under the Union Street, downtown, and Chinatown areas, there are a few others that are exceptionally interesting, both for buying or browsing, and that offer easily transportable items or will handle shipping.

The **San Francisco Mystery Bookstore,** 746 Diamond St., at 24th (tel. 282-7444), is a tiny shop catering solely to detective and mystery fans and at very restricted hours—on Friday from noon to 6 p.m., on Saturday from 10 a.m. to 6 p.m., and on Sunday from noon to 5:30 p.m. The place bulges with books of the genre, mostly paperbacks, but including some rare hardcover first editions. It also has shelves of Sherlock Holmes–related material, movie posters, and exact plaster replicas of the famous Maltese Falcon itself ("The stuff dreams are made of," according to Bogey). The exactitude is guaranteed—it was cast from the original studio mold of the "black bird."

Headlines, 838 Market St., at Ellis (tel. 956-4872), is not in the strict sense of the word a "specialty" shop, except that it specializes in everything. Don't leave town without visiting Headlines. They have picked the best of the most interesting knickknacks you'll see in some time, and they attract some of the most interesting customers. I guarantee it's an experience that will fascinate you, and one that is unique unto San Francisco. There also are Headlines stores at 1217 Polk St., at Sutter (tel. 776-4466), and 557 Castro, at 18th (tel. 626-8061). Hours at the Market Street store are 10 a.m. to 9 p.m. daily; at the other two stores, Sunday through Thursday from 10 a.m. to 9 p.m., on Friday and Saturday to 11 p.m.

The **Magic If Gallery,** 4 Embarcadero Center (tel. 362-4500), has a magical assortment of toys for kids of every age. It's a world of whimsy and of marvelous merchandise handmade by American artists. The price range is considerable—from about $3 on up to $2,000. There are life-size butlers and maids (you've asked for a maid for years, right?), life-size palm trees and sunflowers, and all kinds of soft sculpture. The gallery is open daily from 10 a.m. to 6 p.m. (to 5 p.m. on Sunday).

CHAPTER XIII

TOURS AND EXCURSIONS

□ □ □

Although you could probably spend a lifetime exploring San Francisco, my advice to you is: Don't! Save a while to take in the regions yonder as well. The Bay City is a captivating Circe, but you shouldn't let her ensnare you to the point of ignoring her surroundings.

For San Francisco is set amid the most fascinatingly diverse area in northern California—possibly in the United States. And the contrasts of the region are even more spellbinding than its beauties.

There are silent forests of 1,200-year-old trees and smartly sophisticated seaside resorts. Humming industrial cities and serene, sun-drenched Spanish missions contrast with rolling wine country, wildly rugged mountain ranges, an island transformed into an oceanarium, and two of America's greatest universities.

With San Francisco as either your travel base or your springboard, you can reach any of these points in a few hours or less by car or public transport.

The purpose of this chapter is to give you a glimpse of some of the attractions beckoning beyond Coit Tower . . . how to get there and what to expect. At the end you'll find a selection of package tours, specifically designed to make the going even easier, smoother, and vacation-sized.

ANGEL ISLAND

This is the prettiest of the three islets in San Francisco Bay (the others are Alcatraz and Yerba Buena), and is a federal and state refuge for wildlife.

Now a state park (tel. 435-1915), the 730-acre island has been, at various times, a prison, a favorite site for duels, a quarantine station for immigrants, and a Nike missile base. Today it is popular for picnics, bicycling, and fishing. The park is open from 8 a.m. to sunset.

There are picnic sites with tables, benches, barbecue pits, and rest rooms at Ayala Cove, where you land, and at West Garrison. If you like hiking, miles of trails lead you around the island and to the peak of Mount Caroline Livermore, 776 feet above the bay.

Red and White ferries (tel. 546-2896) sail from Pier 43½ daily. Round-trip fares, including admission to the park, are $8.20 for adults, $5.15 for children 5 to 11; free for under-5s.

Year-round transportation is available from Tiburon, the jumping-off point for the **Tiburon–Angel Island Ferry** (tel. 435-2131). From June to Labor Day, the ferry runs daily from 10 a.m. to 4 p.m. (weekends and holidays till 6 p.m.). The rest of the year, it runs on weekends and holidays only, from 10 a.m. to 4 p.m. Round-trip fares are $5 for adults, $3 for kids. If you bring a bike, there's an extra $1 charge.

OAKLAND

Connected with San Francisco by the giant Oakland Bay Bridge (see Chapter II), this is the largest city of the East Bay and has been variously tagged San Francisco's workshop, bedroom, or bugbear. There is, in fact, about as much love lost between the two towns as between Israel and Lebanon. I could recite some of the "Oakland anecdotes" circulating in San Francisco, but I haven't got the nerve. An A.C. Transit (tel. 839-2882) bus leaves from the Transbay Terminal (Mission and 1st Streets), and the ride over costs $2; round trip is $3. BART also makes the trip from Powell Street to Oakland City Center, for $1.65.

Although Oakland is chiefly a sprawling industrial city of 350,000 busy people, and entirely lacks her rival's unique charm, she boasts a number of outstanding attractions.

At the very center, surrounded by speeding traffic and towering apartments blocks, you'll find **Lake Merritt,** the world's only midtown refuge for wild ducks! The entire region is a recreation oasis and precisely the kind of nature spot every metropolis needs and so very few have.

Adjacent to Lake Merritt, the **Oakland Museum,** 1000 Oak St. at 10th, four blocks east of Calif. 17 (tel. 273-3401), traces the development of the state of California through history, art, and natural sciences. Contained within are the artifacts—clothing, tools, etc.—that man used to shape his environment from the Indian era to the present, as well as California art from the late 1600s on. Environmental and ecological themes are stressed in other parts of the museum. An interesting place to browse is the book and gift shop, which specializes in items related to the California theme. There are terraced court areas and beautiful gardens with sitting areas for visitors. A restaurant and snackbar are on the premises, and there's parking.

Forty-five-minute guided tours leave the gallery information desk at 2 p.m. weekdays; weekend tour times are announced over a public address system. Open Wednesday through Saturday from 10 a.m. to 5 p.m., on Sunday from noon to 7 p.m. Admission is free, except for special exhibitions in the Great Hall, when it's $2 for adults, $1 for seniors.

Right by the shore lies **Lakeside Park,** where you can rent boats or listen to bandstand concerts. But the high spot is **Children's Fairyland** (tel. 452-2259), one of the most imaginative and skillful setups of its kind I've ever seen. You can peer into old Geppetto's workshop, watch the Mad Hatter eternally pouring tea for Alice and the March Hare while the dormouse slumbers, see Noah's Ark overloaded with animal passengers, enjoy the antics of trained sea lions and Willie the Whale spouting in a cavern pool. It's a wonderfully clever mixture of live and mechanical critters (half of which *seem* alive) and almost as astonishing for adults as for kids. Fairytale stories also come alive during puppet-show performances at 11 a.m., and 2 and 4 p.m. Open daily in summer from 10 a.m. to 5:30 p.m.; to 4:30 p.m. in the spring and fall, Wednesday through Sunday; weekends and holidays in winter from 10 a.m. to 4:30 p.m. Admission is $2 for adults, $1.50 for children 12 and under.

At the end of Oakland's Broadway (there seems to be one in every U.S. city) lies **Jack London Square,** dedicated to the memory of the great California writer, a bust of whom stands there. London was an Oaklander, grew up there, and spent most of his time at the Oakland Waterfront. The square itself does little but utilize his name. It's a sprawling place, but there are maps placed in strategic locations to help you find your way around. At 56 Jack London Square, at the foot of Webster Street, you'll find the oddly titled **First and Last Chance Saloon,** where London did some of his writing and much of his drinking. The corner table he used has remained exactly as it was 75 or so years ago. Have a schooner in Jack's memory. You'll see his photos on the walls, looking young and strong and indestructible, ready to tackle the world with his fists as well as his pen.

Also in the square are the mast and nameplate from the U.S.S. *Oakland,* a ship that saw extensive action in the Pacific during World War II. And you'll notice a small rustic cabin. It's the one Jack London lived in while prospecting in the Klondike during the gold rush of 1897.

BERKELEY

From the Transbay Terminal, an A.C. Transit (tel. 839-2882) bus leaves every quarter hour for the **University of California at Berkeley.** Fare is $2; round trip is $3. BART fare to Berkeley is $1.50. Berkeley is actually an East Bay factory town that has achieved fame, glory, and notoriety through harboring an educational institution that has produced a squad of Nobel Prize winners —more than any other university—and spawned some of the worst campus riots in the nation.

You're not likely to see any rioting on campus in the now-tame '80s, but you'll see hordes of students—the university has about 30,000 of them. The campus is strikingly beautiful in the wide-open California style, and you'll admire the graceful, beacon-like Campanile Tower, symbol of the institution.

Telegraph Avenue is the main drag for the student populace, and it seems to be lined in equal numbers by coffeebars and bookshops, overflowing with noisy, but delightfully friendly scholars of both sexes. It's filled with street people selling everything from T-shirts and jewelry to I Ching and tarot card readings. On Telegraph Avenue the '60s has never left.

You might call Berkeley a city with a split personality, or at least two faces. The western part is flat, chock-a-block with factories and garages, and decidedly drab. The eastern portion undulates over a series of hills, with little houses clinging all over them and lush green patches smiling right into the main shopping areas. This is the **university section,** dominated by students and professors and catering to their particular tastes like no other town in the United States.

Just before Telegraph Avenue runs into the university campus, it crosses **Bancroft Way.** This is the hub, the vortex, of student activities, a great many of which seem to take place right at this corner. Stand there for a few minutes and you're bound to have a bunch of leaflets thrust at you, hear an impromptu corner debate or a jingling, rattling Hare Krishna chant, or make friends with several of the swarming puppies that come with the scholars. And you can likely purchase anything from a curried-beef pie to falafel from food stands here while you're being converted to the current cause.

Right across from you is the **Student Union,** as spacious and hectic as the rest of the university. Go to the information desk on the second floor and get yourself a map of Berkeley, a local paper, and should you need it, information about crash pads and free meals in the vicinity. At the corner you'll find **Cal Books,** where the student population gets its textbooks and other school supplies. But as you wander down the avenue, you'll pass more bookstores than are gath-

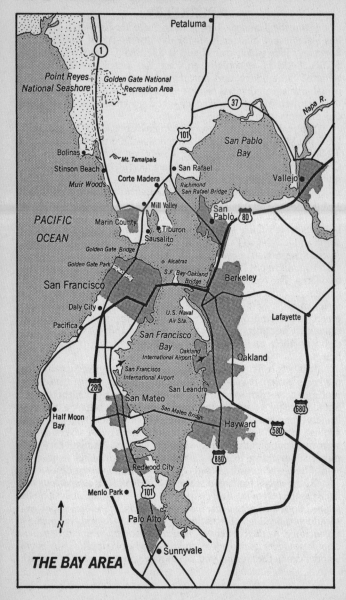

THE BAY AREA

ered on any equivalent thoroughfare anywhere. Let's face it—this is a *reading* town.

WHERE TO STAY: Near the university, the most pleasant place is **Gramma's,** 2740 Telegraph Ave. (four blocks north of Ashby), Berkeley, CA 94705 (tel. 415/549-2145). These charming restored Victorian houses have 29 rooms altogether, all furnished in period style with antiques, floral-print wallpapers, and pretty patchwork quilts on the beds. All have private baths and phones, but no TVs, and larger rooms have sitting areas. Accommodations out back in the restored carriage house overlook a garden and have fireplaces.

Guests are served a complimentary breakfast in the downstairs dining room or on the deck overlooking the garden. Sunday brunch, not included in rates, is also an option.

Rates are $75 to $140, single or double occupancy. Children under 6 are not accepted.

Just one block from the university is the very pleasant **Hotel Durant,** 2600 Durant Ave. (near Bowditch), Berkeley, CA 94704 (tel. 415/845-8981). Built in 1928, it's the only full-service hotel this close to the university. New ownership restored it nicely to keep the best of its earlier days while providing conveniences now expected by vacationers and travelers. The rooms are tastefully furnished; most are quite light, done in pastels, and all have cable TV, movies, radio, and phones. Some of the rooms can be connected for family groups. A new restaurant, Henry's Publick House and Grille, is on the premises and serves complimentary breakfast for hotel guests Monday through Saturday from 7 to 9:30 a.m. Henry's is also open for lunch and dinner.

Rates are $70 to $88, single or double occupancy.

WHERE TO EAT: You can eat on campus Monday through Friday in the building directly behind the Student Union. The least expensive food is available downstairs in the **Cafeteria,** on Lower Sproul Plaza. Adjacent to it are the **Bear's Lair Pub and Coffee House,** the **Deli,** and the **Ice Creamery.** Upstairs at the **Terrace** you can get breakfast, snacks, and lunch. Also on this level of the building is the handsome **Golden Bear Restaurant.** All of the university eateries have both indoor and outdoor dining areas.

Telegraph Avenue has a wonderful array of small restaurants of many nationalities. Walk along reading the posted menus and take your pick.

An extremely popular eatery is **Larry Blake's R&B Café,** 2367 Telegraph, off Durant (tel. 848-0886). For over 45 years this was a mom-and-pop establishment run by Larry and Leona Blake. Now the kids (three of his past employees and one of their friends) have taken it over, and they're running it very well indeed. Students have always favored Blake's nightclub, a dimly lit low-ceilinged basement hideaway with sawdust on the floors and candles in red glass holders on the tables. The walls are lined with celebrity photos. There's live music Tuesday through Sunday night. The house specialty is blues, as you might gather from the R&B tag on the restaurant sign. Above the restaurant is a quiet, more upscale, candlelit cocktail lounge if conversation happens to be your choice for the evening.

The upstairs is also candlelit, has lots of atmosphere, but is not quite the same you-can-cut-it-with-a-knife variety as in the night-club. It also has two no-smoking sections. Food is reasonably priced. At lunch, a boneless breast of chicken on French bread with a salad is available, as well as at least 15 varieties of hamburgers. Lunches range from $4 to $7. Dinner entrees range from $7 to $11, including New York steak, stuffed chicken breast, and broiled Pacific snapper. Dinners include soup or salad, bread, vegetables, and rice pilaf or potatoes. Open Monday through Friday from 11 a.m. to 2 a.m., on Saturday from 10 a.m. to 2 a.m., and on Sunday from 10 a.m. to 10 p.m.

Moving away from the campus, at 1517 Shattuck Ave., between Cedar and Vine, is Alice Waters's extraordinary **Chez Panisse** (tel. 548-5525). Let me put it this way, if you have never heard of this restaurant and its creator, surely you've been on another planet. California cuisine is so much a product of Waters's genius that all other restaurants following in her wake should be dated "A.A.W." (after Alice Waters).

This delightful raw-wood and stucco cottage is entered via a brick terrace filled with flowering potted plants. The provincial interior is equally charming. Downstairs, it's wood-paneled with a fireplace, art deco lamps, and beautiful floral arrangements. Upstairs, the oak bar is adorned with displays of pastries, flowers, or fruit. The café menu is posted daily out front. Offerings include such delights as linguine with mussels, scallops, leeks, garlic, and herbs; braised veal shanks with spring vegetables; and pizza with sausage, olives, fennel, and fontina cheese. Lunch entrees run from $10 to $12. In the genre of a country restaurant, Chez Panisse serves only one five-course dinner each evening. It costs about $55 per person, and reservations are essential (as far in advance as you can—up to one month). Such a dinner might include pan-fried oysters with Chino Ranch curly endive, spinach-and-fennel soup, veal saltimbocca, straw potatoes, salad, and blood-orange ice cream in almond cookie cups.

There is a long wait for the upstairs café since it does not take reservations and the food is superb. The delights include a fabulous calzone, stuffed with mozzarella, goat cheese, and prosciutto. The homemade pastas are just as exceptional. In fact everything is delicious, and even the ice creams and sherbets are homemade. Take the time, and wait.

The upstairs café is open Monday through Saturday from 11:30 a.m. to 11:30 p.m. The prix-fixe dinner is served from 6 to 9:15 p.m. in the restaurant downstairs.

For Berkeley breakfasts I like **Smokey Joe's Café,** 1620 Shattuck Ave., between Cedar and Lincoln (no phone), a traditional Berkeley hangout where the walls are plastered with protest posters, leaflets, and messages. The atmosphere somehow evokes Berkeley's activist past. It's a small place, with pale-yellow walls and seating at the counter or tables.

I especially like Smokey's Mexican breakfast with beans and cheese, tortillas, and a garnish of fresh fruit. Other specialties are great homemade pancakes—you can have them with blueberries or bananas—your favorite omelet, and original creations such as the Holy Mole Frijole Bowl. Prices average about $3 to $5. Open daily from 8 a.m. to 3 p.m.

Should your sweet tooth act up in Berkeley, head for **Cocolat,** a chocoholic's paradise over at 1481 Shattuck, near Vine. Open Monday through Saturday from 10 a.m. to 6 p.m., on Sunday from 11 a.m. to 5 p.m. Cocolat now has a second East Bay location at 3945 Piedmont Ave., in Oakland (tel. 653-3676). You simply can't believe that heaven comes in so many forms of chocolate indulgence. Handmade truffles from an old French recipe are the specialty here, made fresh every day. Then there are chocolates filled with eau de vie (pear, raspberry, quince, kiwi, or Kirsch) which burst as you bite into them, thereby requiring the ultimate joy of plunking the entire bit into your mouth all at once. Each of the shops also offers tortes and cakes. You might indulge in a tricolor mousse—three chocolate mousses in one—or Chocolate Decadence, caressed by whipped cream and slices of truffle surrounded by raspberry sauce. Cocolat also has mail-order gifts to delight the heart of any chocoholic. Many of their chocolate spectaculars do travel well.

Pastries are served at table at four of Cocolat's closest locations: both of the above in East Bay; and in San Francisco at 4106 24th St. (tel. 647-3855), and 2119 Fillmore St. (tel. 567-1223), both open daily.

Just around the corner at 2122 Vine is **Delicktables,** where gelato (Italian ice cream) can be obtained. They also serve soup, sandwiches, cappuccino, espresso, and other desserts. Summer hours are Sunday through Thursday from 10 a.m. to 11 p.m., to midnight on Friday and Saturday. During winter, the shop closes an hour earlier.

TIBURON

Imagine San Francisco reduced to toy dimensions, with just a dash of western stagecoach atmosphere thrown in, and you'll have a fair picture of Tiburon. This decidedly odd seacoast town—or rather village—rambles over a series of green hills and ends up at a spindly, multicolored pier on the waterfront, like a Fisherman's Wharf in miniature.

You can drive the 18 miles from San Francisco via the Golden Gate Bridge and U.S. 101 (get off at the Tiburon Boulevard exit and take 131) or take a Golden Gate Transit (tel. 332-6600) bus for $2.20. But by water it's only a third of the distance and a much more intriguing ride. The **Red and White Fleet** (tel. 546-2896) cruisers leave from Pier 43½, at Fisherman's Wharf, and the 20- to 40-minute crossing (in the summer there's a stop in Sausalito) costs $8 round trip; kids 5 to 11 pay $4.

Tiburon, situated on the peninsula of that name, looks like a cross between a fishing village and a Hollywood mockup of Tombstone in its six-gun days. But it only *looks* that way. In reality it's an extremely plush patch of yacht-club suburbia, as you'll see by both the marine craft and the homes of their owners. This, indeed, is the "good life."

The main street—called Main Street—is lined with ramshackle, color-splashed old frame houses which hide chic little boutiques, expensive antique shops, and art galleries. The streets are narrow, winding, and hilly, leading up to ultramodern villas—in deliberately glaring contrast to the old village atmosphere of the shopping center.

Strangely enough, this contrast creates charm in massive doses —so much so that visitors fall in love with the place almost as soon as they set foot in it. The pace is sleepy, the bay view bewitching, the hill setting glorious—and the living very expensive. The view of the San Francisco skyline and the islands in the bay is almost worth the price.

There's a row of charming waterfront restaurants—nothing garish in Tiburon.

Whether you reach Tiburon by car or by boat, it'll give you a pang of envy for its lucky inhabitants, enjoying city sophistication and village air in one breath. Several hundred upper-bracket business people felt exactly the same way. That's why they live there and commute daily to San Francisco offices, making the 6:15 ferry (from the Ferry Building at the foot of Market) to Windjammer Pier a kind of nautical coach to suburbia.

WHERE TO EAT: Take the 6:15 yourself and you'll be faced with a dizzying choice of well-known eating places.

The liveliest time to visit Tiburon is on Sunday afternoon in the summer, when the weekend boatmen tie up at the open decks of the waterside restaurants and there is much singing, laughter, and general conviviality. The traditional place to tie up, for almost 70 years now, is **Sam's Anchor Café** at 27 Main St. (tel. 435-4527), which boasts two 110-foot piers and a large wooden deck which is filled to overflowing with blithe Sunday spirits from brunchtime on.

Even the owners commute to work in their boats. Sam's is the kind of place where you can take off your shoes and shirt—everyone's home-away-from-home neighborhood bar. During Prohibition days it was a rendezvous point for bootleggers, who used to pull in under the restaurant and bring liquor in through trap doors.

At lunch you might order a bay shrimp, tomato, and cheddar cheese sandwich on a toasted English muffin, or the soup du jour and half a sandwich for $4.25 to $7.25. Dinner might be any one of the fresh seafood specials, or deep-fried oysters served with fresh vegetables. Sourdough bread and butter come with all entrees, which cost $8 to $13. Sam's is open daily from 11 a.m. weekdays, from 10 a.m. on Saturday, and from 9:30 a.m. on Sunday, closing nightly at about 2 a.m.

Tiburon Tommie's Mai Tai, 41 Main St. (tel. 435-1229), is a Polynesian restaurant with all the exotic décor that its name implies. Especially impressive is the upstairs dining area, which is divided into the Maori Room and the Tapa Room Bar. The former, with its peaked ceiling and painted beams, really does look authentic; traveling Maoris will feel right at home. Carvings of Maori gods, a jungle of plants, a canoe, bamboo poles overhead, and a rock fountain further add to the South Seas setting. There's even a waterfall under the stairway. The windows are open to the view of the yacht harbor and San Francisco in the distance, for, while Tommie's has no deck, it stands at the water's edge and offers an excellent vista.

Tommie's serves both Cantonese and Mandarin dishes along with its South Sea specialties. Entrees like crab foo yung and chicken with almonds cost $7 to $12. And there are full-course dinners, for two or more persons, including soup, entree, fried rice, and fortune cookies, for $9 to $15 per person. Open Sunday through Thursday from 10 a.m. to midnight, on Friday and Saturday till 2 a.m. Food is served until 9 p.m.

Christopher's, back down the street at 9 Main St. (tel. 435-4600), is the posh restaurant on Main where, as you might expect, seafood is the specialty of the house. The restaurant has an elegant interior, with redwood-paneled walls, blue-and-gold carpeting, and candlelit, white linen-covered tables at night. Antique ship models add a nautical touch. A large expanse of window allows for lovely views of the bay and the San Francisco skyline, and if the weather is good you can dine outdoors on a terrace.

Luncheon fare, costing $6 to $12, includes a mouthwatering selection of sandwiches and entrees, from a Philadelphia cheese steak sandwich to seafood crêpes with shrimp, scallops, and mushrooms. Dinner is à la carte and entrees range from $13 for a superior calamari steak to $24 for the filet mignon–lobster tail combination.

Christopher's is open for dining from 11:30 a.m. to 9 p.m. Monday through Thursday, to 10 p.m. Friday through Sunday. The bar stays open till 1 or 2 a.m. nightly.

One of my favorite places in Tiburon is the **Sweden House Bakery-Café,** 35 Main St. (tel. 435-9767), a quaint little eatery with gingham-covered walls adorned with copperware and other kitchen things. I love sitting on the terrace, gazing out over the bay and sipping espresso along with a home-baked Swedish pastry (the raspberry-iced, cream-filled napoleon is a great favorite). Full breakfasts are served daily, and not just the usual, run-of-the-mill variety. You can have scrambled eggs with a choice of green onions, tomatoes, cheese, mushrooms, shrimp, or slices of smoked salmon. And combination vegetable omelets are offered too. All are served with the restaurant's own toasted Swedish limpa bread. At lunch there are open-face sandwiches like avocado and bacon with sprouts, or delicious asparagus tips rolled in Danish ham; you can also order such American standards as chicken salad. Garden salads are also an option, and you can have a soup-of-the-day-with-salad combination. Look for the daily luncheon specials too. Everything is very well prepared; prices range from $4 to $7. Sweden House is open Monday through Friday from 8 a.m. to 3 p.m., 8:30 a.m. to 4:30 p.m. on Saturday and Sunday.

While in Tiburon, enjoy a taste of the wine country at the **Tiburon Vintners Wine Shop,** 72 Main St. (tel. 435-3113). Their Victorian tasting room dates to 1888. You may choose from over 45 fine Windsor Vineyards wines, including many award winners, for complimentary sampling. Windsor has been awarded more than 300 medals at prestigious wine-tasting competitions since 1985—the list is impressive. Tiburon Vintners also carries a good selection of wine accessories and gifts—glasses, cork pullers, gourmet sauces, posters, maps, etc. Carry-packs are available (they hold six bottles); as of now, only California and New York residents can have their wines shipped home for them. Ask about personalized labels for your own selections. The shop is open from 10 a.m. to 6 p.m. daily. If you drive to Tiburon, Vintners will validate your parking ticket from the Main Street parking lot next door.

SAUSALITO

Eight miles from San Francisco over the Golden Gate Bridge and along U.S. 101 lies Sausalito. Unlike nearby Tiburon, it makes no attempt to hide what it is—a slightly bohemian, completely nonchalant, and studiedly quaint adjunct to San Francisco, designed for folks who want to have their metropolitan cake and eat it outdoors too. Sausalito has a fascinating community of houseboats just north of the village, which can be reached most gloriously by ferry: both the Red and White Fleet (tel. 546-2815), for $9 round trip, and Golden Gate Transit (tel. 982-8834 or 457-3110), for $8 round trip, offer service to Sausalito. Or you can travel more prosaically by Golden Gate bus (tel. 332-6600) for $2 one way.

With approximately 6,500 residents, Sausalito has an aura rather like St. Tropez on the French Riviera—but minus the starlets as well as the social rat race. It has its quota of near-millionaires and gilt-edged playgirls, but they rub permanently suntanned shoulders with hard-up artists, struggling authors, shipyard workers, and fishermen and their families.

It has swank restaurants, plush bars, and expensive antique stores, but also hamburger joints, beer parlors, and secondhand bookshops, most of them in a row and frequently next door to each other. Above all, it has scenery and sunshine, for once you cross Golden Gate Bridge you're out of the San Francisco fog patch and under blue California sky. And the scenery—steep hills with white houses, a forest of masts on the water below, San Francisco gleaming in the distance—is superb, and gratis.

Sausalito's main street is **Bridgeway,** which runs along the water. Just about everything notable is somewhere on or just off this roadway, which plays the combined role of shopping center and promenade.

SHOPPING IN SAUSALITO: A mecca for handmade, original, and offbeat clothes and footwear, Sausalito boasts many charming shops featuring a wide variety of unusual arts and crafts as well as antiques, gifts, and souvenirs. The shops here are pricey, but the merchandise is original, and what you find on Sausalito's main street, you aren't likely to find on your own. Some of them come and go, but here's a roundup of the interesting establishments I visited when last here.

Strolling Down Bridgeway

Make your first stop at 777 Bridgeway, where there's a fascinatingly undefinable complex of 40 shops, souvenir stores, coffee bars, and gardens known as the **Village Fair.** Leaning against the hillside and spilling over in all directions from what used to be an old warehouse, this is almost a village in itself and could occupy an afternoon's exploring. But don't spend all your time there. You don't want to miss the many interesting shops that can be discovered by prowling through the alleys, malls, and second-floor boutiques reached by steep, narrow staircases along Bridgeway and up the side streets.

Bridgeway's shops are interspersed with several galleries. One worth looking at is the **Quest Gallery,** at no. 777 (tel. 332-6832), which specializes in fine ceramics, contemporary glass, hand-painted silks, woven clothing, art jewelry, and graphics. The shop specializes in California artists, many who are exclusive to this shop and have been featured in major American art shows. Open seven days from 10 a.m. to 6 p.m.

Another lovely shop, at 795 Bridgeway, is the **Stoneflower Gallery** (tel. 332-2995). It is an extension of the Quest Gallery but with a lovely contemporary Southwest décor. The shop specializes in wood, ceramics, and original fiber creations with a southwestern flair. The Stoneflower carries artwork from major American and international artists. Open daily from 10 a.m. to 6 p.m.

There are picnic areas and benches all along Bridgeway, so you might interest yourself in some of that thoroughfare's food shops. The **Venice Gourmet Delicatessen,** at no. 625 (tel. 332-3544), has all the makings for a superb picnic—wines, cheeses, fruits, stuffed vine leaves, mushroom-and-artichoke salad, quiche, delicious sandwiches made to order on sourdough bread, olives, fresh-baked pastries, etc. They now serve pizza at **Giovanni's Pizzaria,** next door to the Venice. They're open every day from 9 a.m. to 7 p.m.

For one-of-a-kind redwood furniture plus fine jewelry, metal sculptures, hand-blown glass, Oriental rugs, and other interesting gifts, visit the **Burlwood Gallery** at 721 Bridgeway (tel. 332-6550). There are lots of fun and interesting things here; it's well worth browsing. Open daily from 10 a.m. to 6 p.m.

The **Sausalito Country Store,** 789 Bridgeway (tel. 332-7890), sells oodles of wonderful handmade country-style goods. Many of these items—ceramic, stuffed, and painted-wood animals, aprons, and baskets—are made by local artists and artisans. Open daily from 10:30 a.m. to 6 p.m.

Princess Street

Turn right off Bridgeway onto Princess Street and look into **Pegasus,** 30 Princess (tel. 332-5624), vendors of lovely leather clothing, some so soft they seem to be made of flowing fabric and in colors sure to add excitement to a wardrobe. Along with jackets, coats, and even leather blouses, there are handsome leather belts, and purses. The shop also offers ruggedly good-looking jackets for men in award-winning designs. In addition to their off-the-rack items, the people at Pegasus offer their styles customized to ensure a perfect fit. Open Monday through Saturday from 10:30 a.m. to 5:30 p.m., on Sunday from 11 a.m.

Farther up the street you might want to rummage through the various and sundry goods at **Sausalito Salvage,** a thrift shop at no. 19 (tel. 332-3471). You'll find every kind of bric-a-brac here, along with old books, clothing, and jewelry, and you also get the satisfaction of knowing that the money you pay for your treasures goes to one of over 25 charitable organizations. Open on Monday from 1 to 4 p.m., Tuesday through Friday from 10 a.m. to 4 p.m., and on Saturday from 10 a.m. to 1 p.m.

Caledonia Street

If you have energy enough to push on farther, new shops, pubs, and restaurants are mushrooming on Caledonia Street, which runs parallel to and one block inland from Bridgeway. This street may be as busy as the main drag by the time this book is in your hands, but, as yet, the strollers are mainly natives, and the baseball game in the schoolyard helps remind you that this tourist-thronged town on woody hillsides has real people in residence.

Its most notable shop, in my hungry opinion, is the **Stuffed Croissant,** at no. 43 (tel. 332-7103). Here you can get anything from a nosh to a meal. There are all sorts of gourmet sandwich croissants filled with almond chicken salad or a scrumptious roast beef barbecue with garlic and onions, bagels, plus a soup of the day. For your sweet tooth there are croissants stuffed with fruits—strawberries and cream cheese, or apples, raisins, and cinnamon, as well as pain au chocolat—and a fantastic variety of delicious fresh muffins, like honey bran, pumpkin raisin, carrot pineapple, poppy seed, banana nut, and blueberry. All these goodies cost a mere $1.50 to $4 each. There's always a variety of coffees brewing (including cappuccino and espresso), and juices, tea, and mineral waters are available. Open daily from 7:30 a.m. to 10 p.m.

WATCHING THE BAY AT WORK: While shopping and browsing occupy most visitors to Sausalito, few know what a fascinating exhibit is located at 2100 Bridgeway, at the **Bay Model Visitors Center** (tel. 332-3871). Here is a 1.5-acre model of San Francisco Bay, where the Army Corps of Engineers can make water behave in the model as it does in the bay and observe just what these changes in water flow will mean. Here you can see the impact of pollution, view the Sacramento and San Joaquin Rivers flowing into the bay, and even see the swift flow of water around Alcatraz. Rangers are usually available to answer questions. Guided tours are available by reservation for groups of ten or more. Admission is free; open Tuesday through Saturday from 9 a.m. to 4 p.m. in the winter. Summer hours are 9 a.m. to 4 p.m. Tuesday through Friday, 10 a.m. to 6 p.m. weekends. (*Note:* The model is most interesting when it's actually in operation, and that happens only when a test is being conducted. It pays to call before you go, and ask about testing.)

WHERE TO STAY: The **Sausalito Hotel,** 16 El Portal, Sausalito, CA 94965 (tel. 415/332-4155), is a pleasant hostelry located in the center of the shopping area between Bridgeway and the bay shore.

All the rooms are furnished with pieces that antique lovers among you will ache to own. Beds with massive wooden carved headboards, great wooden dressers, delicate flowered glass lamps, and period armchairs abound. For all this Victorian lushness, the rooms are remarkably uncluttered, with restfulness enhanced by views of the park or bay. There's no radio or telephone to disturb you, but be warned: some of the rooms open right onto public areas and can get noisy, especially on weekend nights.

The largest, most expensive room, and the only one with a fireplace, is named after the Marquis of Queensbury. Sleeping here is especially enjoyable because you drift off dreamily in the great bed once owned and slept in by Gen. Ulysses S. Grant. The huge, ornately carved dresser also belonged to the general.

Continental breakfast is served informally in the diminutive lobby and can be either eaten there or taken to your room.

Private or shared baths are happily not in the Victorian style, barring the antique wall mirrors.

Of the 15 rooms, five come without private bath. Bathless rooms cost $75 to $85; rooms with private bathroom rent for $95 to $150.

DINING IN SAUSALITO: **Ondine,** 558 Bridgeway (tel. 332-0791), is one of the most magnificent restaurants in the Bay Area. From this second-floor vantage point, the view of San Francisco through the huge plate-glass windows is spectacular, almost too spectacular because it tends to distract you from the food, which deserves your close attention. Specialties here include roast duckling à l'orange, roast pheasant Vladimir with vodka and sour-cream sauce, rack of lamb with an exquisite sauce, and chicken glazed with marsala in a delicate truffle sauce, garnished with avocado. Dinners that include soup, salad, dessert, and beverage are served until 7 p.m. and priced from $18 to $23. On the high side in price, but also in quality and ambience, Ondine is open daily from 11:30 a.m. to 3 p.m. for lunch, and 5 to 11 p.m. for dinner. Reservations are advised, and jackets are required for men at dinner.

HIDEAWAY BY THE BAY. Sooner or later most visitors to Sausalito look up and wonder at the ornate mansion on the hill. It's part of the **Casa Madrona,** a hotel whose entrance is on lower ground at 801 Bridgeway, Sausalito, CA 94965 (tel. 415/332-0502). The mansion was built in 1885 by a wealthy lumber baron named Barretti. The epitome of luxury in its day, the mansion slipped, with the passage of time, into decay. It was saved by a Frenchman, Henri Deschamps, who converted it to a hotel and restaurant. Now owned by John Mays, it has undergone even further changes. The mansion began slipping again—this time, literally—so more repairs and renovations were made, and a rambling New England–style building was added to the hillside below the house. The hotel, a certified historical landmark, now has 32 rooms, suites, and cottages; the 16 newest units were each decorated in unique and pleasant style by 16 local designers. "1,000 Cranes" is Oriental in theme, with lots of ash and lacquer. "Artist's Loft" is reminiscent of a rustic Parisian artist's studio, complete with easel, brushes, and paint. "Summer House" is decked out in white wicker, and "Château Charmant" evokes the genteel French countryside. Up in the mansion, the rooms are also decorated in a variety of styles; some even have Jacuzzis. Amenities include quilts, telephones, and baskets of luxury shampoos, soaps, bath gels, etc., in the bathroom. TVs and radios are available on request. The new rooms have fireplaces and sundecks overlooking the water; many mansion rooms have bay views and some have fireplaces.

The **Casa Madrona Restaurant** (tel. 331-5888), located in the mansion with breathtaking views of the bay, serves California nouvelle cuisine for lunch and dinner Tuesday through Saturday, and affords an excellent wine list including a number of fine French wines. Guests only can partake of a daily continental breakfast served here.

The two rooms with shared bathroom at the Casa Madrona rent for $65; other rooms cost $85 to $135. Cottages let for $155, and the Madrona Villa, a three-room suite, costs $305. All rates are for single or double occupancy; an extra person in a room pays $10. There's a two-night minimum stay on weekends.

About a mile from the center of Sausalito, not far from the Bay Model Visitors Center, is another terrific restaurant. **Guernica,**

2009 Bridgeway (tel. 332-1512), is a French-Basque place, named for the Basque town of the same name in northern Spain. It's operated by a French Basque, Roger Minhondo, who runs the place with a firm but friendly hand. The atmosphere is homey; Roger himself and maître d' Gary greet regulars by name and welcome first-timers with a smile. In its decade of operation, Guernica has developed quite a large following, both in Sausalito and in San Francisco.

The small dining room is tastefully decorated, with walls in stone, brick, wood, and white stucco, large wood and leatherette booths, white-clothed tables with flowers and candles. On one wall there's a large print of Picasso's *Guernica*. Classical music plays softly in the background.

You can begin with an appetizer of artichoke hearts or escargots. For $12 to $19, you can get a complete dinner with soup, salad, entree, and warm, crispy rolls. Some of the entrees from which you can choose are poulet du chef (chicken with a delicious mushroom stuffing and a port wine sauce), fresh scallops in crème sauce, and medallions of veal with mustard sauce. If you're eating à deux, you can enjoy rack of lamb or chateaubriand. With 24 hours' notice, Guernica will also prepare beef Wellington or paella valenciana for a minimum of four. The desserts at Guernica are terrific. In season, there's a superb strawberry tarte. You can also get chocolate mousse or peach Melba.

Guernica is open Monday through Thursday from 5 to 10:30 p.m., on Friday and Saturday till 11 p.m., and on Sunday till 9:30 p.m. Reservations strongly advised.

SAUSALITO NIGHTSPOTS:
During the week, the action in Sausalito's lively bistros begins to pick up about 6:30 p.m. as commuters get back from San Francisco and local businesses close. On weekends, figure an hour earlier. Most of the spots are on Bridgeway, or nearby.

The **Bar with no name,** easy to overlook at 757 Bridgeway (tel. 332-1392), is a delightful tavern with oak paneling inside and a garden in the rear. A meeting place with an almost legendary reputation, the bar attracts earnest chess, backgammon, and Scrabble players, local folk, yacht skippers, poets, and, of course, tourists. The No Name is so called because the four partners who opened it some 30 years ago couldn't agree on a name. The current owner is a cat named Cinderella. It's a low-key kind of place with just about the best ambience for relaxed hanging out of any bar I've ever seen. It's much like some of the old Greenwich Village bars in Manhattan. There's a shelf of books that you can read and take home to finish; the owner finds that people who take them also bring in new ones. Well-chosen taped music—jazz, classical, etc.—is always playing in the background, and several evenings a week there's live music (usually jazz). Order a Ramos Fizz—eggwhite, gin, orange Curaçao, sugar, lemon, orange flower water, and cream—it's the house specialty. Open seven days a week from 10 a.m. to 2 a.m.

MUIR WOODS AND MOUNT TAMALPAIS

Also in Marin County, but in silent, majestic contrast to the bustle of the seacoast towns, lies one of America's most enchanting nature preserves. **Mount Tamalpais** is the great landmark of the county, its outline towering over the entire scenery. At its foot nestle the **Muir Woods**.

Be advised that in driving to and from Muir Woods the secondary road is a steep series of S-curves with very few places to pull over. So be sure to start with ample gas, firm brakes, and good tires. This is not the place to get a flat.

You get to **Muir Woods National Monument** via a well-marked turnoff from U.S. 101 past Sausalito. Admission is free; hours are 8 a.m. to sunset. There's a Visitors Center, gift shop, and snackbar; I suggest that you have a bite to eat before heading up to Muir Woods.

There, amid the quiet grandeur of the forest, you'll see the world-famous California redwoods. Although these magnificent trees have been successfully transplanted to five continents, their homeland is a 500-mile strip along the mountainous coast of southwestern Oregon and northern California, where they grow inland "as far as the fog flows"—about 30 miles.

The coast redwood—or *Sequoia sempervirens*—is the tallest tree on earth, the largest-known specimen towering 367.8 feet. It has an even larger relative, the *Sequoiadendron giganteum* of the California Sierra Nevada, but the coastal variety is stunning enough. There is no other forest like it anywhere in the world—soaring like a wooden cathedral up to the sky while spreading over a lush green carpet of ferns underfoot.

You can drive the 2,600 feet to the top of Mount Tamalpais, or take one of two clearly marked trails (one gentle, the other fairly rough) to the summit. The mountain offers a special picnic camp and some wonderful forest rails undulating for miles beneath the spreading green canopy above. The redwoods range from months-old seedlings to 1,200-year-old elders that were fully grown when Charlemagne ruled France. And from the peak you get a 100-mile sweep in all directions, from the foothills of the Sierras to the western horizon.

What is known as Marin today, incidentally, was actually the first "New England." In June 1579 Sir Frances Drake sailed his sturdy *Golden Hinde* into the bay named after him. One of the first acts was to order a "plate of brasse, fast nailed to a great and firm post" claiming his discovery for his tough and level-headed sovereign,

Queen Elizabeth I of England. He then named the land "Nova Albion."

However, this turned out to be one of the rare historical instances when the English were unable to follow through their exploration by occupation—they were too busy elsewhere on the globe. Instead, the Spaniards arrived two centuries later and made Marin part of their empire "over which the sun never set"—until it did.

For a bus tour of Marin County, see the tour section at the end of this chapter.

LARKSPUR

North of the highly developed tourist towns of Tiburon and Sausalito, Marin County opens into vistas of housing developments and rolling hills. In places, the marshes of the upper bay can still be seen within a short distance of U.S. 101.

Continuing north on 101, take the Larkspur/Corte Madera turnoff, proceed west on Tamalpais Road, which turns into Magnolia Avenue, and you'll soon arrive in Larkspur (it's also reachable by ferry from San Francisco). Does it look familiar? If so, it's probably because so many period movies have been shot here.

A walk through the town reveals drugstores, banks, and other shops, unique only in that they have not changed in style from the '30s. Just three blocks south of town is a delightful creekside shopping center painted daffodil yellow and grass green.

The real reason to visit Larkspur, however, is to dine at the **Lark Creek Inn,** 234 Magnolia Ave. (tel. 924-7766). On the banks of Lark Creek, this charming Victorian mansion (established in 1888) has been lovingly restored by Victor and Roland Gotti, owners of the resplendent Ernie's in San Francisco (see "Luxury Restaurants" in Chapter VI). Under their guidance the interior has been re-created with great attention to authenticity. In the oak-furnished dining room, the print pattern on the lampshades and drapes attractively echoes the period reproduction wallpaper, and large windows and skylights provide plenty of sun for many potted plants.

At lunch mainly salads, omelets, and sandwiches are served, for $6 to $12. There are also hot entrees like breast of chicken with wine, lemon butter, tomato sauce, and jack cheese, or veal medallions with capers, for $10 to $13. Dinners are more elaborate at $14 to $18, with entrees like veal samana ($17.50)—named for the chef, it consists of slices of white veal wrapped around avocado slices and asparagus spears served in lemon-butter sauce—and prawns sautéed in Dijon mustard, shallots, and cream. There is an extensive wine list. Lunch is served from 11:30 a.m. to 2:30 p.m. Tuesday through Saturday; dinner, from 5:30 to 9:30 p.m. Tuesday through

Sunday; Sunday brunch is on from 11 a.m. to 2 p.m. Closed Monday. Reservations advised.

A ROMP IN THE HILLS. The Renaissance Pleasure Faire (tel. 892-0937) held annually in Marin County, 27 miles north of the city, is a happy event that takes place on five weekends from late August through the end of September, including Labor Day.

Located in a small grotto of hills and valleys shaded by oak trees, the atmosphere is one of enormous Elizabethan gusto helped along by period costumes of entertainers, artisans, and—to a lesser extent—you, the paying participant.

A handbill for a previous year's fair is an accurate description of what you'll find to do. It reads: "Join the Grand Call O' the Faire Procession at Noon from the Meadow. Cheer the Queen at 3 p.m. See Jugglers, Fire-Eaters & Street Puppet Shows. Carouse in the Ale & Wine Gardens. Discover Fine Hand-Crafted Wares 'mongst 200 Colorful Stalls. Enjoy a Great Variety of Gourmet Foods. Play Pitch-the-Hay, Tug-O-War and Other Rustic Games. Try your Skill at the Many Craft Activity Stalls."

It's a great way to spend a Saturday or Sunday afternoon, and if you take the children you'll have a hard time prying them away.

To get to the fair, drive over the Golden Gate Bridge, along U.S. 101 past San Rafael, and turn off at the Vallejo exit. Go along Calif. 37 for two miles to the Black Point exit and you're in the parking area. Parking is free. Admission for adults is about $15; children under 12 pay $5.50.

POINT REYES NATIONAL SEASHORE

Some 35 miles north of San Francisco on Calif. 1 is a lovely stretch of shoreline. It's a 67,000-acre park of sand beach and scrubland, home to birds, sea lions, and a variety of tidepool creatures. There are three distinct areas of interest that you can visit. Facing the Pacific is **Point Reyes Beach.** It gets the full brunt of ocean tides and winds, and the water is much too rough to swim, surf, or even wade in. It's a lovely stretch of shore to walk along, though, when the winds aren't too biting.

Along the south coast is another stretch of sand, named **Drake's Beach** after the English explorer who visited here. The waters here are as tranquil and serene as the Point Reyes waters are turbulent. San Franciscans and Marin residents find the beach here an ideal spot to sun and picnic; occasionally a hearty soul ventures into the quiet but cold waters of Drake's Bay.

The main road of the park, Sir Francis Drake Boulevard, which passes by Point Reyes Beach and branches off to reach Drake's Beach, leads right out to **Point Reyes** itself. The **Point Reyes Lighthouse** is one of the best places on the West coast to watch for whales since the point juts out almost 15 miles from the mainland. As they migrate from Alaska to the lagoons of Baja, California—an annual round trip of 10,000 miles, one of the longest mammal migrations known —these magnificent creatures pass by Point Reyes heading south in December and January, and in March on their return trip north. The last of the group are the mothers with their newborn calves. If you plan to drive out to the lighthouse to whale-watch, be sure to arrive early since there's a limited amount of parking space. And if possible, come on a weekday. During January the lighthouse is open daily; in February and March it's open Thursday through Monday. If you come on a weekend or holiday, it's wise to park at the Drake's Beach Visitor Center and take the free shuttle bus to the lighthouse. If you want to enjoy yourself, be sure to dress warmly—it's often quite cold and windy—and don't forget to bring binoculars if you have them. Before you leave for the lighthouse, call the Visitor Center (tel. 415/669-1534) for a weather and whale-activity report.

But whale watching, as spectacular as it is, is not the only interesting activity the Point Reyes National Seashore offers. There are excellent ranger-conducted tours: you can walk along the Bear Valley Trail, where you'll see the wildlife and inhabitants of the ocean's edge; get a good look at the birds and some of the very secretive waterfowl of Fivebrooks Pond; explore tidepools; view some of North America's most beautiful ducks in the wetlands of Limantour; hike to the promontory overlooking Chimney Rock to see the sea lions, harbor seals, and sea birds; or take a guided walk along the San Andreas fault to look at the site of the epicenter of the famous 1906 earthquake and learn about the regional geology. And this is just a sampling. Since available tours and their lengths vary seasonally, you can either call the ranger station (tel. 663-1092) and have pencil and paper handy, or ask to be sent a copy of the *Park Paper,* which includes a schedule of activities and much other useful information. Many of the tours are suitable for the handicapped. Two important "no-no's"—pets are not permitted on any trails, and no swimming or wading is permitted at the outer Point Reyes beaches: *surf and rip tides are extremely dangerous.*

If all the sea air at Point Reyes gives you an appetite, treat yourself to the remarkable gastronomic glories of the **Station House Café** on Main Street (tel. 663-1515) in the tiny town of Point Reyes Station. How often do you find a real community restaurant, complete with locals, that is a gourmet's paradise with nongourmet prices? Make note of the following—the café is open daily except Tuesday from 8 a.m. to 9 p.m. (to 10 p.m. on Saturday).

The café has a traditional menu, in addition to which it features a different special menu each week. There are two breakfast specials, four at lunch, and five dinner specials. For breakfast, served from 8 to 11:30 a.m., you might be offered dill crêpes filled with smoked salmon and topped with a subtle parmesan sauce, or Indian scrambled eggs with cream cheese and green onions over curried rice with a spicy tomato sauce. For the ultra-conservative, the regular menu offers a fine selection of omelets, Belgian waffles, eggs, pancakes, etc.

Specials at lunch, served from 11:30 a.m. to 5 p.m., might be fettuccine with fresh local mussels steamed in white wine and butter sauce, or two-cheese polenta served with fresh spinach sauté and grilled garlic-buttered tomato. From the regular menu, the local Johnson's oysters are delicious raw, steamed, or fried, as is the café's famous Niman-Schell beefburger served with country fries. (Mr. Niman and Mr. Schell raise a limited quantity of organically fed beef of an exceptionally superior quality sold only locally and to restaurants in San Francisco.) Rounding out the delicious choices are homemade chili, steamed clams, fresh soup made daily, or fish and chips, among others.

Among the dinner specials, served from 5 to 9 p.m., you might savor a Niman-Schell sirloin with shiitake mushrooms and shallots and creamed spinach, or perhaps chicken breast with sherry and currant-cream sauce with acorn squash, and wild rice custard. The regular dinner menu offers the items listed at lunch plus garlic-fennel sausage with polenta, liver and onions, fettuccine with leeks, shiitake mushrooms, and chicken in a Parmesan cream sauce. As for the desserts—all homemade—there are always apple pie, Indian pudding, strawberry shortcake, cheesecake, and the special of the week. The café also has an extensive list of fine California wines, plus local and imported beers.

Breakfast specials average $4 to $6.50; lunch, $4 to $8.50; dinner specials are $6 to $15. The food at the Station House Café is exceptional, delicious, splendidly prepared and served—it draws regulars from San Francisco. Don't miss it.

MARINE WORLD AFRICA USA

About 10 miles south of the Napa wine country, and a bit less than 30 miles northeast of San Francisco off Interstate 80 (exit at Calif. 37), is the 160-acre Marine World Africa USA, 1000 Fairgrounds Dr. in Vallejo (tel. 707/643-ORCA for a recorded announcement). It's less than an hour's drive up I-80, or you can have the fun of taking the **Red and White Fleet** (tel. 546-2896 in San Francisco, or toll free 800/445-8880 in California) high-speed catamaran from Pier 41 at Fisherman's Wharf, pass Alcatraz and the Golden Gate Bridge, and be there in 55 minutes. The round trip, including admission, is $35 for adults, $30 for seniors (over 60), and $25 for kids 4 to 12.

Marine World Africa USA is the interesting conjunction of two distinct outfits: Marine World, which specializes in aquatic attractions; and Africa USA, which features animals of land and air in spectacular shows and innovative habitats; some even stroll the park with their trainers, meeting visitors face to face.

When you plan your visit to Marine World Africa USA, count on participation in the shows—it's a big part of your enjoyment and education as a visitor. Throughout the day a variety of events are scheduled. There's a **Killer Whale Dolphin Show** where seven rows of wet-area seats are saved for guests who want a thorough drenching. In the **Sea Lion Show** you can be a recipient of one of the many kisses handed out by some of the oldest and largest performers in the country.

When you cross the bridge over the waterfall, heading through the trees and past the flamingos, you enter Africa. At the **Elephant and Chimpanzee Show** young elephants kick beach balls to the spectators. The **Parrot and Predatory Bird Show** is remarkable in its beauty and in the skill of the birds. And the Wildlife Show at the **Ecology Theater** teaches us what a precarious foothold wildlife has on the earth. You'll leave the **Tiger and Lion Show** with a new understanding of what's required to work with 14 lions and tigers as a group. In the **Small Animal Petting Corral** you can make a friend of a llama for the handful of food you can buy there. Or if the spirit of adventure is in your soul, take a ride on an Asian elephant or a dromedary.

You may be sorry you're not a child again when you see the **Gentle Jungle,** the unique playground that combines education, fun, and adventure. It's one of the most innovative play areas of its type. Among other things, children can crawl through burrows in the prairie dog village and pop up into Plexiglass domes so they see the world as these cute little animals view it. The **Whale-of-a-Time World** combines education, fun, and adventure.

And finally there's a 55-acre lake (once a golf course) that is the stage for a **Water Ski and Boat Show.** Daredevil athletes jump, spin, and even hang-glide while wearing waterskis.

A wide variety of fast food is available at the restaurant plaza, everything from burgers and pizza to nachos and chicken. Prices are moderate, averaging about $6 to $7 for a light bite. Or you can bring your own food—there are barbecue facilities on the grounds.

Marine World Africa USA is open daily during the summer (Memorial Day through Labor Day) from 9:30 a.m. to 6 p.m.; it's open Wednesday through Sunday the balance of the year with hours to 5:30 p.m. during the spring and fall, to 5 p.m. during winter. Admission is $17 for adults, $11 for children 4 to 12 and seniors over 60, and free for under-4s. Credit cards are accepted. The price covers all shows; dromedary and elephant rides will add $3. Tickets to Marine World Africa USA are available through Ticketron. All shows and attractions are handicapped-accessible except the elephant and dromedary rides and the Whale-of-a-Time Playground. Some pathways are too steep for easy access, but alternative routes are available.

Note: The best way to cope with the full schedule of shows is to get there early, make up your own itinerary from the leaflet and map given to you at the entrance—and then stick to it. Otherwise you'll find yourself missing parts of each presentation and feeling frustrated.

THE WINE COUNTRY

Most of the delicious California wines you've been enjoying with your meals in San Francisco hail from a warm, narrow valley starting about 55 miles north of the city. You get there by heading first north on U.S. 101, then turning east on Calif. 37 to Calif. 29, and continuing to Napa. From then on . . . well, take it easy.

All over Napa and Sonoma, you can pick up a very informative —and free—weekly publication called the *Wine Country Review*. It will give you the most up-to-date information on wineries and assorted events in the wine country. Be sure to get a copy and peruse it before making the rounds.

There are a number of interesting events that go on each year in the Napa Valley. A small sampling would include the **Napa Valley Wine Auction**, sponsored by the Napa Valley Vintners Association and usually held in June. This is the most important annual auction, one a wine connoisseur would not want to miss. In July, Calistoga holds an old-fashioned **Napa County Fair**, complete with rides, food, etc. At the end of July or the beginning of August there's a **Napa Town & Country Fair** at the Napa Fairgrounds. Let's just say that there's always much to see and do in the valley throughout the year. The Napa Chamber of Commerce (see below) will be glad to answer any questions you might have or to send you a calendar of events for the month or the year.

NAPA VALLEY WINERIES: Make your first stop in the Napa Valley the **Napa Chamber of Commerce**, 1556 1st St., in downtown Napa (tel. 707/226-7455), where you can pick up more information on the local vineyards, as well as listings of antique dealers, walking tours, etc. As you drive through Napa Valley, you'll see the welcoming signs put out by rows of wineries, most of which not only take visitors on conducted tours but also offer them samples of their product, most free. And a few of those visits can affect your driving in no uncertain manner. In September and October— when the grapes are being pressed—the very air in the valley seems intoxicating.

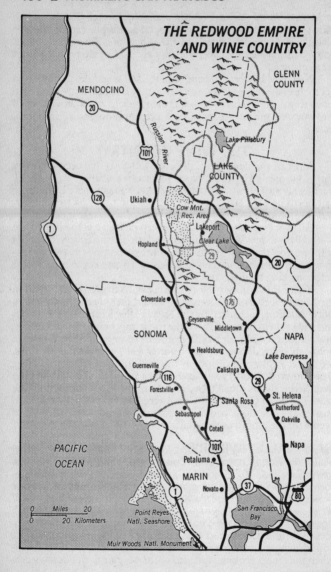

THE REDWOOD EMPIRE AND WINE COUNTRY

GLENN COUNTY

MENDOCINO

Russian River

Lake Pillsbury

LAKE COUNTY

Ukiah

Cow Mnt. Rec. Area

Lakeport

Clear Lake

Hopland

Cloverdale

Geyserville

Middletown

NAPA

SONOMA

Healdsburg

Lake Berryessa

Guerneville

Calistoga

Forestville

St. Helena

Santa Rosa

Rutherford

Sebastopol

Oakville

Cotati

Napa

Petaluma

MARIN

Novato

PACIFIC OCEAN

San Francisco Bay

Point Reyes Natl. Seashore

Muir Woods Natl. Monument

0   Miles   20
0   20 Kilometers

For the most part, we'll saunter (by car) north along Calif. 29, though a few of the Napa Valley vineyards I've included are a bit off the main road. But you'll enjoy the diversion—the beauty of the valley is striking whatever the time of year, and especially in the fall season. Throughout Napa, Yountville, St. Helena, and Calistoga, the colors are breathtaking as the leaves on the vines change to gold, rust brown, deep maroon—all in preparation for the next season of grapes.

Napa Valley now has about 150 wineries, and an exceptional selection of fine restaurants and hostelries at all price levels. It's a good idea to plan on spending more than one day if you'd like to tour even a small segment of the valley and its wineries. And if you do spend a weekend, or better yet a week, plan in advance and bear in mind that the summer is quite busy.

Most of the wineries en route conduct their tours from 10 a.m. to 5 p.m. daily. And there's considerably more to them than merely open vineyards. There are the huge presses (they don't tread the grapes in these 'ere parts) and an elaborate system of pipes and vats that the wines have to flow through and get blended in before being allowed to mellow gracefully in giant oak casks in the deep cellars.

Napa Valley's fame began with cabernet sauvignon and, except for the white chardonnay, more acreage is devoted to the growth of this grape than any other.

We'll begin in Napa with **Stag's Leap Wine Cellars,** 5766 Silverado Trail, Napa, CA 94558 (tel. 707/944-2020). For the most part, the Silverado Trail parallels Calif. 29 and you can get there by going east on Trances Street or Oak Knoll Avenues, then north to Stag's Leap Wine Cellars. The man who has guided the destiny of this now-famous winery and attracted the attention of France's noted wine experts is Warren Winiarski. A hill hides the group of buildings at its foot that comprise Stag's Leap. The first building of the group, which once housed the entire operation, still offers a summary view of winemaking from start to finish. Undoubtedly one of the best-known wines is the Cabernet Sauvignon Cask 23, under Winiarski's distinguished Stag's Leap Vineyard label. (Winiarski also offers good-value wines under the Hawk Crest label.) Sales hours are 10 a.m. to 4 p.m. daily; you can taste selected current releases then too. Tours are by appointment.

Now back to Calif. 29 and its intersection with California Drive, where you'll find **Domaine Chandon,** California Drive, Yountville, CA 94599 (tel. 707/944-2280). The firm produces about 750,000 cases annually of champagne-method California sparkling wines. Founded in 1968, this is a modern winery. You can take a tour here to find out all about the making of sparkling wines. There's also a small exhibit here on the vineyard's parent company,

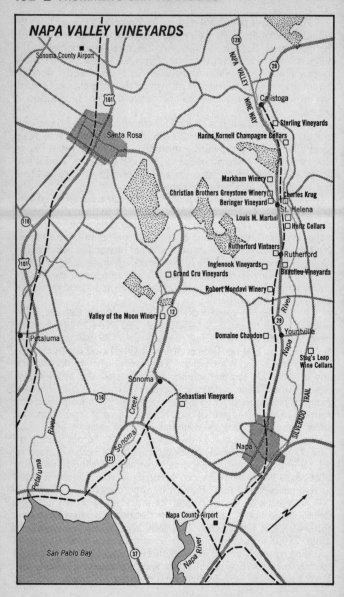

NAPA VALLEY VINEYARDS

Moët et Chandon, and the history of sparkling wines. November through April, guided tours depart Wednesday through Sunday from 11 a.m. to 5 p.m., leaving every hour on weekdays and every half hour on weekends. May through October the tours depart daily. When you've seen the place, you can enjoy a glass of one of Domaine Chandon's products in the Salon for a few dollars or dine in their excellent restaurant (see below); there's also a shop to browse through. The salon and shop are open from 11 a.m. to 6 p.m.

Continuing on Calif. 29 up to Oakville and you arrive at the **Robert Mondavi Winery,** 7801 St. Helena Hwy. (Calif. 29), Oakville, CA 94562 (tel. 707/963-9611). This is the ultimate hi-tech Napa Valley winery, housed in a magnificent mission-style facility. Almost every conceivable processing variable in their wine making is computer controlled—fascinating, especially if you've never watched the procedure before. Sales hours are 9 a.m. to 5 p.m. After the guided tour, you can taste the results of all this attention to detail with selected current wines. The Vineyard Room usually features an art show, and you'll find some exceptional antiques in the reception hall. During the summer the winery has some great outdoor jazz concerts.

Farther north on Calif. 29 you will reach Rutherford and the **Inglenook Vineyards,** 1991 St. Helena Hwy. (Calif. 29) opposite Rutherford Cross Road, Rutherford, CA 94573 (tel. 707/967-3300). Inglenook's history dates back to 1887 when the vineyards were bought by Gustav Niebaum. They stayed in the family's hands until 1964, were sold to Allied Growers, and subsequently were purchased by Heublein, which set about to build the prestige of the wines. The original winery, designed and built by Captain McIntyre, the architect of several neighboring wineries, is now the tasting room and starting point for tours. Sales hours are 10 a.m. to 5 p.m. daily, during which time you can taste current releases. Guided tours available.

A bit farther on is the **Beaulieu Vineyard,** at 1960 St. Helena Hwy. (Calif. 29), Rutherford, CA 94573 (tel. 707/963-2411) founded by a Frenchman named Delatour. The original winery looks as French baronial as a turn-of-the-century transplant can be. The winery is now substantially larger than when first built, but you can still see the complete tradition-oriented process of wine making from start to finish—beginning with the crusher, step by step on to the bottling and then the tasting, the last step being yours. Sales hours are 9 a.m. to 4 p.m. Tasting of selected current products is possible during sales hours. Guided tours begin at 11 a.m., the last at 3 p.m. The Garden Restaurant, next to one of the tasting rooms, has concerts in the summer.

The **Flora Springs Wine Co.** is at the end of West Zinfandel Lane, off Calif. 29 at 1978 W. Zinfandel Lane, St. Helena, CA 94574 (tel. 707/963-5711). While this handsome stone winery dates back to Napa Valley's early days, the Flora Springs label first appeared in 1978. The owners, the Komes family, have vineyards throughout Napa Valley and select choice lots for their own label. They are especially known for their sauvignon blanc and chardonnay, as well as cabernet sauvignon.

Flora Springs offers an excellent two-hour "familiarization seminar" that almost everyone interested in wines would enjoy. And best of all, it's tailored to all levels of enophiles. Limited to ten participants, the course is held on the second and fourth Saturday of each month at 10 a.m. The program begins in the vineyards where you'll see a good-growing vine and taste the grapes. While the grapes are being crushed, you taste the must (just-pressed juice) and ultimately see how it becomes a beautiful, clear wine. Then you are taught how to evaluate wines: you'll blind-taste different ones and learn to distinguish between them, trying an older and a younger wine, for example, to see what happens with aging. You will also learn to pair wines with different foods. There is a fee of $20 to cover the imported wines that are part of the ten-wine tasting. The two hours will be among the most interesting and enjoyable you'll ever spend. Make reservations by calling Fritz Draeger (tel. 707/963-5711) or by writing to him at the above address.

Be sure to stop at **Beringer Vineyards,** 2000 Main St. (Calif. 29, just north of the business district), St. Helena, CA 94574 (tel. 707/963-7115), if only to look at this remarkable Rhine House and view the hand-dug tunnels carved out of the mountainside, the site of the original winery.

Beringer Vineyards was founded in 1881 by the brothers Jacob and Frederick. The family owned it until 1970 when it was purchased by the Swiss firm of Nestlé, Inc. In true Swiss fashion, the business has prospered. It is the oldest *continuously* operating winery in the Napa Valley. What about Prohibition? you might ask. Beringer made "sacramental" wines during the dry years.

The modern working winery on the opposite side of the road is not open to the public, but you can get a general look at it from the Rhine House. Sales hours are 9 a.m. to 4:30 p.m. Tasting of current products is conducted during sales hours in the manor house. Tours are conducted by very knowledgeable guides.

Just beyond the Beringer Vineyards, still on the same side of the road at the north end of St. Helena, is the showplace of the **Christian Brothers,** P.O. Box 391, St. Helena, CA 94574 (tel. 707/963-0763). In 1987 the Christian Brothers resurrected the body and soul of what had been known as Greystone Cellars—

originally built at the turn of the century to be the largest stone winery in the world. Greystone now has a very detailed and informative visitors' tour through a portion of the first floor of this splendid building; it covers many aspects of wine making from cooperage to wine aging, discussing the vines at Greystone and pointing out the subtleties of tastings. Sales and tour hours at Greystone are 10 a.m. to 4 p.m. Tasting of selected products is offered after the tour.

Most of the process of wine making goes on at the winery just south of St. Helena, but as it is not designed to accommodate visitors, the winery is not open for tours.

Spring Mountain Vineyards, 2805 Spring Mountain Rd., (about 1½ miles west off Calif. 29 via Madrona Avenue and Spring Mountain Road), St. Helena, CA 94574 (tel. 707/963-5233), has probably the most unique claim to fame of any Napa Valley vineyard—it is the setting for the TV program "Falcon Crest." While the grand house was built in the late 19th century, Spring Mountain Vineyards as a working winery is housed in a new structure. The cellars were built in the early 1980s, though the label goes back to 1968. Tours of the winery are free; however, if you're a "Falcon Crest" fan who would like to take a guided tour of the grounds around the house, there is a fee. Sales hours, during which there are tastings, are 10 a.m. to 5 p.m. daily; the last tour of the winery is at 4:30 p.m. Free tours of the grounds are every half hour.

Sterling Vineyards, at 1111 Dunaweal Lane, Calistoga, CA 94515 (tel. 707/942-5151), is just south of the town of Calistoga and approximately half a mile east of Calif. 29. Sterling Vineyards is probably more startling in appearance than any of its neighbors. Perched on top of an island of rock it looks much more like a Greek or even an Italian mountaintop monastery than a Napa winery. Reaching this isolated facility is relatively easy—just take the aerial gondola. However, if you have any infirmity that makes walking or climbing difficult, this is not your cup of tea (or glass of wine). Gravity moves the wine and the visitors. You will go downstairs to fermentors, then down to the aging cellar; you'll climb farther down to the final aging cellar, then up to the reserve cellar, and finally up to the top of the rocky perch where you'll be rewarded in the tasting room. The very informative tour is guided by signs, not humans, so you can set your own pace. (It was kind not to employ a tour guide to make these arduous rounds several times daily.) The winery has changed hands more than once since its founding in 1969; its current owner is the Seagram Classic Wine Company, which produces over 100,000 cases per year. Sales hours and tasting times are 10:30 a.m. to 4:30 p.m. daily; however, the winery is closed to visitors on Monday and Tuesday during the winter.

For a detailed description of the above and many other wineries, get the tour guide, *California Is Wine Country,* handed out by the **Wine Institute** at 165 Post St. (between Grant and Kearny Streets), San Francisco, CA 94108.

NAPA: If you're touring the wine country, you might want to make your base its commercial center, the town of Napa. The gateway to the valley, Napa rose at the juncture of two streams; it was served by ferries and steamboats as early as the mid-1800s, and later by the Napa Valley Railroad. The valley is just 35 miles long, so if you stay in Napa and want to dine, wine, shop, or sightsee in Yontville, Rutherford, or St. Helena, you won't have very far to travel.

Where to Stay and Dine

To go the way of elegance in Napa is to stay at the **Silverado Country Club & Resort,** 1600 Atlas Peak Rd., Napa, CA 94558 (tel. 707/257-0200, or toll free 800/532-0500). It's north on Calif. 29 to Trancas Street, and east to Atlas Peak Road. Silverado is a 1,200-acre resort lavishly spread out at the foot of the hills. The resort has 280 spacious accommodations ranging from very large studios with a king-size bed, kitchenette, and a roomy, well-appointed bath, to one-, two-, or three-bedroom cottage suites, each with a wood-burning fireplace. Brown carpeting in the rooms sets off the pastel-striped spreads and drapes. The setting is superb: the cottage suites are in private, low-rise groupings, each sharing tucked-away courtyards and peaceful walkways. This arrangement allows for a feeling of privacy and comfort despite the size of the resort.

The main building and center of the resort looks more like an old southern mansion, pillars and all, than a California country resort. Lace curtains, white bentwood chairs, white tables, and gray carpeting complete the picture. Silverado offers exceptional resort services, including eight swimming pools and the largest tennis complex in northern California: 20 superlative Plexi-paved courts with a mini-clubhouse, canvas-topped review decks, and sport shop. You say you don't play tennis anymore but have switched to golf? Silverado has two 18-hole courses, occupying some 360 acres, very cleverly designed by Robert Trent Jones, Jr. The South Course is 6,500 yards, with a dozen water crossings (how many balls do you plan to take?); the North Course, 6,700 yards—somewhat longer, but a bit more forgiving. Obviously there is a staff of pros on hand.

Silverado has three restaurants to accommodate your every taste (well, almost). The Royal Oak is the quintessential steak restaurant, with high-back chairs, carved-wood tables, and exposed beams and brickwork. Vintner's Court offers California cuisine in a chandeliered salon with a view of the surrounding eucalyptus and beautifully groomed flower beds. The Silverado Bar & Grill is a large indoor terrace/bar which overlooks the North Course and serves breakfast, lunch, and cocktails.

Rates at Silverado range from $165 for a studio to $190 for a one-bedroom suite, single or double occupancy. Two- to three-bedroom suites are $325 to $365. Special packages are in effect at various times of the year, so be sure to ask.

And now let's look at the other end of the scale—the ever-handy, low-cost **Motel 6,** at 3380 Solano Ave., Napa, CA 94558 (tel. 707/257-6111). From Calif. 29, turn west on the Redwood Road turnoff and go one block to Solano Avenue, then half a block south and there you'll find Motel 6. The location is excellent since you are close to Calif. 29 and just across the street from a pleasant mini-mall. Rooms are simple, comfortable, and clean. Free TV and feature movies are included in the rate, and now every Motel 6 room has a phone. Local calls are free and there is no motel service charge for long-distance calls. Rooms are air-conditioned and there is a small pool. Rates are $30 for one person, and $6 for each additional adult. One other important feature: The managers of this Motel 6 are pleasant, helpful, and chock-full of useful information (but, then, I found that to be true of most people in the Napa Valley —it must be the air).

YOUNTVILLE: Yountville is casual nouveau posh (and advancing on chi-chi), but undoubtedly the most charming village along Calif. 29. Of less historical interest than St. Helena or Calistoga, it is nonetheless an interesting jumping-off point for a wineries tour or for the simple enjoyment of the beauties of the valley. What's more, it has several lovely places to stay, interesting places to shop, and excellent to superb restaurants at various price levels. And Yountville is walkable—you can easily take a very enjoyable stroll from one end of town to the other.

At the center of the village is **Vintage 1870** (tel. 707/944-2451), once a winery (from 1871 to 1955) and now a gallery with specialty shops featuring art, antiques, wine accessories, country treasures and collectibles, contemporary furnishings, gifts, clothing, music boxes, and chocolates. It is also home to three restaurants and to the Keith Rosenthal Theatre and gallery, where for 15 minutes you can absorb a multi-image film presentation of the valley's four seasons and see the interior of Spring Mountain's famous "Falcon Crest" mansion. The *San Francisco Examiner* has called photographer Keith Rosenthal "the Ansel Adams of the wine country." Admission to see the film is $3 for adults, $2.50 for seniors, $1 for children under 12. One of the most intriguing shops I found in the complex was the Napa Valley Trading Company, with antique and contemporary furnishings, weather vanes, pied and silver-gray zebra finches (live and absolutely beautiful), stuffed kittens (fabric), and paper hot-air balloons, to name just a few of the many items you'll want to take with you.

And if you've always wanted to try real hot-air ballooning, this may be the place to indulge your airy whim. **Adventures Aloft,** P.O. Box 2500, Vintage 1870, Yountville, CA 94599 (tel. 707/255-8688), is located at Vintage 1870 and is Napa Valley's oldest hot-air balloon company with full-time professional pilots. Groups are small and the flight will last about an hour. If you're a late sleeper, this may not be your bag since Adventures Aloft flies in the early, sunrise hours; it's then that the winds are gentle and the air is cool, which makes for an especially enjoyable trip. If you need reassurance about flying, be advised that modern balloons are operated by licensed pilots under the supervision of the Federal Aviation Administration.

Where to Stay and Dine

There are four notable accommodation choices in town. The **Vintage Inn,** 6541 Washington St., Yountville, CA 94599 (tel. 707/944-1112, or toll free 800/982-5539, 800/351-1133 in California), built on an old winery estate in the center of town, is very much the contemporary luxury country inn. The exterior is a brick-and-board construction; the reception lounge has a cathedral ceiling with exposed beams, brick fireplace, deep-brown couches, and shuttered windows, giving a sense of the handsome, warm look of the guest rooms. Each room has a fireplace, an armoire concealing the TV, oversize beds, a Jacuzzi, wine bar, refrigerator, and either a patio or veranda. The inn also provides nightly turn-down service. If you insist on exercise other than walking through the lovely village and its shops, the inn has a 60-foot pool heated year round, as well as an exercise room with a sauna, and tennis courts reserved for the use of the guests. A complimentary champagne breakfast is served daily in the Vintage Club, as well as afternoon tea.

November through April, rates for singles range from $99 to $119; doubles, from $109 to $129; mini-suites, from $129 to $139. May through October, singles are $119 to $149; doubles, $129 to $159; mini-suites, $159 to $169. The extra-person charge is $12 per night.

Burgundy House, 6711 Washington St., Yountville, CA 94599 (tel. 707/944-2855), offers rooms in a small fieldstone house. All are country French in décor with antique furnishings. There are no TVs or phones, and some rooms share a bath. All rooms are air-conditioned. Rates are $72.50 to $90.

Continental breakfast and wine (both complimentary) are served in a breakfast room with a fireplace or in a pretty little garden. Children are not accepted.

Under the same ownership, and just down the road a piece, is

Bordeaux House, 6600 Washington St., Yountville, CA 94599 (tel. 707/944-2855). Accommodations here are surprisingly contemporary (very un-wine country) with grasspaper-covered walls, Lucite furnishings, and beds on carpeted platforms. The amenities are also more up-to-date. Your room will have a private bath, and a TV; all have a fireplace. Guests may avail themselves of complimentary continental breakfast and evening wine over at Burgundy House. Children are welcome.

Rates range from $84 to $135.

Finally, there's the **Magnolia Hotel,** 6529 Yount St., Yountville, CA 94599 (tel. 707/944-2056), with 12 rooms in a beautifully restored old building (from 1873 to be exact) as well as in a new wing (the latter with fireplaces and sundecks). All rooms are individually decorated in cluttery Victorian motif with floral carpeting, and all have private bath but no phone or TV. A decanter of complimentary port is in each room. On-premises facilities include a large swimming pool (heated May through October) and a Jacuzzi.

Rates—including a full hot breakfast daily—are $95 to $165, single or double occupancy. A secluded suite overlooking the pool and garden (suitable for four) is $275. No smoking is allowed indoors.

As to where to eat in Yountville, there are several excellent choices. The ambience at **The Diner,** 6476 Washington St. (tel. 707/944-2626), is friendly, warm, and unpretentious. Done in shell pink, with track lighting overhead, the restaurant features a functioning Franklin stove, a collection of vintage diner water pitchers, as well as some interesting photos of what I assume to be local personalities. Seating is at the counter or in wooden booths.

For breakfast and lunch, everything I tried on the extensive menu was delicious and the portions were huge. House specialties range from huevos rancheros served with fried potatoes, a breakfast burrito with eggs scrambled with homemade chorizo, garlic, jalapeños, and cream cheese, to the less exotic, but equally delicious French toast and a wide range of eggs and pancakes. Fresh fruit with yogurt or cottage cheese is also available. The Diner's selection of natural, baked-on-premises breads usually includes raisin-walnut, whole wheat, cottage dill, and sourdough rye (with a starter descended from San Francisco's famous Larraburu Bakery, circa 1873).

Luncheon specialties include a superior carne asada as well as several other toothsome Mexican dishes. For more staid tastes, there is quite an assortment of hamburgers, sandwiches, salads, and homemade soups. Sundaes, espresso, cappuccino, and a variety of drinks from fresh-squeezed orange juice and natural-fruit sodas to domestic and imported beer and wine by the glass are all available.

Dinners are exceptional variations on the Mexican theme. Don't pass by the enchiladas with chicken, green chiles, and cream cheese, topped with crème fraîche and jack cheese. And the Tostada Grande—heaped with beans, cheese, lettuce, avocado, turkey breast, tomatoes, sour cream, and salsa—defies any appetite. Burgers, homemade soups, and salads are available at dinner too. If you still have room for dessert, flan, chocolate torte, or New York cheesecake are among the offerings (price range: $2 to $3.25). Service at the Diner is attentive, helpful, and friendly—indeed characteristic of all Napa Valley restaurants and inns.

Breakfast is served from 8 a.m. to 3 p.m.; lunch, from 11 a.m. to 3 p.m.; dinner, from 5:30 to 9 p.m. Prices at breakfast range from $3.50 to $6; lunch, $3.25 to $8; dinner, $5 to $8.50. Open daily except Monday.

Now the setting for the talents of Chef Sally Schmitt and her creative American menu, the **French Laundry,** 6640 Washington St., at Creek Street (tel. 707/944-2380), was in truth once a laundry. There is no sign to indicate that this historic old building might be anything but a country home, nor is an address visible, so look closely for the very small sign that indicates the cross street.

At the French Laundry you'll feel as though you are an honored guest in a private home. Infinite care has been taken with every detail of cuisine and décor, from the perfectly arranged flowers, the inviting fireplace, lovely fabric tablecloths, still-life paintings and historical prints.

A different five-course prix-fixe dinner (about $42 per person) is offered at the French Laundry each evening. It is difficult to get a reservation, but if you succeed, you're here for a relaxing evening. Your meal begins with a choice of three appetizers—perhaps sautéed sweetbreads and shiitake mushrooms in lemon cream, artichokes with garlic mayonnaise, or smoked trout with red-onion compote. Next comes a soup course, followed by an entree such as suprême of chicken with rosemary and orange, or pork loin with mustard-caper sauce. A simple green salad with a selection of perfectly ripe cheeses at room temperature follows. The meal is capped by a choice of at least three desserts. Sally Schmitt specializes in fruit desserts: a fall favorite of mine is gingered figs with crème anglaise, or the cranberry and apple küchen with hot cream sauce. The coffee is a special house blend, and as you might expect, there's an extensive and well-chosen wine list.

Dinner is served Wednesday through Sunday (there's only one seating, but times of arrival are spread from 7 to 8:30 p.m.). Remember, reservations are essential. A meal at the French Laundry is an experience you'll savor.

Heading back onto Calif. 29 (at this point known as the St. Helena Hwy.) and proceeding a bit north, you come to **Mustards**

Grill, 7399 St. Helena Hwy. (tel. 707/944-2424), a close relative of the Fog City Diner in San Francisco, Tra Vigne in St. Helena, and Rio Grill in Carmel. Look for the humorous bronze sculpture of a gentleman in bowler on the west side of the road. As you enter a barn-like structure, you'll see beamed cathedral ceilings, a black-and-white tile floor, track lighting, and a small bar. The main dining room is on two levels, and there's an airy glass-enclosed outer dining area for a simulated al fresco experience.

The atmosphere is light, festive, and relaxed, as you might expect it to be in wine country. Mustards is a favorite with local winemakers and growers. The blue-jeaned, white-shirted young servers are friendly and very knowledgeable. Specials of the day are listed on a blackboard along with featured local wines ranging from $3.50 to $5 by the glass. You can bring your own bottle of wine, as many diners seem to do, but the restaurant does charge a $5 corkage fee. I'd guess that more wine per table is consumed here than in any San Francisco restaurant.

While you review the dining possibilities, half of a sliced warm, crusty baguette arrives with sweet butter. Among the starters are such gems as a cornmeal pancake with Tobiko caviar and sour cream, warm goat cheese with sun-dried tomatoes and chives, and Chinese chicken salad. Sandwiches, apart from a sizable hamburger or cheeseburger, also include a rib-eye steak with horseradish cream, or smoked ham and Jarlsberg cheese grilled with tomato chutney. Entrees are reasonably priced and range from wood-burning-oven specialties—barbecued baby back ribs, pork chops with Thai marinade, or quail—to such items from the grill as Sonoma rabbit, New York steak with shiitake mushroom ragoût, gulf prawns, lamb chops with braised eggplant, or fresh fish. For dessert, the chocolate-pecan cake with chocolate sauce is a chocoholic's delight. I found the caramel custard with pistachios and cream irresistible. And Mustards has some of the best coffee I've ever tasted.

Back to basics: entree prices range from $9.90 to $17.50; appetizers and sandwiches, from $4 to $8. Dessert will add another $3 to $4. Open daily from 11:30 a.m. to 10 p.m.; at lunch, you can dine at the bar. Reservations are necessary for lunch and dinner.

Backtrack a bit on Calif. 29 to California Drive, just south of the Yountville Cross Road, turn west into California Drive, and there you will find **Domaine Chandon** (tel. 707/944-2892), one of California's most exquisite restaurants.

This outpost of the French champagne house of Möet has been making sparkling wines to French standards with great success for several years. The winery building is a low ultramodern stone-and-concrete structure that seems like part of the hillside. A creek shaded by large trees contributes to the idyllic setting. Tours of the winery, including displays and explanations of the champagne process, are given daily, but the excellent restaurant is by far the best reason to visit.

Domaine Chandon forsakes the usual old-fashioned wine-country quaintness for understated modern elegance. Its multi-level interior consists of several dining rooms with arched fir-paneled ceilings. It is one of the most dramatic and beautiful settings in the wine country—almost stark with rows of trees, potted plants, and dark-green chairs providing the color. Large picture windows allow for vineyard views during the day, and at night candlelight adds flattering warmth.

At lunch (which can also be enjoyed al fresco), you can begin with a salad of Belgian endive and radicchio. Entrees cost $14 to $17 and change daily, but might include ahi tuna served in a sauce of butter, fish juices, and Chandon Napa Valley Brut. There are lovely pastries and fruit tarts for dessert.

Dinner might start with chanterelle soup made with Oregon wild mushrooms and continue with salmon in champagne and sorrel sauce or sweetbreads with truffle juice and herbs for $22 to $26. Need I say, the wine list is impeccable.

Domaine Chandon is open for lunch from 11:30 a.m. to 2:30 p.m. and for dinner from 6 to 9 p.m. Wednesday through Saturday from November to April; the same hours daily from May through October. Reservations are essential; you can phone them in daily between 10 a.m. to 5 p.m., no more than two weeks in advance of your visit.

OAKVILLE: Driving north again on St. Helena Hwy. (Calif. 29) you soon come to the Oakville Cross Road. There you will find the **Oakville Grocery Co.,** 7856 St. Helena Hwy., Oakville, CA 94562 (tel. 707/944-8802). Stop! Its name, its location, and its exterior disguise one of the finest gourmet food stores this side of Dean and DeLucca in New York City. You'll find the very best of breads, cheeses, pâtés, fresh foie gras (American and French), smoked Norwegian salmon, smoked sturgeon, fresh caviar, smoked pheasant, and an exceptional selection of California wines. (If you find the wine decision difficult, there are sampler sets to help you along.) Special bottles such as the 1983 Stag's Leap Wine Cellars "Cask 23" cabernet, or the 1985 Long Vineyards chardonnay, are also available in limited quantities. Oakville Grocery can ship wines by the case anywhere in the United States. Remember, you can charge liquor purchases in California; major credit cards are accepted here.

The Oakville Grocery Co. will prepare a picnic basket lunch for you if you give them 24 hours' advance notice. Delivery service is available to some areas.

RUTHERFORD: From Oakville, take the Oakville Cross Road

east to the Silverado Trail; turn north to Rutherford Hill Road, then east on up the hillside to the French gem of Napa Valley—the **Auberge du Soleil,** at 180 Rutherford Hill Rd., Rutherford, CA 94573 (tel. 707/963-1211). This elegant hideaway with its glorious French country restaurant is nestled in a hillside olive grove overlooking the lovely valley. It's a peaceful spot, air fragrant with eucalyptus, to rest and to eat brilliant classic French and California nouvelle cuisine.

At the auberge's restaurant, a magnificent fireplace (large enough to roast a whole pig), huge wood pillars, banquettes with rainbow-striped cushions, white tablecloths, and fresh flowers combine to create an elegantly rustic—or is that rustically elegant?—ambience. Light opera plays in a room that opens out to a wisteria-decked terrace with white umbrellas, pink-clothed tables, and attractive carved-wood chairs.

At lunch the appetizers include chicken-and-leek sausage with bell-pepper vinaigrette, as well as crab cakes with cucumber-and-mint sauce. Ask about the soup of the day too: I've had a superb and unusual black-bean soup and a pumpkin/sweet potato blend (with a tad of juniper flavor) that I'd love to take home by the gallon. The bread brought to table with sweet butter is deliciously hot. Among the lunch entrees are such excellent seafood dishes as sautéed prawns with tomato-and-dill sauce and grilled salmon with scallions, garlic, and sweet potatoes, as well as a delicious fettuccine with sun-dried tomatoes, porcini mushrooms, and poussin. The desserts are superb: my choice was a delicious puff pastry with fresh fruits and caramel sauce. Luncheon entrees average $13 to $17; appetizers, $5 to $8; desserts, $6.

Dinner at the Auberge du Soleil is a four-course, prix-fixe affair ($52). You might begin with the fish-and-shellfish dumplings (quenelles) with meunière sauce, the wild-mushroom ravioli, the tuna carpaccio, or the pan-fried, hazelnut-coated goat cheese with cassis vinaigrette. The soup of the day is followed by an enticing list of entrees. I find it difficult to pass over the rack of lamb, but the valley squab with truffles and marrow is truly enlightened cuisine. Somewhat more standard tastes might be pleased by the chicken suprême prepared with herbs and wild rice, or grilled New York cut with horseradish sauce, served with grilled eggplant and tomatoes. An extraordinary dark-chocolate sac with tangerine mousse and raspberry sauce, a hot apple tart with apricot sauce, or, in fact, any of the other delights, should satisfy all dessert palates.

Each dish, lunch and dinner, is a work of art. Reservations are necessary, and weekends are often booked a month in advance. The restaurant is open daily for lunch from 11:30 a.m. to 2 p.m., and for dinner from 6 to 9 p.m.

The Auberge du Soleil has 36 rooms, probably the most elegant in the valley, each with fireplace, television, wet bar, and decks overlooking Napa Valley. One-bedroom rooms and suites range from $205 to $330; two-bedroom suites are $500. Room rates include a continental breakfast and the use of swimming and tennis facilities. Note: Even if you are staying at the inn, it is suggested that lunch and dinner reservations at the auberge restaurant be made in advance of your arrival.

ST. HELENA:
Reminiscent in some ways of the south of France, with its tall plane trees arching over the roads, St. Helena also suggests feudal England, with its mansions overseeing the vineyards and valleys from hillside perches. Many of the buildings in the main part of town date to the 1800s; the modern wares in a variety of shops are also worth a look. It's a friendly place, with some excellent restaurants and inns.

Where to Stay and Dine
One of the most romantic hostelries I've ever seen is the **Wine Country Inn,** two miles north of St. Helena at 1152 Lodi Lane, St. Helena, CA 94574 (tel. 707/963-7077). Set on a hillside overlooking the vineyards, it has 25 air-conditioned rooms decorated in New England inn style. Many have fireplaces, balconies, or patios, and though all have private bath, there are no TVs or phones. The rooms are just lovely, with country antique furnishings, stitchery hangings on the walls, and patchwork quilts on the beds. And to add to the aura of quiet relaxation, the inn now has an elegant pool and a Jacuzzi. A buffet-style continental breakfast—with homemade breads—is included in rates. Children under 13 are not accepted.

Rates: $105 to $126 single, $115 to $156 double.

Tra Vigne, 1050 Charter Oak Ave., at Main Street (Calif. 29) (tel. 707/963-4444), is one of the most attractive restaurants I've ever seen. Its chic neoclassical Italian look, its innovative, informal Italian-American food, and its attentive, knowledgeable, and friendly service are an unbeatable combination.

You approach the restaurant, which looks like a small Roman forum, from a splendid outdoor patio. To the right, as you enter, is a comfortable bar that extends the entire length of the wall, and to the rear of the dining room is the ultra-contemporary pizza oven. An artistic arrangement of dried flowers, salami, bread, garlic, and cheese hangs over the entry to the kitchen.

Whether you go for a drink, an unconventional pizza, lunch, or dinner, Tra Vigne is worth seeing. And the prices are most reasonable. Appetizers go from the hearty homemade minestrone or the pizzetta con aglio (small pizza with garlic) to the smoked prosciutto with persimmons and mascarpone cream. Pasta ranges from a deliciously simple shell-shaped variety with fresh tomato-and-tarragon sauce, to delectable ravioli filled with homemade ricotta, spinach, and red chard. Want an adventurous pizza? Consider Pizza Rustica, with pancetta, sautéed red chard, roasted sweet peppers, and Parmesan; or Pizza al Gamberi, with prawns, yellow tomatoes, Bel Paese, Parmesan, and pesto. Tra Vigne also has fresh fish daily, braised rabbit with mustard, sage, and juniper (a Tuscan specialty of the house), roasted quail wrapped in pancetta with chervil vinaigrette, and a superb 16-ounce T-bone steak served with fennel-roasted potatoes. For dessert, the poached pear in merlot custard with chocolate-walnut grissini is above reproach, but you won't go wrong either with the rich coffee caramel custard with Sambuca crème anglaise. Entrees are $6.75 to $11.25 for pasta, and $8.25 to $14.25 for the meat and fish dishes (the T-bone steak is $17.25). Pizza (all are one-person size) is $7.25 to $9.25. Appetizers cost $3.25 to $10.25 for the antipasto misto for two. Desserts average $4.

Tra Vigne has an excellent selection of California and Italian wines, and a choice of several fine grappas in a broad price range.

Tra Vigne is open daily: Sunday through Thursday from noon to 9 p.m., on Friday and Saturday to 10 p.m. Reservations are suggested.

CALISTOGA:
Sam Brannan became California's first millionaire by building a hotel and spa to take advantage of the area's geothermal springs. His entrepreneurial instincts combined "California" with the name of popular East Coast resort "Saratoga": Calistoga was born in 1859 and incorporated in 1886, attracting the newly wealthy from San Francisco. Today Calistoga still has a main street about six blocks long, with no building higher than two stories; it looks for all the world like a set for a somewhat updated western. At the northern end of lush wine country, near Old Faithful and the Petrified Forest, the town remains popular. Calistoga is a delightfully simple place to relax and indulge in mineral waters, mud baths, sulfur steambaths, Jacuzzis, massages—and of course, wines.

Where to Stay and Dine
The **Mount View Hotel,** 1457 Lincoln Ave. (near Fairway), Calistoga, CA 94515 (tel. 707/942-6877), offers 25 art deco rooms and nine glamorous suites named after movie idols of the past—like the Carole Lombard (it has peach-colored walls and light-green carpeting) and the western-themed Tom Mix. Amenities include private baths and phones in all rooms; no TV. Facilities also include a heated swimming pool and Jacuzzi.

A continental/nouvelle cuisine restaurant on the premises serves breakfast, lunch, dinner, and Sunday brunch. Typical dinner entrees here are rack of lamb with whole-grain mustard and fresh fish specials of the day, for $10 to $22. A prix-fixe dinner is $30. There's an extensive California wine list, reasonably priced, and well balanced for any menu. A cocktail lounge (the scene of nightly piano music) adjoins.

Rates are $65 to $90 a night, single or double, and $120 to $145 for suites, including a full American breakfast. A special package—"The Suite Life"—includes a suite for two evenings, champagne, and a dinner for two for $205.

Another Calistoga choice is **Dr. Wilkinson's Hot Springs,** 1507 Lincoln Ave., Calistoga, CA 94515 (tel. 707/942-4102). It's a typical motel with 42 rooms, mostly distinguished by the mud baths on the premises. A mud-bath treatment takes about two hours. This rejuvenating process costs $32, $15 additional if you include a half-hour massage. There's also a hot spring on the premises, and none of these healthful facilities is limited to guests. Be sure to reserve your spa visit four to six weeks in advance. Motel rooms at Dr. Wilkinson's have color TVs and phones and drip coffee makers. Rates are $48 to $69 single, $52 to $80 double. Lower weekly rates are also available. Facilities include two outdoor and one indoor pool.

If you've never had a mud bath before, you might well wonder what it is and how it feels. Although mud baths are not recommended for people with high blood pressure or for pregnant women, all others may enjoy their benefits. The bath is composed of local volcanic ash, imported peat, and naturally boiling mineral hot springs water, all mulled together to produce a thick mud at a temperature of about 90° to 100°F. Once you overcome the hurdle of deciding how best to place your naked body into the stone tub full of mud, the rest is pure relaxation—you are in the bath, surprisingly buoyant, for about 10 to 12 minutes. A warm mineral-water shower, a mineral-water whirlpool bath, and a mineral-water steamroom visit are followed by a relaxing blanket wrap to cool your delighted body down slowly. All of this takes about 1½ hours; with a massage, add another half hour. The outcome is a rejuvenated, revitalized, squeaky-clean you.

In addition to Dr. Wilkinson's Hot Springs, other spas providing similar services are the **Lincoln Avenue Spa** at 1339 Lincoln Ave. (tel. 707/942-5296), **Golden Haven Hot Springs Spa** at 1713 Lake St. (tel. 707/942-6793), and the **Calistoga Spa Hot Springs** at 1006 Washington St. (tel. 707/942-6269). All spas offer a variety of other treatments such as hand and foot massage, herbal wraps, acupressure facelift, skin rubs, herbal facials, etc. Appointments are necessary for all of the above services, and you should phone at least a week in advance.

And for a delightful meal in a combination deli and treasurehouse of wines, wend your way to the **All Seasons Market** at 1400 Lincoln Ave. (tel. 707/942-9111). You may choose to eat in or gather picnic provisions. However, don't overlook the luncheon and dinner specials here and the fresh desserts. Recent luncheon entrees included a mesquite-grilled chicken sandwich served with homemade bread and salad, and fettuccine with prawns served with cucumber, bell peppers, and tomatoes in virgin olive oil and white wine. Entrees range from $5.50 to $7.50. The menu also includes homemade soup, and an appetizer and salad of the day. The All Seasons Market is open daily: Monday through Thursday from 9 a.m. to 6 p.m., weekends to 10 p.m. The Market serves breakfast, lunch, and dinner on weekends; the balance of the week, lunch is served from noon until 4 p.m., then dinner until closing.

Seeing the Sights

Before you head off to see the Old Faithful Geyser and Petrified Forest, stop at the **Calistoga Depot,** at 1458 Lincoln Ave. (tel. 707/942-6333), which now houses a variety of shops and the Calistoga Chamber of Commerce. The depot occupies the site of the original railroad station built in 1868; alongside it sit six restored passenger cars dating from 1916 to the 1920s.

If you decided against ballooning in Yountville, Calistoga may have something to lighten your spirits. The **Calistoga Soaring Center,** 1546 Lincoln Ave. (tel. 707/942-5592), is the largest and most active soaring site in the country. You can take a glider ride (they're available for one or two persons) with a federally licensed commercial glider pilot. Sailplanes are built, certified, and maintained to the same standards the government requires of engine-driven aircraft. Twenty minutes of quietly soaring like an eagle above beautiful Napa Valley is $74.50 for one person, or $94.50 for two. Trips can be arranged any day of the week from 9 a.m. till sunset.

The **Old Faithful Geyser of California,** 1299 Tubbs Lane (tel. 707/942-6463), has been blowing off steam for as long as anyone can remember. The hot (350°F) water spews out every 40 minutes, day and night; the performance lasts about three minutes, and you'll learn a lot about the origins of geothermal steam. One of the few geysers in the world that performs at regular intervals, Old Faithful's deviations from the normal pattern generally seem to relate to earthquakes within 500 miles from the area. You can bring a picnic lunch with you and catch the show as many times as you wish. Old Faithful is situated between Calif. 29 and Calif. 128 (there are signs directing you to it from downtown Calistoga). Admission is $2.50 for adults, $1.50 for children under 12; under 6, free. The geyser area is open year round: from 9 a.m. to 6 p.m. in summer, to 5 p.m. the rest of the year.

Also in Calistoga, off Calif. 128 at 4100 Petrified Forest Rd., is the **Petrified Forest** (tel. 707/942-6667). Don't expect to see thousands of trees turned into stone; however, you can see many interesting specimens of redwoods that have become petrified through the infiltration of silicas and other minerals in the volcanic ash that covered them after the eruption of Washington's Mount St. Helens. Earlier specimens—petrified seashells, clams, and marine life—indicate that water covered the area before the redwood forest. Admission is $3 for adults, free for children under 10. The Petrified Forest is open daily: from 9 a.m. to 6 p.m. in the summer, 10 a.m. to 5 p.m. the rest of the year.

SONOMA

Not far from Napa Valley, but deserving a day's outing in itself, Sonoma is 45 miles north of San Francisco. To get there, follow the directions to Napa, but instead of continuing on Calif. 37, make a left on Calif. 121, then head north on Broadway, following the signs.

Rich in California history, much of the area is still preserved as it was in the mid-1800s when a brilliant Mexican army officer, Gen. Mariano Guadalupe Vallejo, was in charge of the Sonoma mission. So many historical monuments and landmarks are intact in Sonoma that it's almost as though time had stood still.

The center of town is the **Plaza**—a lovely park, the largest town square in California, and the site of City Hall. The Bear Flag Monument in the Plaza marks the spot where the crude Bear Flag was raised in 1846, signaling the end of Mexican rule. The Bear Flag was later to become the state flag.

Before you begin your explorations of the area, stop in at the **Sonoma Valley Visitors Bureau,** 453 1st St. East, Sonoma, CA 95476 (tel. 707/996-1090), right in the park for brochures, maps, etc. The bureau is open daily: weekdays from 9 a.m. to 5 p.m., on Saturday to 4 p.m., on Sunday to 3 p.m.

The major sights in town are organized into a walking and driving tour in a pamphlet available at the Visitors Bureau. With the help of this pamphlet, you can "follow the golden line" on the street to historic spots in and near Sonoma Plaza. Highlights include a wing of the **Casa Grande,** General Vallejo's first home in 1836, a Mexican-style adobe; the Victorian-style **Vallejo Home,** which the general built in 1852 about a half mile northwest of the Plaza; **Sonoma Barracks,** erected in 1836 to house Mexican army troops; the **Swiss Hotel,** originally another adobe of Vallejo's, later a hotel and restaurant, where you can still dine today; **Mission San Francisco Solano de Sonoma,** founded in 1823, the last of the 21 missions on the Royal Road; the **Blue Wing Inn,** an 1840 hostelry built to accommodate tourists and new settlers while they built homes in Sonoma (John Frémont, Kit Carson, and Ulysses S. Grant were guests); and the **Toscano Hotel,** a fascinating accommodation filled with early relics. Many of these landmarks offer guided tours of their interiors.

In addition to historic sights, Sonoma has many wineries to explore. Some 15 of them have public tours and/or tastings conducted daily from 10 a.m. to 5 p.m., and several others offer tours by appointment. Picnic areas are an added feature at several. The Visitors Bureau can provide you with a detailed wineries map. A *Visitors Guide to Sonoma Valley* is available by sending $1.50 to the bureau at the above address.

A final suggestion: Although Sonoma has plenty of restaurants, the Plaza park is a lovely place for a picnic, complete with tables. You can get all the fixings at the **Sonoma Cheese Factory,** 2 Spain St. (tel. 707/996-1000), where an extraordinary variety of imported meats and cheeses is sold, and caviar, gourmet salads, pâté, plus the Monterey Jack they make. They'll be happy to make up sandwiches for you; purchase a small bottle of wine to drink it down. While you're there, you can watch a narrated slide show about cheesemaking. Open from 9:30 a.m. to 5:30 p.m. seven days a week.

About five miles north of Sonoma (a mile west of Glen Ellen on London Ranch Road) is **Jack London State Park** (tel. 707/938-5216). This 800-acre memorial includes a museum built by his wife in 1919 to display a considerable collection of objects and memorabilia from London's varied activities and interests. You can also see the cottage, ranch buildings, and the ruins of the Wolf House, destroyed by fire before the Londons moved in. The graves of the writer and his wife, Charmian, are on the property. The park is open daily from 8 a.m. to the closing hour posted at the station entrance; the museum, from 10 a.m. to 5 p.m. There is a charge of $3 per car.

RUSSIAN RIVER WINE ROAD: This section of Sonoma County is a bit more off the beaten track than Napa or southern Sonoma, but it contains equally beautiful scenery. The meandering roads going north from Guerneville to Cloverdale pass quiet farms and tree-lined creeks, and the 100-mile stretch is home to about 57 of California's wineries, many of them offering tasting rooms and tours.

Some highlights follow. For more detailed information on the area, send $1 to **Russian River Wine Road,** P.O. Box 127, Geyserville, CA 95441 (tel. 707/433-6935).

To begin your Russian River tour, turn off U.S. 101 at River Road, proceed west to the Healdsburg Road turnoff, and make a right at the 62-acre **Mark West Vineyards,** 7000 Trenton-Healdsburg Rd., Forestville (tel. 707/544-4813). Production in this family-owned and -operated vineyard and winery is limited to six distinctive varietals, but although it's small, Mark West boasts a lovely setting and picnic grounds. Tours, tasting, and retail sales are offered daily from 10 a.m. to 5 p.m.

Just north of Mark West Winery, make a left turn on Eastside Road and rejoin River Road going toward Guerneville. This leads to **Korbel Champagne Cellars,** 13250 River Rd. (tel. 707/887-2294), a leading producer of premium California champagne which celebrated its centennial in 1982. Its classic brick champagne cellar was constructed in 1886, and the picturesque brandy tower was added in 1889. Korbel offers an extensive tour (daily from 9:45 a.m. to 3 p.m.) that provides an opportunity to see how they produce their classic méthode champenoise champagne. The wine shop is open daily from 9 a.m. to 5 p.m.; the tasting room, from 9 a.m. to 4:30 p.m. (May to September, everything is open a half hour later).

Farther north, about halfway along the road to Calistoga, you'll see the **Alexander Valley Vineyards,** 8644 Calif. 128 (tel. 707/433-7209), located on the original 1840s homestead of Cyrus Alexander. Tastings and sales are weekdays from 10 a.m. to 5 p.m., on weekends from noon to 5 p.m. Tours are by appointment.

A relative newcomer to the area is **Dry Creek** in Healdsburg (exit from U.S. 101, and go west on Dry Creek Road for about three miles to Lambert Bridge Road; tel. 707/433-1000). Founded in 1972, Dry Creek has reached a production level of 75,000 cases each year under the expert guidance of David Stare, whom you're likely to meet in the tasting room. Open daily from 10:30 a.m. to 4:30 p.m.

Continue north to **Geyser Park Winery,** 22281 Chianti Rd., west of U.S. 101 at the Canyon Road exit (tel. 707/433-6585). Geyser Park was founded in 1880 and produces some fine bulk wines. There are hiking trails and picnic areas here, but tours are by appointment only. The tasting room is open daily from 10 a.m. to 5 p.m.

Where to Stay

Although this area is not as crowded with tourists as the rest of the wine country, advance reservations are still advisable at all accommodations.

Madrona Manor, 1001 Westside Rd., Healdsburg, CA 95448 (tel. 707/433-4231), was built in 1881 as a majestic three-story Victorian summer home surrounded by acres of wooded and landscaped grounds. It's not too hard to find: take the second Healdsburg exit (the first says Healdsburg Avenue), go north to the first stop sign, then turn left under the highway. This is Mill Street, which takes you through the countryside and ends at the Madrona Manor's entrance. Follow the drive up to the main house.

This inn is truly a family enterprise. John and Carol Muir are the owners and innkeepers, their two sons preside over the kitchen and hotel maintenance, their daughter is the pastry chef, and their son-in-law is the groundskeeper. They've done wonders with banker John Paxton's 1881 summer home overlooking Dry Creek Valley.

There are 20 rooms situated throughout four buildings on just under eight acres. The main house, a Victorian jewel with a gabled mansard roof, has nine guest rooms filled with period furnishings and décor. The gingerbread-trimmed carriage house has eight rooms with hand-carved rosewood furnishings from Nepal and decorated with prints and artifacts from the Muirs' travels abroad. Another house has two more rooms, and there's a lovely honeymoon cottage furnished with white wicker and a sunken bathtub for two. All rooms have private bath, air conditioning, and a working fireplace. And there is a swimming pool behind a citrus grove.

The public rooms—lobby, music room, parlor—are also charming. Dining in the Madrona Manor Restaurant is a memorable experience. The California-cuisine menu changes nightly, allowing chef Todd Muir, trained by Chez Panisse's Alice Waters, to use the freshest ingredients available to create his dishes. The menu is à la carte or prix fixe (at $42.50 per person) daily. Sunday brunch, like dinner, is open to the public; a full daily breakfast is served only to guests. Suffice it to say that the food is heavenly at any meal.

Rooms at the Madrona Manor are $85 to $120, single or double; suites cost $125 to $135. And, wonder of wonders, children and pets are allowed.

An excellent choice is the **Ridenhour Ranch House Inn,** 12850 River Rd., Guerneville, CA 95446 (tel. 707/887-1033), just down the road from Korbel champagne cellars. Innkeeper Rick Jewell keeps this charming hostelry open from mid-February through November. The inn has eight quaintly decorated Victorian-style rooms named after local fauna—Madrone, Maple, Oak, Laurel, etc.— furnished with antiques and lovely patchwork quilts. There is a family room with TV and phone, plus complimentary sherry and port in your room. There's also a hot tub for the use of guests. Children over 10 are welcome at the inn with their parents.

Rates are $55 to $90, single or double occupancy and include a full breakfast.

Where to Dine

In addition to the **Madrona Manor** restaurant (described in the hotel listing above), you might try **Catelli's, The Rex,** on U.S. 101, at Geyserville Avenue, in the town of Geyserville (tel.

707/857-9904), which serves good home-cooked garlic-laced Italian fare prepared by Richard Catelli. Lunch often seems to be convention time for local winemakers. (The restaurant has been a family operation since 1938.)

Entrees include homemade ravioli, chicken sautéed with mushrooms, rabbit sautéed with herbs and wine, and linguine with white clam sauce. All dinners, which cost $9 to $14, include homemade soup and salad. For dessert try the amaretto mousse.

Open weekdays for lunch from 11:30 a.m. to 2 p.m. and nightly from 5 to 9 p.m. for dinner.

CONDUCTED TOURS AND PACKAGE HOLIDAYS

The following conducted tours are run by the **Gray Line** (tel. 415/558-9400), and represent samples of many others operated by that company. Departure times given are from the Gray Line Terminal, 1st and Mission Streets, although a shuttle bus leaves Union Square a half hour before each departure time.

San Francisco Deluxe: This tour of the city includes Golden Gate Bridge, Mission Dolores, Golden Gate Park, the Presidio, museums, Civic Center, Fisherman's Wharf, and other points; it lasts 3½ hours. Departures year round begin at 9 a.m. daily (there are more tours in the summer). The cost is $20.50 for adults, $10.25 for children ages 5 to 12.

Muir Woods and Sausalito: This is a trip to the redwood country, returning via Sausalito. It includes a leisurely stroll through Muir Woods. Departures daily year round begin at 9 a.m. and tours last 3½ hours; the cost is $20.50 for adults, $10.25 for children.

You can add a 1½-hour harbor cruise to either of these tours for a total of $26.50 for adults, $13.75 for kids.

THE SIERRA CLUB

This, of course, is a nationwide—in fact, worldwide—organization of nature lovers, protectors, and enjoyers, but San Francisco boasts the national headquarters at 730 Polk St. (tel. 776-2211).

The triple functions of the organization are to study nature, to preserve it, and to get out into it as often as possible. The club therefore arranges lectures and courses, maintains huts and wilderness lodges, helps to clean up beauty spots, combats air and water pollution, and gives members an opportunity to enjoy nature trips throughout the year at reasonable prices.

CHAPTER XIV

FARTHER AFIELD

□ □ □

Americans take to the road like fish to water, preferring the automobile—and their own pace—to all other vacation styles. Thus this chapter, which takes the last one a step farther, covers all those important sights within reasonable reach of the city by car. (For car rentals, see Chapter III).

THE TIMBER TRAIL

Are you tired of the city—however beautiful—and do you yearn to escape the crowds and traffic? Aim north, right up the coast, where natural beauty is at a maximum and people at a minimum.

Take off from San Francisco via the Golden Gate Bridge, pausing at **Vista Point** for one glorious panorama of what you are leaving. First stops can be Sausalito, Tiburon, and Muir Woods—all covered in detail in the previous chapter. Then get on the freeway, U.S. 101, and wend your way to San Rafael (about 14 miles).

SAN RAFAEL: Take the first turnoff entering town and you can spend a while visiting a charming replica of **Mission San Raphael Archangel,** founded in 1817.

Continue north on 101 for two more miles for a startling contrast of ultramodern with antique. Turn right after topping Puerto Suello Hill to inspect the **Marin Civic Center,** one of the last works of the late great Frank Lloyd Wright.

Opened in 1962, the handsome Byzantine-domed center spans the gap between two gentle knolls. In gold, buff, and blue, it echoes the famed architect's dictum that buildings should blend with nature. The center is open to the public, and its interior wells and arching skylights are spectacular and well worth a visit.

The next 40 miles or so will be over the U.S. 101 freeway and not terribly interesting. Next stop is Little River.

LITTLE RIVER: Plan to stay at least one night in the vicinity of Mendocino. Just before you reach it, in Little River, there are two charmingly antiquated inns. The **Little River Inn,** Little River, CA 95456 (tel. 707/937-5942), is the quainter: a rambling Maine-style mansion built in 1853 by pioneer Silas Coombs. Where Silas once oversaw lumbering, shipbuilding, and shipping operations, a great-grandson and his wife maintain a quiet country retreat. The original mansion is only one building among the inn complex—others are more modern. But, personally, I prefer the old attic rooms with their grandmother rockers, thick quilts, and dome windows looking out toward the sea. Attic double rooms in the inn cost $56. Fireplace cottages are $85; rooms in the contemporary Hilltop Annex are $72. Winter rates (mid-week from November 15 to April 15) are 20% less, excluding weekends and holidays. Modern amenities include a dining room (entrees run $14 to $20) with a bar, a nine-hole regulation golf course, and two night-lit championship-caliber tennis courts.

Somewhat more expensive is the **Heritage House,** Little River, CA 95456 (tel. 707/937-5885), on the sea side of the road. This, too, is a New England-style farmhouse. But the outbuildings that have been built around it, which provide the "cottage" accommodations, are all inspired by early-day buildings and institutions and named such things as "Scott's Opera House," "Country Store," "Bonnet Shop," "Ice Cream Parlor." Most are outfitted with antiques from old houses in the area. Rates are $105 to $260 single, $125 to $280 double, MAP (including breakfast and dinner).

MENDOCINO: It's barely two miles from the inns to Mendocino (once known as Meiggsville, also as Big River), today recognized as a center for the arts on California's northern coast.

Around 1853 Harry Meiggs came to Big River in search of a wrecked cargo of Chinese silk. Instead he found another kind of wealth under the redwood bark. Meiggs helped denude the Oakland hills to get lumber for fast-growing, faster-burning San Francisco in the Gold Rush days. Big River's giant trees represented a fortune. So he built the region's first sawmill beside the inlet and shipped cargoes of lumber back to the new city.

Meiggs later overreached himself and had to flee to South America, where he built the first railroad across the Andes and ultimately made a new fortune. As a legacy, he had started a lumber boom that lasted more than half a century in Mendocino.

The New England woodsmen who followed him to the California coast built a town at Big River, much like the rockbound ports in Maine. Steeply pitched roofs—slanted to shed snow that never falls in Mendocino—remind one of harsh New England winters. Adding flavor are saltbox cottages and enclosed water towers. Most of them still stand, adorned with new paint by new owners.

Food and Lodging

As the port grew in importance, coastal ships from Seattle and San Francisco made regular calls at Mendocino. Along Main Street sprouted a dozen hotels. On steamer day, each sent a carriage down to the wharves. A lone survivor of these enterprising hostelries is the **Mendocino Hotel** (formerly the Central House), at 45080 Main St., Mendocino, CA 95460 (tel. 707/937-0511 or toll free 800/ 548-0513), whose look evokes the day when prosperous lumbermen nicknamed $20 gold pieces "Big River Bits." It's a delightful place to stay, fully modern and totally renovated in a Victorian motif. The 50 rooms are all decorated in period-style furnishings and wallpapers with modern amenities like cable TV and phone. Some 25 of the 50 rooms are located just across the road in four small, handsome buildings, one of which is called the Heeser House, built in 1852 by one of Mendocino's pioneer families. Each room contains photographs and memorabilia reflecting the history of the town and its founders, and 22 out of these 25 have fireplaces. A lovely English country garden surrounds the buildings. The hotel offers room service, and there is a nightly turndown accompanied by homemade chocolates. And there's a fine restaurant on the premises. Rooms range from $65 to $210 (for suites), single or double; lower rates are for those rooms without a private bath.

Another lovely place to stay is the **MacCallum House,** Albion Street (P.O. Box 206), Mendocino, CA 95460 (tel. 707/ 937-0289), located directly behind Main Street. The house was a wedding gift to young Daisy Kelly MacCallum in 1882. It was turned into a gorgeous hostelry a few years ago. Many of the furnishings were left by Daisy MacCallum, who was the town matriarch until her death in 1953. The inn's 20 rooms are situated throughout six buildings (including a carriage house, barn, and water-tower building). Six of the rooms have private bathroom. Rates are $55 to $135 a night, and include a generous continental breakfast. Also located in the main building is the **MacCallum House Restaurant,** a lovely establishment that serves exquisite California cuisine.

Mendocino Sights

There are several art galleries along Main Street, where prints or pottery can be bought. Farther north, at 45200 Little Lake Rd., is the **Mendocino Art Center,** founded by a Bay Area art teacher and now the center of the coast's artistic renaissance. Many of the town's 1,000 residents include potters, painters, sculptors, weavers, and musicians. Art festivals and exhibits are held, and there is a popular school partially under University of California sponsorship.

One authentic artifact is the wooden statue atop the ancient **Masonic Hall,** beside Calif. 1. It was carved from a single redwood log in 1869 by the cabinetmaker "Prince" Albertsen, and depicts a maiden shadowed by Father Time, complete with scythe.

A walk down Mendocino's wide streets takes you past weathered picket fences and the homes of long-dead lumber barons. The disused red **Baptist church** is among the better-preserved buildings. The collapse of lumber prices around the turn of the century caused a mass exodus from the town, and this also left Mendocino without the compulsion to rip down its unused structures. As a result, they form a cluster of attractive and authentic relics, sitting ready for the artists and shop owners to move right in.

Pick up a *Mendocino Gallery and Shop Guide* from any shop as soon as you arrive in town. It will lead you to such places as the **Mendocino Art Center,** where arts and crafts workshops are held throughout the year, and locally produced items are available for sale or rental, to the **Melting Pot** for handcrafted candles, oil lamps, pottery, etc., to the **Soup Kitchen,** a general store peddling wooden toys among their nautical antiques (bikes for rent also). (Names and contents shift with the mobile population.)

Six miles north of town at 18220 North Calif. 1 in Fort Bragg (tel. 707/964-4352), there is the **Mendocino Coast Botanical Gardens,** a charming 17-acre clifftop, semiformal to native garden. The garden features rhododendrons, fuchsias, azaleas, heather, perennials, and a multitude of flowering shrubs among the redwoods and along the rugged coast. Open daily from 9 a.m. to 6 p.m. Admission is $5 for adults, $3.50 for seniors, $3 for those aged 12 to 17, free for those under 12.

FORT BRAGG: Ten miles north is Fort Bragg. Like Little River and Mendocino, Fort Bragg also has a historic building which now serves as a bed-and-breakfast inn. The **Grey Whale Inn,** 615 N. Main St., Fort Bragg, CA 95437 (tel. 707/964-0640 or toll free 800/382-7244 in California), is a handsome four-story redwood building that was a hospital from the early 1900s until 1971. It has no hospital feel now, however: it's spacious and elegant, attractively furnished with some antiques and modern amenities like a color TV with VCR in the theater room, and a pool table in the recreation room. The Fireside Lounge is a great gathering place for guests. There are 14 guest rooms, all with private bath. Each room offers its own special features—some have an ocean view, or a fireplace, or a whirlpool tub; some have a private deck or a shower with wheelchair access. Rates—which include a buffet breakfast of homemade bread or coffeecake, juice or fresh fruit, and a selection of hot beverages, cereals, brunch casseroles—are $55 to $90 single and $65 to $135 double. Off-season rates, November through March, are half price for the second consecutive night on nonholidays. If you're in the area during whale-watching season, you can take one of the local boats to get a view of the gray whales. March sees Fort Bragg's annual Whale Festival.

From Fort Bragg, you can take your first foray into the big-tree grovelands. And the best way to do this is by hopping a strangely named **"Skunk" train,** at the foot of Laurel Street in Fort Bragg, to Willets, 40 miles inland.

The "Skunks" are self-powered diesel cars which were at one time powered by gas. So potent were the gas fumes that people used to say "You can smell 'em before you can see 'em," and dubbed them, affectionately, "Skunks." With windows front and side, they're wonderful for sightseeing.

The trains take you through country that is wild and inaccessible to cars. You'll travel through towering redwoods, the view changing with every turn. You'll cross 31 bridges and trestles, plunge into two deep tunnels, and twist through serpentine turns so sharp they have earned the Skunks the distinction of riding the crookedest railroad track in the world!

The diesel trains stop for natives and to deliver the mail. Running all year round, the round trip takes six to eight hours, which allows ample time for lunch in Willets before returning on the afternoon train. In summer you can take a half-day trip. A small railroad station on Laurel Street gives out schedules of both. Round-trip fares are $22, $18 one way; the half-day fare is $18, and children pay half price. For further information and a time schedule, phone 707/964-6371.

A redwood attraction in Fort Bragg itself is the **Georgia-Pacific Corporation's Tree Nursery** at 275 N. Main St. (tel. 707/964-5651). It's open March to November: weekdays from 8:30 a.m. to 4:30 p.m., weekends from 10 a.m. to 4 p.m. In addition to all the trees and an interesting and informative visitor center, there's a picnic area and self-guided nature trail. Also check out their logging museum, donated to the city of Fort Bragg, open Wednesday through Sunday from 8 a.m. to 4:30 p.m. Admission is free.

More redwoods? Hop in the car and head north to **Garberville** on U.S. 101 (Calif. 1 and U.S. 101 converge at Leggett).

YOSEMITE NATIONAL PARK

You might call Yosemite National Park and Yosemite Valley breathtaking, spectacular, incredible, awesome, humbling—all of which adjectives are accurate and none of which even begins to describe the magnificence of this country and the many faces of its beauty. Yosemite Valley is a glacier-carved canyon with crashing waterfalls (come in May and June and see), dramatic domes, and sheer walls of granite extending thousands of feet upward from the valley's flat floor.

The evolution of Yosemite Valley began with glaciers moving through the canyon that the Merced River had carved with repeated geological rises of the Sierras. The ice worked its way through weak sections of granite, bypassing the solid portions—what you now see as El Capitan is a good example of such a rock mass—and substantially widening the canyon. When the glacier began to melt, the moraine (the accumulated earth and stones deposited by a glacier) dammed part of the Merced River to form Lake Yosemite in the new valley. Sediment ultimately filled in the lake, which accounts for the flat floor of Yosemite Valley. This same process, on a much smaller scale, is even now occurring with Mirror Lake at the base of Half Dome.

The Ahwahneechee Indians had been living in the valley for several thousand years when their first contact was made with non-Indian people in the middle of the 19th century. Members of the Joseph Reddeford Walker party were probably the first non-Native Americans to see Yosemite Valley as they crossed over from the east side of the Sierra in 1833, though they did not come into contact with the Ahwachneechee. With the later encroachment of visitors and indiscriminate abuse of the environment and the threat of potential private exploitation (it was ever thus), President Lincoln granted Yosemite Valley and the Mariposa Grove of Giant Sequoias to California as a public trust. Federal legislation created Yosemite National Park in 1890. And by 1913 a different problem arose—the auto was permitted into Yosemite.

Still, with tender loving care, the valley has survived. It remains a sensual blend of open meadows, wildflowers (1,400 species), woodlands with Ponderosa pine, incense cedar, and Douglas fir. Wildlife from monarch butterflies and a world of birds (223 species) to mule deer and black bear flourish in the protected environment.

Today Yosemite Valley is a focal point of activities in one of America's most spectacular national parks—and the logical place to begin your visit. Though occupying only seven of the 1,200 square miles that make up the park, the valley offers campgrounds, lodgings, shops, and restaurants. Visitors who are in the valley for the day only are encouraged to use the day-use parking at Curry Village. A free shuttle-bus system travels on a continuous loop through the eastern portion of the valley and is quite convenient for visiting any of the above amenities.

There is an entrance fee to the park, but no one minds paying it after seeing how well the National Parks Service keeps its end of the bargain. At each of the four entrances—Calif. 120 on the northwest, Calif. 140 toward the west, Calif. 41 on the south, and Calif. 120 on the northeast (open in summer only)—rangers are stationed to check you in and out. As of this writing, the entrance permit still costs only $5 per car (no charge for seniors 62 and over). If you plan to stay longer than seven days, it might be worth your while to purchase an annual Golden Eagle Passport—for $25 you get free entrance to all national parks that charge fees—or an annual Yosemite Passport for $15, which allows you to leave and enter the park at will for the year your permit is valid.

I'd recommend that you make your first stop at the **Visitor Center** in Yosemite Village. Rangers are generally on duty here from 9 a.m. to 6 p.m. during April and May, 8 a.m. to 7 p.m. in the summer, 8 a.m. to 6 p.m. in September and October, and 9 a.m. to 5 p.m. in the winter. They will provide you with information about park features, services, activities, and regulations. Books and maps are on sale here too.

While the valley offers a multitude of activities such as hiking, bicycling, ice skating, and tours, you'll want to leave the valley often to explore the park's natural bounties. There are 800 miles of trails you can cover by horse, mule, or foot only, most leading into a wilderness of mountain peaks, forests, meadows blanketed with wildflowers, lakes, and streams. The higher elevations are under a heavy mantle of snow more than half the year and offer access only on skis or snowshoes. There are also 216 miles of paved road which you can traverse by car, and the rangers can give you a recommended road tour. You'll want to know, too, how to reach the museums, the sequoia groves, the inspiring granite summits, and the waterfall bases —and what to do if a begging deer or squirrel approaches you for a handout (absolutely nothing). Although some of Yosemite's deer seem tame, they are wild and unpredictable, and capable of inflicting serious injury with their antlers or hoofs.

Note: National parks have toughened rules on drinking to cut down on drunk driving. New regulations outlaw open containers of alcoholic beverages in a car, specify a strict blood-alcohol level, and set penalties for anyone who refuses a Breathalyzer test. The regulations are being enforced by the local police and by the park service's 2,800 rangers.

WHERE TO STAY: The Yosemite Park and Curry Company manages a wide variety of accommodations in the park. In Yosemite Valley there's **Yosemite Lodge,** which offers hotel rooms and cabins (with or without bath). Prices range from $34 to $76.25 in season and during holiday periods, single or double occupancy. Off-season rates are $18.75 to $57.25 in season, reservations should be made a year in advance—it's that popular. On the sprawling premises are a coffeeshop, cocktail lounge, dining room, and cafeteria, as well as several shops and a swimming pool. It's a short walk to Yosemite Falls or the Merced River.

More rustic is **Curry Village,** also in the valley. In addition to hotel rooms and cottages (priced $34 to $60.50), there are bathless tent cabins (used in summer only) for $24.75 a night. All rates are for single or double occupancy. A cafeteria, hamburger stand, ice-cream stand, cocktail lounge, and swimming pool are open in summer. Also on the grounds are a bike-rental stand, a mountaineering school, and a convenience store.

For an elegant stay in Yosemite Valley, you'll want to choose the **Ahwahnee Hotel,** a National Historic Landmark hotel, built in the 1920s. In season, make your reservations a year in advance or you may be disappointed. It's well worth visiting, even if you don't stay here. The public rooms are mostly wood-paneled, and decorated in art deco Indian designs. The Indian motif is also used in the guest rooms, which cost $150 single, $155 double. The Ahwahnee has a lovely formal dining room; diners are expected to dress for dinner. Even if you're staying in the hotel, reserve for dinner as early as possible. It's a very popular place.

If you want to stay at the south end of the park, the **Wawona Hotel,** also a National Historic Landmark hotel, is open from mid-April to October and at Christmas. It resembles a southern mansion, and offers rooms both with and without bathroom for $73 and $60 respectively. Amenities here include a swimming pool, tennis courts, golf course, horseback riding, lounge, and dining room.

You can write or phone for **reservations** to the Yosemite Park and Curry Company, 5410 E. Home Ave., Fresno, CA 93727 (tel. 209/252-4848).

If you want to rough it a bit more, there are several **campgrounds** scattered throughout the park. You can reserve campsites up to eight weeks in advance through any Ticketron outlet or by writing the Ticketron Reservation Office, P.O. Box 2715, San Francisco, CA 94126.

And for those who want to sleep in the backcountry, a **wilderness permit** is needed. You can get them in advance (reservations are accepted from February 1 through May 31) by mail only through the Backcountry Office, P.O. Box 577, Yosemite National Park, CA 95389. Only 50% of the permits are available this way; the other half can be obtained up to 24 hours in advance of your hike at ranger stations throughout the park.

THINGS TO DO: As soon as you reach the valley, stop at the Visitor Center and request a copy of the free leaflet called "The Yosemite Guide," brochures on Yosemite and saddle trips, plus a map of the park. With these in hand, you'll be well equipped to make the most of your visit. The pamphlets are also obtainable at Yosemite Lodge or the desk of your hotel.

On a typical summer day in Yosemite you have your choice of the following activities: you can fish in well-stocked lakes (California license required), you can bike ride through the valley—some three miles of roads on the valley floor are set aside for bikers and hikers only. You can hike—trails are marked and you can follow them from the valley floor to the top of a waterfall or granite peak, or strike out on foot for the High Country. Seven-day hiking trips are led through the Tuolumne Meadow "loop" by a ranger/naturalist guide. You can ride over the park trails by renting a horse at the stables in the valley, at Wawona or Tuolumne Meadows, or White Wolf Lodge.

During nonsummer days your choice of organized activities diminishes. The stables aren't open and you can't get into the High Country except on your own two thickly booted feet. But you can certainly enjoy the exquisite Yosemite scenery. A drive or walk around the valley floor takes you within view of spectacular Yosemite Falls (there's an easy half-mile walk to its base, along a paved walkway), as well as impressive rock formations like El Capitan and Half-Dome Rock. There's also a comfortable car drive you can take that will cover at least the bare highlights of this grand national estate.

Start from the valley and take the **Wawona Road.** You will come to a parking lot along the left side of the road, marked **Bridalveil Fall.** Park here and climb up the short trail to the rocky base of the fall. It's a memorable experience, standing that close to the brutal force of thousands of gallons of water, crashing down from a height of 620 feet above you. Back at the car, continue up the Wawona Road to **Inspiration Point**—close to the site where the first band of men discovered Yosemite Valley. Park at the turnoff and trot out the camera. You'll never find words to describe this view to the folks at home, so you might as well record it. Pass through the **Wawona Tunnel** then, and on to the Glacier Point turnoff. If you have time, take the left-hand road up to **Glacier Point** for an overall view of the spectacular valley; if not, just continue south past the Calif. 41 entrance to the end of the road at the **Mariposa Grove of Giant Sequoia.**

After exploring Yosemite in all its grandeur, you can leave the valley via Calif. 140, take Calif. 99 north at Merced, meet Calif. 50 at Manteca, and follow it to the Oakland Bay Bridge. From Merced to San Francisco, you travel on superhighways all the way, prodigiously provided with foodshops and lodgings.

Ecological Transportation Note: Travel to Yosemite without driving (and distributing those polluting fumes) by catching AMTRAK's daily rail service out of Oakland (tel. toll free 800/872-7245). The scenery en route is worth getting your hands off the wheel to fully enjoy. The train leaves you in Merced from whence you proceed by bus. Be sure to check the Merced bus schedule so that you can synchronize your arrival time with that of a bus.

SOUTH ALONG THE SHORE

A visit to the **Monterey Peninsula** is a full weekend's outing, though many will prefer adopting a more leisurely approach in order to completely enjoy this area's offerings. As you head south from San Francisco, take U.S. 101, California's main north-south freeway, and in about 40 miles you'll reach the exit to **Palo Alto.** This is the campus town of **Stanford University,** a magnificently landscaped school—"The Harvard of the West"—which you are welcome to visit. About 15 miles farther and you come to the junction of Calif. 17 and U.S. 101. If you'd like to make a stopoff at **Santa Cruz**—San Francisco's closest beach resort—turn right on Calif. 17 and follow it to the coast. From Santa Cruz you can then take Calif. 1 along the coast to **Monterey.** If you don't wish to visit Santa Cruz, simply continue down U.S. 101 through Morgan Hill and San Martin, where the **San Martin Winery,** alongside the highway, invites visitors to stop and sample the wine. When you reach **Salinas,** you can follow the signs to the Monterey turnoff and go directly out to the peninsula, where Monterey, Pacific Grove, and Carmel are all clustered on one small, jutting piece of land.

GREAT AMERICA: A fun excursion with the kids (or without them, for that matter) is a theme park just 45 miles south of San Francisco, Great America. To get there, just take U.S. 101 and get off at the Great America exit in Santa Clara (they make it easy). You'll find yourself at a spectacular $50-million, 200-acre amusement park with more than 30 major rides, a gigantic wooden roller coaster, the Grizzly, plus live shows and special attractions, games, arcades, and more.

Like Disneyland, Great America is divided into theme areas: Yukon territory; a rural American town circa 1920; an 18th-century New England Whaling village; 1850s New Orleans; and a turn-of-the-century country fair and exposition. American history is the park's overall theme.

For thrill seekers there's the Demon, the only roller coaster in California to turn you upside down four times, speed through steaming tunnels, and plunge into a blood-red waterfall. Other super-thrill rides are the Sky Whirl, a triple-armed Ferris wheel 110-feet high; Yankee Clipper and Logger's Run, two side-by-side flume water rides with 60-foot slides (you *will* get wet); and the Tidal Wave, one of the world's tallest roller coasters. And now there's Rip Roaring Rapids, a new $5-million white-water-raft ride—yet another way to get wet as you brave a quarter mile of churning water. It's wild and fun, but not scary. For the total coward (I'm one) Great America has just the thing—they've refurbished my favorite ride, the Columbia, the tallest carousel in the world and certainly one of the handsomest. Or you can share the kiddies' Blue Streak roller coaster.

In between the rides, you can give your stomach a rest and watch one of the many shows presented daily. They range from full-scale musical revues, puppet shows, and Smurf Woods, to a variety of animal acts. Or you can try to win a stuffed animal at the arcade games—9,500 are won daily. And strolling through the park you'll see Fred Flintstone, Yogi Bear, Huckleberry Hound, Barney Rubble, and for the first time, George Jetson and his faithful dog, Astro.

Since you're going to spend the day, and probably don't want to bog yourself down with picnic fare, you'll be glad to know that there is a choice of some 23 family-priced restaurants and snackbars on the premises. Fried chicken with sourdough muffins and apple dumplings, seafood, burgers, hot dogs, and french fries are just a small sample of the eats sold in profusion daily.

Finally, in addition to scheduled acts, you might see a marching band, barbershop quartet, puppet show, parade, or even a fireworks display. There's much more, but I'll leave a few surprises for you.

A one-price admission includes everything except food, merchandise, and arcade games. General admission is $18 for adults; seniors over 55 pay $11.50; kids 3 to 6, $9; and children 2 and under go in free.

Great America usually opens about mid-March and closes in October. During the spring and fall it's open only on weekends and holidays from 10 a.m. to about 6 p.m. From May 31 through Labor Day, Great America is open daily from 10 a.m. to about 9 p.m. For further information, call 408/988-1800 (recording) or 408/988-1776. There's plenty of parking, and the fee is $4 per car.

SAN JOSE: There are several reasons to allow time in your itinerary for a day's visit to San Jose. Just 48 miles south of San Francisco (via U.S. 101), it's chock-full of visitor attractions.

You might want to visit the various museums centered around **Rosicrucian Park.** They include an **Egyptian Museum** full of rare Egyptian, Babylonian, and Assyrian antiquities, a full-size replica of an Egyptian tomb, sarcophagi, and such-like. There's also an **Art**

Gallery offering eclectic exhibits of international artists, a **Science Museum** exploring subjects ranging from physics to space travel, and a **Planetarium** presenting seven different shows yearly. It's open daily from 1 to 4:45 p.m. Adults pay $3 for the planetarium, and those under 18 pay $2. There's no admission charge for the Science Museum, but for the Egyptian Museum or the Art Gallery, admission is $3 for adults, $2 for those under 18. The two latter attractions are open on Saturday, Sunday, and Monday from noon to 5 p.m., and Tuesday through Friday from 9 a.m. to 5 p.m.

Another local sight is the **San Jose Historical Museum,** Senter Road at Phelan Avenue, which, along with the lovely **Japanese Friendship Garden,** a baby zoo, and a children's play area, is set in **Kelly Park.** The museum's exhibits deal with local history—historical San Jose re-created with 21 buildings including a bank, post office, stable, etc.—and it's particularly nice to stroll around the grounds after you visit the museum.

Winchester Mystery House

I've been saving the best for last. Winchester Mystery House, 525 S. Winchester Blvd. (tel. 408/247-2101), is not to be missed. The former home of Sarah L. Winchester, widow of the son of the famous rifle manufacturer, it is a bizarre monument to one woman's insanity. Probably many people are as eccentric as she was, but few have a fortune ($20 million plus an income of $1,000 a day!) with which to indulge their foibles.

The guilt-ridden Mrs. Winchester believed that the ghosts of all the people killed by Winchester rifles were out to get her. She was especially afraid of the Indians. Terrified at the idea of death, and unable to enjoy her immense wealth and freedom, she consulted a seer who told her that she would never die if she kept a building project ceaselessly going. The result was this unique and bizarre dwelling that cost $20 million to build. It began as an eight-room house, and when Sarah died at the age of 82 it was a sprawling, 160-room mansion occupying six acres. The work went on for 38 years, seven days a week, 365 days a year, 24 hours per day!

The house contains many superb examples of Victorian architecture, and the rooms are palatially furnished. There are doors inlaid with silver and bronze, priceless Tiffany stained-glass windows, exquisite West African mahogany paneling, parquet flooring, gorgeous hand-carved fireplaces, etc.

Most interesting, however, are the many oddities that were designed to foil the evil spirits. Mrs. Winchester's methods were incredibly complex. For instance, in the entire house there are only two mirrors but 50 fireplaces, in spite of the fact that ghosts hate mirrors (according to ancient lore) and would prefer to enter or leave a house via the chimney than the front door. So why did she court ghosts these ways? Ah—these hospitable considerations were for the *friendly* ghosts and spirits, whose protection Sarah Winchester felt she required. A third lure for friendly spirits was an enormous bell that tolled at midnight, 1 a.m., and 2 a.m.—spook rush hour. No simple arrangement this—it required a labyrinthine arrangement known only to one loyal Japanese servant who carried an expensive watch and three of the best chronometers money could buy. And every day he checked his chronometers by calling an astronomical observatory.

While offering every possible hospitality to friendly spirits, Mrs. Winchester had many ruses to confound the evil ones. There are flights of stairs that go up to the ceiling; doors that open to a wall; and staircases with steps two inches high which you have to ascend, descend, and ascend again to climb to a height of about seven feet. The number 13—dangerous to evil spirits—is repeated frequently; 13 palm trees line the driveway, windows have 13 panes, chandeliers have 13 globes, etc. And everywhere there is a profusion of light—chandeliers, candles, etc.—to entice the good spirits and ward off the bad.

She was a tortured soul. One day she descended to her cellar to choose a vintage wine, only to come shrieking upstairs that she had seen the imprint of a black hand on the wall. No one could convince her that it had been there for years and was the handprint of one of the original workmen. She was sure it was a message from the spirits warning her against alcohol. She locked the room, and walled it in so thoroughly that no one has been able to find it to this day!

I could go on and on with fascinating stories, but I'll let you find out the rest when you visit Winchester House. Guided tours take place daily between 9 a.m. and 5:30 p.m. in summer; closing times change seasonally. Admission for the one-hour house tour is $10 for adults, $8.50 for seniors age 60 and over, and $6 for children to 12. Included in the price is admission to the garden and outlying buildings, plus the Winchester Rifle and Antique Products Museums. The Winchester Rifle Museum obviously has a large collection of Winchesters, but as its name suggests, it also displays many rifles, some dating back to the 1800s, many very exotic. The Antique Products Museum has many items made by the Winchester company in the early 1900s—knives, roller skates, fishing tackle, tools, flashlights—products not commonly associated with the name of Winchester.

MONTEREY AND THE MONTEREY PENINSULA: Monterey has figured in the history of California from the time of the Spanish occupation to its position as the capital of the state. Monterey was the home of California's first theater and of Robert Louis Stevenson in 1879, and is the site of the oldest government building on the West Coast. But the most colorful part of its past rests with its literary fame. Monterey, Point Lobos, Carmel, and that long Salinas Valley are Steinbeck Country—all of it—every blade of grass, every cramped chicken coop bitingly familiar to that author's many avid readers.

Mack and the boys lived down on **Cannery Row** in a place called the Palace Flophouse. The old building is gone now. In fact the only thing that still stands from those wistful days, aside from a few quite corrugated canneries, is **Doc's Laboratory**—a small, gray building with crooked steps, just below what is now called **Steinbeck Circle.** When Steinbeck traveled home with Charley in 1961, he found the Row still there, but so different. In the 1940s he had written: "Cannery Row in Monterey in California is a poem, a stink, a grating noise, a quality of light, a tone, a habit, a nostalgia, a dream." In the 1960s he returned to the street he had given fame and said, "The beaches are clean where once they festered with fish guts and flies. The canneries which once put up a sickening stench are gone, their places filled with restaurants, antique shops, and the like. They fish for tourists, now, not pilchards, and that species they are not likely to wipe out."

It's true that Cannery Row is touristy. The entrepreneurs have moved in and upped the real estate value of the old waterside slum. They've planted sweet antique shoppes where Dora's girls once plied their profession, and laden the shaky wooden wharf with direct-import gifts. But there's no reason you have to go as a tourist. You can skulk down there, sans camera and in wrinkled jeans, scuff barefoot along the rocky shoreline, and give only one furtive glance toward Doc's house. Go down at dawn, at the "hour of the pearl," when the fishermen are just putting off from the docks, and you'll find that Cannery Row has not yet lost all its magic.

As for the rest of Monterey City, it's not large, but it is historic. As the one-time capital of California, it has flown three flags; Spanish, Mexican, and American. Many of the century-old buildings of its heyday still stand, and you can see them by following the **Path of History,** a red line painted on the pavement to guide you from historic house to museum.

A pamphlet and map of this tour are available from the **Monterey Peninsula Chamber of Commerce,** 380 Alvarado St., between Franklin Street and Del Monte Avenue (tel. 408/649-1770). Many of the historic buildings are open to the public. Two of the most interesting, each fitted out with museum displays, are the **Old Custom House,** across from the entrance to Fisherman's Wharf, and the **Stevenson House,** 530 Houston St., near Pearl Street. The Custom

House is the oldest government building in California and was built under the Mexican regime. Here, the flag of the United States was raised on July 7, 1846. The Stevenson House was erected as a family home in the 1830s. Robert Louis Stevenson lodged there in 1879, and the top floor now contains a good collection of Stevenson's effects. (Just as a point of interest, according to Steinbeck and others who know this land, the terrain on **Point Lobos,** just south of Carmel, is amazingly similar to that of Treasure Island in the book.)

At the shore end of Alvarado Street, Monterey's **Municipal Wharf** invites visitors with good seafood restaurants, gift shops, and fishing boats to rent. **Cannery Row** is just below the Wharf, bounded vaguely by Drake and David Avenues, along the shore en route to Pacific Grove, the adjoining town.

There are several free publications covering current happenings, where to go, food and lodging, and providing maps of the Monterey Peninsula and Cannery Row. *This Month* and *Key* are among the most complete. Both are available at most hotels and shops.

Monterey is also the gateway to the excitingly beautiful **Monterey Peninsula**—northern California's playland for golfers. In the area surrounding the city, there are sea views and scenic drives, ghostly cypress trees, and Seal Rocks. But most of all, there are golf courses. The famed **Pebble Beach Golf Links** is here, on which the AT&T National Pro-Amateur Golf Tourney is held every February. Of the many golf courses on the Monterey Peninsula and nearby areas, four are open to the public—the Laguna Seca, Pacific Grove, Rancho Canada, and Del Monte golf courses. Greens fees range from about $15 to $30 (plus cart) for 18 holes. In addition to the AT&T Pro-Am Tournament at Pebble Beach, the Monterey Peninsula hosts the **Laguna Seca GT races** in May, the **Carmel Bach Festival** in July, the oldest continuing **Jazz Festival** in September, and the **Monterey Grand Prix races** in October.

One of the easiest and most enjoyable ways to see Monterey is to be taken around. **Steinbeck Country Tours** (tel. 408/625-5107) provides one of the most popular tours of the area, encompassing the entire Monterey Peninsula in three to four hours. You are picked up at your local hotel (in Monterey, Pebble Beach, Carmel, or Pacific Grove) and taken on an informative trip around the peninsula, including the original 17-Mile Drive, Cannery Row, Pacific Grove, and Carmel. Steinbeck Country Tours also has regularly scheduled tours from the Monterey Peninsula to Hearst Castle. The castle tour, via Big Sur, is an all-day affair, leaving at 8 a.m., returning at 6:30 p.m., and including a wine tasting at a local vineyard. For reservations with Steinbeck Country Tours, call two to three days in advance or ask the guest representative at your hotel to make reservations. The cost of the Monterey Tour is $20, and well worth the price; the Hearst Castle tour is $45.

Monterey Bay Aquarium

Whatever else you may want to see in Monterey, don't miss the Monterey Bay Aquarium at the west end of Cannery Row, 886 Cannery Row (tel. 408/375-3333), the largest exhibit aquarium in the nation. Its $50-million cost was financed by David Packard at the behest of four local marine biologists, including his daughter, who was brought up on the criteria of Ed (Doc) Ricketts, the marine biologist and prototype for "Doc" in Steinbeck's *Cannery Row*.

Statistics alone simply do not do justice to this spectacular living gallery of the sea. The building, on the site of the old Hovden sardine cannery, houses an astounding display of more than 5,000 sea creatures that literally surround you. You step into an enchanted new world and stand by the bottom of a three-story kelp forest, visible through an acrylic-windowed tank holding over 300,000 gallons of sea water, with seaweed waving gently as though moved by tidal surges. Sit down and quietly watch the hundreds of creatures slowly moving back and forth—the greenlings, sand sharks, jacksmelts, rockfish—and you feel like a scuba-diver in an underwater cathedral. The sea otters, including the four orphans rescued by the staff, are the delightful clowns of the aquarium. Feeding time for the otters is an acrobatic event you don't want to miss.

There are exhibits of coastal streams, tidal pools, a beach with sea birds that inhabit the salt marsh and sandy shore, and even a touching pool where you can stroke a living bat ray or a sea star.

The sea life you see here is representative of the plants and creatures that abound in Monterey Bay and the Pacific. The aquarium borders on the submarine Monterey Canyon, one of the largest in the world—wider and deeper than the Grand Canyon.

The aquarium is designed to be visited on a self-guided tour, but there are guides to help you throughout. There's much to see, so allow two to three hours for your visit. A café on the premises provides lunch—you cannot bring in food or beverages. The aquarium is open daily (except Christmas) from 10 a.m. to 6 p.m. Admission is $8 for adults, $6 for seniors over 65 and students, and $4 for children 3 to 12 years. Children under 3 are admitted free.

The 17-Mile Drive

The whole family will enjoy a tour of the 17-Mile Drive. This private road circumscribes the Del Monte Forest and the famed Pebble Beach Golf Course and offers some of the most magnificent seascapes you are likely to see (especially if you don't intend to continue down the coast on Calif. 1). Three gates lead into the road, one on the Monterey side of the peninsula—take Lighthouse Avenue to 17-Mile Drive road, which leads you to the Lighthouse Gate. A second gate is located off Calif. 1 about halfway between Monterey and Carmel, at Carmel Hill. The third gate is in Carmel, and you can enter at Monterey and exit in Carmel at the coast, about two blocks north of the main Ocean Avenue. The road toll is $7 per car. At the gate you will be given—on request—a map of the drive. Inside the forest you may picnic at designated areas and you can fish on Anshell Beach. But most people go just for the views, so whatever you do, take your camera. The huge, jutting **Seal and Bird Rocks,** two close-to-shore boulders inhabited by thousands of gulls, cormorants, and gyrating seals, are probably the most photographed rocks in California.

One comment, however: While the 17-Mile Drive is admittedly beautiful, it is no more stunning than the coastline south of Monterey, in the **Big Sur** area, all of which is free to be enjoyed.

Monterey Food and Lodging

In your exploration of the 17-Mile Drive, you'll pass the luxurious **Lodge at Pebble Beach,** Pebble Beach, CA 93953 (tel. 408/624-3811), of which the above-mentioned Pebble Beach Golf Links is part. Though a long stay here could wreak havoc on your budget, you might want to spend a few nights at these posh digs while seeing the Carmel/Monterey area. In addition to the golf course, there's a beach, a heated swimming pool and sauna, fishing, 14 tennis courts, horseback-riding facilities, and 34 miles of bridle and hiking paths. Of course, the rooms are fitted out with every possible amenity; many even have wood-burning fireplaces. Single or double accommodations cost $210 to $270.

If you're a guest at The Lodge and want to play 18, you're given priority in booking tee time at the famous Pebble Beach Golf Links. The cost of a round is $115 for guests, $150 for others.

If you can't stay, you might at least want to dine at the lodge's posh French restaurant, **Club XIX** (tel. 408/625-8519). It's extremely elegant, with oak-paneled walls, burgundy and forest-green carpeting and tablecloths, and fresh flowers in silver vases at every table. During the day you'll enjoy views of the golf course and bay; at night it's candlelit and romantic. A dinner at Club XIX might begin with an appetizer of foie gras with truffles, followed perhaps by a soup called velouté Bongo-Bongo—a creamy blend of oysters, spinach, herbs, and cognac. For an entree you might select stuffed quail in a potato nest with brandy sauce or poached Monterey salmon, and finish off the feast with a soufflé Grand Marnier. If you're averse to spending $18 to $33 for an entree, come at lunch when lighter dishes are a more reasonable $8 to $14.

Club XIX is open daily for lunch from 11:30 a.m. to 4:30 p.m., and for dinner from 6:30 to 10 p.m. Reservations are advised.

In the fall of 1987 the Lodge opened the Inn at Spanish Bay, a deluxe 270-room, full-facility resort alongside the Links at Spanish Bay (a golf course designed by Tom Watson and Robert Trent Jones, Jr.).

The Monterey Bay Aquarium is at one end of Cannery Row, and the new and very grand **Monterey Plaza Hotel** stands at the opposite end, at 400 Cannery Row, Monterey, CA 93940 (tel. 408/646-1700, or toll free 800/631-1339, 800/334-3999 in California). The hotel overlooks Monterey Bay and the Pacific and is just a short scenic stroll to the aquarium. The 290 luxurious rooms and suites at this $60-million resort showcase the surrounding sea. Anticipate the grand and you'll find it here. Beds are not king-size, but emperor-size. Rooms are furnished in natural wood tones, dark leathers, and designer fabrics in tones that vary from room to room. Armoires conceal the TV, desk, and drawers. As you might expect, bathrooms have telephones, his-and-hers bathrobes, extra-thick towels. Terraces overlook the bay and its spectacular sunsets.

The hotel provides a recreation director, as well as a concierge, and can arrange entry to several local golf clubs, tennis courts, sightseeing, and transportation as well as the usual services. Singles and doubles are $130 to $200; suites run $300 to $850; $25 for each extra person.

The hotel's restaurant, **Delfino's,** features northern Italian cuisine, of the Emilia-Romagna region. Delfino's conveys a feeling of old-world elegance—wide polished ceiling beams, cloth-covered banquettes with dolphin prints, linen at lunch, wine leather chairs with light walnut wood. The menu is à la carte, and dinner entrees range from $13 to $26 for homemade pastas to magnificent medallions of veal. With salad, and perhaps wine, dinner for two will probably range from $80 to $120. The food is as superior as the service, and all is graced by the sweeping view of the bay and its inhabitants.

Delfino's is open daily from 7 to 11 a.m. for breakfast, noon to 2:30 p.m. for lunch, and 6 to 10 p.m. for dinner. On Friday and Saturday evening the restaurant is open to 10:30 p.m. On Sunday, Delfino's has a superb Champagne Buffet Brunch from 10:30 a.m. to 2:30 p.m. for $18.50. Reservations are always advised for dinner.

The **Monterey Bay Inn,** 242 Cannery Row, Monterey, CA 93940 (tel. 408/373-6242, or toll free 800/424-6242 in California), overlooks Monterey Bay from its perch above the water. And it provides special facilities for scuba-divers, if you're geared for it.

The inn has 47 spacious rooms surrounding an atrium, each elegantly decorated in coral, bone, and seafoam-green fabrics with light-toned woods. Photographs of the area decorate the walls to give the rooms a feeling of thesea and a bit of Monterey history. Apart from the usual amenities, each room also has a dry bar and refrigerator, handy full-length mirrors on the sliding closet doors, and luxurious terrycloth robes (not for the taking). A sauna and hot tub are conveniently located at the atrium terrace. The adjacent park affords access to the beach for scuba-divers and beach loafers.

Single and double rooms range from $105 to $155, depending on the view; suites, from $155 to $175. All rates include continental breakfast and use of the health club. Parking is conveniently located beneath the inn.

There's no question that bargains are few and far between in this popular haven for tourists, but one or two can be found in Monterey if you plan in advance and don't pick weekends such as that of the Grand Prix or the Monterey Jazz Festival.

Truly luxurious accommodations at a reasonable rate are what you'll find at the **Way Station,** 1200 Olmsted Rd., Monterey, CA 93940 (tel. 408/372-2945), just off U.S. 68. This attractive redwood motel, beautifully landscaped and set among pines and well-groomed grounds, is conveniently situated near the Monterey airport, but not a sound of air traffic interferes with your comfort. Guest rooms convey the feeling of a town house rather than a motel. Rooms are done in tones of brown or blue, and carpeting is plush with an inset of beige. Handsome historical prints give a decorator touch. High ceilings add to the luxurious feeling of spaciousness. At one corner of the room there is a circular table, and above, a conveniently placed chandelier. Comfortable leather chairs are on wheels. Several rooms have balconies with sliding doors and screens, comfortable for lounging; others have bay windows facing the beautiful landscaping.

Rates are $75 for singles, $88 for doubles, $110 for the luxury suites. Each additional person pays $10.

Adjoining the Way Station is **Papa's Restaurant** (tel. 408/372-5430). Entry is past the bar into a handsomely proportioned room with high, beamed ceilings, ceiling fans, huge potted plants, and carpeting to match the landscape. Booths are separated by frosted-glass panels with designs of the stagecoach of early California. Service is friendly and attentive. Touches like the thin slice of lemon in the glass of water reflect the thought given to the preparation and presentation of the food.

The quantity of food is in keeping with the proportions of the room—very large and tastefully done. Breakfast is served all day and includes such toothsome dishes as carabaccia, poached eggs with vegetables, for $5.75, and pancakes covered with fresh fruit at $4.50. The salad bar has an exceptionally large number of choices and includes hot baguettes or sourdough bread, all for $5.50. And any time after 11 a.m. you can order a prime rib sandwich on baguette au jus with the day's salad for $6.25. At dinnertime look for the pasta dishes, such as tortellini with sauce Alfredo for $9.50. Seafood specials change daily. Prices range from $8 to $12, including soup or salad. If you have a taste for the unusual, try the stuffed chicken breasts con salsa Pappa at $9.75.

Top off your dinner with homemade cheesecake with blueberry or peach sauce. Papa's also has a fine selection of California and Italian wines, some by the glass. The restaurant is open daily from 7 a.m. to 11 p.m.

Need I remind you of **Motel 6,** 2124 Fremont St., Monterey, CA 93940 (tel. 408/646-8585), where rates range from $30 for one person to $36 for two adults. Reservations for summer months should be made at least six months in advance.

One note about this particular Motel 6 and very cool weather (as does occur even in glorious Monterey)—there is no central heating and the small wall heater in the rooms has no temperature control other than "On" or "Off," operated manually. The choice, then, is to stay cool or overheat during the night.

As noted before, Cannery Row is geared to tourists, which nearly always means a concentration of restaurants. One of my favorites is the **Whaling Station Inn,** 763 Wave St., between Prescott and Irving Avenues (tel. 408/373-3778). It's entered via a rustic cocktail area, and its barnwood walls are hung with framed photos and paintings. The interior is similar in motif, but an added elegance is achieved by mauve linen tablecloths, mauve napkins wound in the drinking glasses, and long white taper candles in wrought-iron holders. There's an antique hutch in one corner, and sumptuous-looking desserts are prominently displayed.

Your dinner includes artichoke vinaigrette, homemade soup, fresh locally grown vegetables, and salad. Among the entrees are a hearty bouillabaisse, veal rollatini—filled with prosciutto and imported cheeses and sautéed in wine sauce—and filet mignon or fresh fish broiled on the open hearth on oakwood and mesquite charcoal for $17 to $24. The homemade desserts, prepared daily by the inn's own pastry chef, are as good as they look. A selection of California—and especially Monterey—wines is available for your delectation.

Open daily from 5 to 10 p.m. Reservations advised. There is free parking and valet service on weekends.

Another suggestion: If you're out on the Wharf, buy picnic fixings and dine al fresco. The **Little Gourmet Shop** (no. 20)—look closely for it, it's easy to miss—makes up great sandwiches on sourdough bread or pita stuffed with imported meats and cheeses. They also sell salads, Greek pastries, a variety of goodies, and small bottles of wine.

PACIFIC GROVE: The best-kept secret on the Monterey Peninsula is the little town of Pacific Grove. It's a charming little place on the peninsula's north point. Founded in the 19th century, it was the site of a Chautauqua-like religious and educational summer tent community; before long, people settled in permanently. Many of the town's picturesque **Victorian houses** date from this era.

Pacific Grove is nicknamed **"Butterfly Town, U.S.A.,"** for the proliferation of Monarch butterflies here. Every fall, the butterflies migrate from as far away as Alaska to spend the winter. They're particularly partial to the Monterey pine, and in season can be seen by the thousands clinging to the needles of those trees. Two spots in town are well known for their "butterfly trees"— Washington Park, bordered by Sinex, Short, Alder, and Rosemont Streets; and the Butterfly Grove Motel at 1073 Lighthouse Ave. Visitors are welcome to stop in at either site, but beware: there's a $500 fine for molesting butterflies. Pacific Grove is proud and protective of its beautiful residents.

Another famous aspect of Pacific Grove is **Marine Gardens Park.** It's a stretch of shoreline along Ocean View Boulevard on Monterey Bay and the Pacific, famous not only for its earth-bound flower gardens but also for its tidepool beds of hundreds of varieties of seaweed. At the midpoint of Ocean View Boulevard, on the very point of Pacific Grove, is the **Point Pinos Lighthouse,** the oldest working beacon on the West Coast. It's been warning sailors off the rocky Monterey shore since 1855, when the town site was nothing more than pine forest.

Make your first stop the **Pacific Grove Chamber of Commerce** at the corner of Forest and Central Avenues (tel. 408/373-3304) for information on these and other points of interest in town. (You can also write ahead to P.O. Box 167, Pacific Grove, CA 93950.)

Pacific Grove Food and Lodging

One of the most charming of Pacific Grove's Victorian houses is now—lucky us!—a charming hotel. The **Gosby House Inn,** 643 Lighthouse Ave. (three blocks from Forest Avenue), Pacific Grove, CA 93950 (tel. 408/375-1287, or toll free 800/342-4888), is a yellow beauty built by cobbler J. F. Gosby in the 1870s as a boardinghouse for Methodist ministers in town for the Christian Seaside Resort Conference.

The charms of the Gosby House embrace you as you enter the door. A member of the friendly staff is always around to welcome you and help you check in. (They'll also help with restaurant recommendations and reservations, golf and tennis arrangements, travel plans—anything you need. And someone's on call throughout the night, in case of emergency.) There are 22 rooms here, all quaintly decorated with flower-print wallpaper, antiques, quilts, lacy pillows. There are phones on request but no TVs here to break the tranquility—you'll find you don't miss them at all. All but two of the rooms have private bath with tub or shower, stocked with shampoos, conditioners, bath gels, and soaps. (The other two rooms share a bath in the hall.) Nine rooms have fireplaces.

Guests gather in the dining room or parlor every morning to partake of a scrumptious breakfast. You can dig into muffins hot from the oven, yogurt, granola, cereal, egg dishes, juices, fruits, coffee, tea, and an ever-changing assortment of foods. In the evening, there's wine, sherry, hors d'oeuvres, and cake. And if you're still hungry after dinner somewhere on the peninsula, there's a good-night snack of milk and cookies to enjoy before going to your room and your turned-down bed.

Rooms at the Gosby House rent for $90 to $135, single or double. No smoking, please.

Also in Pacific Grove is a sister inn of the Gosby House, the **Green Gables Inn,** at 104 Fifth Ave. (off Ocean View Boulevard), Pacific Grove, CA 93950 (tel. 408/375-2095). There are ten rooms here, all as charming as those at the Gosby House. All the rooms in the carriage house have private bath; some rooms in the main house share a bathroom. The house is gorgeously decked out in Victorian splendor. A number of the rooms have ocean views; some also have fireplaces. Until a few years ago the Green Gables was the residence of innkeepers Roger and Sally Post, who also own the Gosby House, the Cobblestone Inn on Junipero Street between Seventh and Eighth in Carmel (tel. 408/625-5222), the Petite Auberge and the White Swan Inn in San Francisco.

Rooms at the Green Gables rent for $100 to $145, including breakfast and evening wine. No smoking is allowed.

Another of Pacific Grove's handsome inns is a stately and beautifully renovated 1904 mansion, the **Pacific Grove Inn,** 581 Pine Ave. (at Forest), Pacific Grove, CA 93950 (tel. 408/375-2825). This impressive structure is just two blocks from historic Main Street and five blocks from the beach.

A magnificent entrance hall and staircase lead to ten elegant and charming rooms, all quite light and airy (with Victorian touches), including two suites. Each has contemporary amenities including a private bath, TV, phone, and queen- or king-size beds. The proprietors are most helpful and gracious, and can supply you with a wealth of local architectural and historical data.

Room rates range from $50 to $80; suites are $90 and $100. A full, homemade breakfast is $4.50.

What more can you ask of a restaurant than good food, a well-appointed bar, good service, moderate prices, daily hours, a handsome setting, and a delightful view. **The Tinnery,** at 631 Ocean View Blvd. (tel. 408/646-1040) in Pacific Grove, has them all. The contemporary interior décor is sea gray with wood paneling—a perfect complement to the bay. Large black-and-white photographs of cannery operations are attractive reminders of one segment of Monterey's past. Indirect track and recessed lighting, banks of white mums dividing the dining rooms, ceiling fans, ficus trees, light-wood chairs, a large fireplace—all add to the welcome feeling of warmth in the Tinnery. A large expanse of window affords a broad view of Lovers Point Park and Monterey Bay. The roomy restaurant lounge, set apart from the main dining room, affords a comfortable spot for cocktails before dinner, and also has a limited menu for late dining until 1 a.m. There is live entertainment nightly until 1 a.m.

The Tinnery serves breakfast from 8 to 11 a.m. The crêpes Normandy—French pancakes with apples, cream, and brandy—while not your usual breakfast fare, are delicious. Lunch is served from 11 a.m. to 5 p.m. and dinner from 5 to 11 p.m. Choices range from a delicious selection of sandwiches and burgers, salads, and soups, at $4.50 to $9, to somewhat grander fare such as teriyaki beef kebab or Monterey Bay snapper for $11. Dinner entrees are sufficiently varied to satisfy whatever your tastes may be. The Tinnery serves a superior prime rib for $16, and the Chinese chicken with snowpeas and ginger sauce at $10 is a good choice. All dinners are served with salad, vegetables, garnishes, and fresh-baked bread. It's one of the best buys in town. The Tinnery also has a children's menu for breakfast ($3.50), lunch ($4.50), and dinner ($4.50). And to add to your meal, there's a good selection of California wines.

And when you leave the Tinnery after breakfast or lunch, turn left and walk down (or drive, if you must) about 100 feet (bring your camera). Directly below the narrow park bordering Ocean View Boulevard you'll see dozens of harbor seals perched on the rocks being viewed by you and by the black cormorants inhabiting the bayfront.

For another terrific dinner in Pacific Grove, try **Fandango,** 223 17th St., off Lighthouse Avenue (tel. 408/373-0588), just a short walk from the Gosby House. The restaurant is located in a long, thin building perpendicular to the street. Inside there are several rooms, all slightly different, all very pleasant, whether you choose to be seated in the dining room with fresh flowers and fireside dining or in the terrace room with its delicate fragrances from the wood grill.

The restaurant features a new menu with an excellent selection of provincial Mediterranean specialties. Appetizers can be ordered à la carte, beginning with a plate of assorted tapas for $3. Two very popular entrees you don't want to overlook include the seafood paella, long a specialty of the house, and the authentic North African couscous. The recipe for the couscous has been in the Bain family (the new and very gracious owners/operators) for 150 years, and they import the spices to maintain the authenticity of the dish. Among the other excellent Mediterranean dishes are the cassoulet maison, the cannelloni niçoise, and the Greek-style lamb shank. There is also a good choice of pasta and fresh seafood dishes. Fandango has a very nice international wine list from which to choose, and their desserts are out of this world. The list begins with a lovely caramel custard or chocolate mousse and graduates in calorie count up to more spectacular choices including a Grand Marnier soufflé and profiteroles.

Dinner entrees range from $12 to $18. A prix-fixe dinner for $21 includes tapas, soup or green salad, and a choice of paella, couscous, cassoulet, or lamb shank, plus dessert. The Fandango also serves lunch (light entrees and sandwiches for $5 to $10) and Sunday brunch. The restaurant is open Monday through Saturday from 11 a.m. to 2 p.m. and 5 to 10 p.m., on Sunday from 9 a.m. to 2:30 p.m. There's plenty of free parking (a real plus). Reservations are advised.

CARMEL: With its narrow streets, its English-village architecture, and an air of not having quite awakened to the 20th century, Carmel is a must on any California visitor's itinerary and makes an exceptionally charming spot for a dinner, a weekend, or a romantic honeymoon. Since 1906 the town has been a haven for artists and writers—seldom, however, of the struggling variety—and reflects, as a whole, the proprietary interest of its residents. No storefront or dwelling can be erected without the approval of the town's artistic referees. No tree may be removed without specific permission of the police. The town is a carefully executed oasis in a practical era. You'll find few sidewalks, street lamps, or street signs marring the effect of tumbled gardens and rock-walled homes, and might even have difficulty identifying the gas stations under their wooden eaves. What you will find are charming international restaurants, delightfully cozy hostelries, and a magnificent wind-tossed beach.

For information, stop by the **Carmel Business Association** in Vandervort Court (second floor), on San Carlos between Ocean and Seventh (tel. 408/624-2522). The staff is friendly and welcoming, and full of facts about Carmel. The office is open Monday through Friday from 9:30 a.m. to 4 p.m.

Carmel Food and Lodging

The **Quail Lodge**, 8205 Valley Greens Dr. (off Carmel Valley Road), Carmel, CA 93923 (tel. 408/624-1581), is a pastoral resort set on 250 acres of lakes, woodlands, and meadows. Graceful bridges arch duck- and swan-filled lakes and ponds, and the exquisite grounds contain the prestigious Carmel Valley Golf and Country Club. You'll find complimentary champagne in your room, and a free newspaper is delivered daily. The accommodations are sumptuous, luxurious, and lovely—especially the upstairs rooms and cottages with cathedral ceilings. Among the facilities here are four tennis courts, two swimming pools, obviously an 18-hole golf course, a sauna for men, shops, a beauty salon, and airport limo.

A posh restaurant on the premises, **The Covey,** serves dinner nightly. The beautifully appointed restaurant overlooks a fountain on the lake. The ambience is warm and elegant, and the adjoining fireplace lounge is delightful for after-dinner drinks. The menu is refined European cuisine. Nonguests can, of course, dine here too. Jackets are required for men, and reservations are essential.

Rates in season (February through November) at the Quail Lodge are $185 to $260, single or double; suites, $265 to $800. Third person in room $25 extra.

Of course, few of us can afford long idylls at such prices. Fortunately for the less well-heeled, there are some excellent choices right in the heart of town.

A different kind of quaintness is offered at the **Normandy Inn,** Ocean Avenue (between Monte Verde and Casanova), Carmel, CA 93921 (tel. 408/624-3825). Here the rooms are housed in a shingled Tudor structure, and they are charming and homey, with ruffled bedspreads, shuttered windows, old-fashioned maple furnishings, and print wallpapers. There's a heated swimming pool on a terrace lined with trees and a great number of potted plants. All have switchboard phones and color TV, and about a quarter have a fireplace.

Rates for single rooms are $59 to $120; for doubles, $81 to $120. Cottages (accommodating two to eight persons) are priced at $120 to $219. Reserve far in advance.

A third choice, also quaint, is the **Pine Inn,** at Ocean Avenue and Monte Verde Street, Carmel, CA 93921 (tel. 408/624-3851). Here the décor is opulent Victoriana. Even the lobby has plush furnishings, a blazing fireplace, stained-glass panels, and red-flocked wallpaper. Each room is beautifully furnished in turn-of-the-century motif; some even have brass beds. All have color TV, direct-dial phone, and tub-shower bath. The Pine Inn also boasts the beautiful **Gazebo Restaurant.** Rates are $75 to $155 per night for one or two people for a wide variety of accommodations including double, twin, queen-size, and king-size beds.

Carmel harbors as many charming village restaurants as places to stay, but one of the most delightful is the **Tuck Box English Room,** on Dolores Street, near 7th Street (tel. 408/624-6365). In September of 1987 the Tuck Box was fire-bombed in the early hours of the morning. It's since been rebuilt to look exactly as it did before, with perhaps a few more tucks here and there, a new hardwood floor and a light-gray interior with charcoal trim. It's still just about everybody's favorite place for breakfast, locals and visitors alike. In this shingle-roofed, stucco cottage you can also enjoy lunch or a traditional afternoon tea (complete with hot buttered scones and homemade marmalade). The dining area is tiny, with a beamed ceiling, table bases that match the beams, stone fireplace, and red-and-white-checked curtains in the front window. You can also dine outside at a few tables on the patio. At breakfast you can have freshly squeezed orange juice for $1.50; and fresh fruit, bacon and eggs, with homemade muffins or scones, for $3.85. Lunchtime, the menu lists a choice of two or three entrees—for example, shepherd's pie, which is served with salad, vegetable, muffin or scone, at $4.40. For dessert there's homemade pie or cake with real whipped cream.

The Tuck Box is open from 8 a.m. to 4 p.m.; closed Monday and Tuesday.

Moving right along from English-village to French-provincial tea rooms, we come to the **Pâtisserie Boissière,** in Carmel Plaza on Mission Street, between Ocean and Seventh Avenues (tel. 408/624-5008). Like the Tuck Box, it features a provincial interior—white stucco walls, low-beamed ceiling, antique maple sideboard, Louis XV–style chairs, and a tiled fireplace. Scrumptious pâtisseries are on view in a glass display case. There's more seating in a skylight café with a garden décor. You can dine on a simple but perfect ham or Camembert sandwich on crusty French bread, have tea or coffee with one of the pastries, or opt for the more filling entrees. These include shrimp curry or chicken in white wine sauce with tomatoes and olives, both served with rice. Entrees cost $7 to $12 at lunch, about $1 more at dinner. Open daily from 9 a.m. to 10 p.m.

If you've been to the Fog City Diner in San Francisco, Mustards in Yountville, or the Tra Vigne in St. Helena, you'll recognize the sweet smell of success at the **Rio Grill,** at Calif. 1 and Rio Road in the Crossroads group of shops (tel. 408/625-5436)—brought to you by the same folks who put together the above-noted establishments (all recommended earlier in this book).

While you are waiting to be seated in the modern, southwestern-style dining room or in one of the cozy dining alcoves, you can watch the action in the Rio Grill's lively lounge or look at the cartoons above the bar of such famous locals as Bing

Crosby and Clint Eastwood. The scene is fun, but you really come for the food, which is as impressive, attractive, and deliciously casual as the décor. You might start with one of the homemade soups that the Rio Grill offers daily, or choose the richer rabbit quesadilla with ancho chili and roasted tomatillo salsa. Then it's on to entree (or sandwich) heaven: a half slab of barbecued baby back ribs from the wood-burning oven perhaps, fresh fish from the grill, or maybe a skirt steak with sesame, soy, and ginger marinade. A different pasta is offered each day, as are hamburgers and cheeseburgers, but consider the joy of a grilled eggplant sandwich with roasted red peppers, Fontina cheese, and watercress. Leave room for dessert; I had trouble deciding between the caramel-apple bread pudding and the caramel custard with pistachios and cream.

Prices are moderate. Entrees go for $9 to $15, with most in the $10 area. Appetizers, soups, salads, and sandwiches are in the $3 to $8 range. The most expensive item on the menu is a delectable Rio Grill sweatshirt for $20.

Service is young, friendly, knowledgeable and helpful. A good selection of wines covers a broad price range.

Rio Grill is open daily. Both the lounge and dining room are closed from 4 to 5 p.m., but otherwise the lounge serves food Monday through Saturday from 11:30 a.m. to 10 p.m. and on Sunday from 11 a.m. to 11 p.m.; and the dining room serves Sunday through Thursday from 11 a.m. to 10 p.m., on Friday and Saturday to 11 p.m.

Almost everyone knows that Clint Eastwood owns a restaurant in Carmel, its name mocking the quaintness of its many competitors. The **Hog's Breath Inn,** San Carlos Street, between Fifth and Sixth Avenues (tel. 408/625-1044), is always mobbed, partly because it's a very comfortable hangout, and partly because you never know when Clint Eastwood, the owner and former mayor of Carmel, is likely to drop in. Entered via a brick walkway, it has several dining and drinking areas. You can sit outdoors on a stone patio in director's chairs pulled up to tree-trunk tables, and there are two brick fireplaces to keep you warm. The main restaurant is dark and rustic with farm implements, dried flower arrangements, and celeb photos hanging on the walls. Another structure on the property is a very small but equally rustic pub, with a brick fireplace in the corner and two wild boars' heads mounted on the wall; a TV over the bar broadcasts sporting events.

Lunch at Hog's Breath, which costs $7 to $12, might consist of the fresh catch of the day, or a sirloin steak sandwich on whole-wheat toast, both of these served with the soup du jour. Dinner entrees—such as double cut of prime rib—come with soup or salad, baked potato or rice, and a vegetable for $14 to $20.

Open seven days, the Hog's Breath serves lunch Monday through Saturday from 11:30 a.m. to 3 p.m., Sunday brunch from 11 a.m. to 3 p.m.; dinner hours are 5 to 10 p.m. nightly, and the pub and patio stay open until 2 a.m. Reservations are taken for large parties only.

Some of the finest French fare in California is offered by André Françot at the award-winning **L'Escargot,** Mission Street at Fourth Avenue (tel. 408/624-4914). And while I'm heaping on praise, let me also say that the interior is the most beautiful in Carmel. Housed in a stucco, shingle-roofed building, it features leaded-glass windows, a beamed ceiling, cream-colored walls hung with copperware, maps of France, and menus of famous French restaurants. Banquettes and chairs are upholstered in provincial French fabric, decorative plates are ranged on a high shelf, and an oak centerpiece is used to display desserts, wines, and a big pot of fresh flowers. There's also a single rose in a pewter vase on every table, and here and there a dried flower arrangement. The entire effect is exquisite —intime, warm, cozy, and romantic.

You might begin with an appetizer of escargots de Bourgogne, or the smoked salmon (cured and smoked by André). The choice is not an easy one—among the other offerings are also braised fresh artichoke bottoms with herbs and a lovely puff pastry with wild mushrooms. As for the entrees, priced from $15 to $19.50, the house classic chicken with cream, foie gras, and truffles is still a vibrant memory. But anything you order will be superb. Other choices include a specialty of the chef, aiguillette de canard (breast of duck roasted with a special sauce); fresh scallops sautéed with orange-lemon butter; and one of my favorites, sweetbreads with cream, madeira, and mushrooms. L'Escargot has an extensive list of French and California wines. And don't pass up the desserts, each a masterpiece—say, the exquisite chilled Grand Marnier soufflé, which has the consistency of a delicate, light ice cream; the tarte tatin, an elegant cousin of an apple tart lightly caramelized in puff pastry and served warm with whipped cream; or the classic mousse au chocolat.

L'Escargot is open Monday through Saturday from 6 to 9:30 p.m. Reservations are advised.

Another of my favorite Carmel eateries is **Casanova,** on Fifth Avenue, between San Carlos and Mission Streets (tel. 408/625-0501). Belgian owners Gaston and Walter Georis designed Casanova to look like a provincial French farmhouse.

The menus change seasonally. The luncheon choices range from $6 to $9, including an excellent linguine (homemade) with scampi, scallops, mushrooms, garlic, and tomatoes, served in a copper pot; and calamari sautéed in white wine and caper sauce served with fresh pasta and salad. Lunches include either soup or salad and homemade grissini bread. Dinners are served with a soup or pasta appetizer. Among the entree choices, priced at $18 to $26, are rack of lamb in red wine and truffle sauce with apple-and-mint compote and fresh filet of sole in white wine, mushroom, and parsley cream sauce. And you're sure to find the perfect accompanying wine from among over 650 the restaurant stocks.

Casanova is open for breakfast the year round from 8 to 11 a.m.; for lunch Monday through Saturday from 11:30 a.m. to 3 p.m.; and for Sunday brunch, from 10 a.m. to 3 p.m. Dinner is served nightly from 5:30 to 10:30 p.m. Reservations for large parties only.

Index

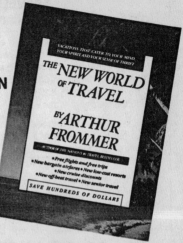

NOW, SAVE MONEY ON ALL YOUR TRAVELS!
Join Frommer's™ Dollarwise® Travel Club

Saving money while traveling is never a simple matter, which is why, over 27 years ago, the **Dollarwise Travel Club** was formed. Actually, the idea came from readers of the Frommer publications who felt that such an organization could bring financial benefits, continuing travel information, and a sense of community to economy-minded travelers all over the world.

In keeping with the money-saving concept, the annual membership fee is low—$18 (U.S. residents) or $20 U.S. (Canadian, Mexican, and foreign residents)—and is immediately exceeded by the value of your benefits which include:

1. The latest edition of any TWO of the books listed on the following pages.

2. A copy of any Frommer City Guide.

3. An annual subscription to an 8-page quarterly newspaper *The Dollarwise Traveler* which keeps you up-to-date on fastbreaking developments in good-value travel in all parts of the world—bringing you the kind of information you'd have to pay over $35 a year to obtain elsewhere. This consumer-conscious publication also includes the following columns:

> **Hospitality Exchange**—members all over the world who are willing to provide hospitality to other members as they pass through their home cities.

> **Share-a-Trip**—requests from members for travel companions who can share costs and help avoid the burdensome single supplement.

> **Readers Ask . . . Readers Reply**—travel questions from members to which other members reply with authentic firsthand information.

4. Your personal membership card which entitles you to purchase through the club all Frommer publications for a third to a half off their regular retail prices during the term of your membership.

So why not join this hardy band of international Dollarwise travelers now and participate in its exchange of information and hospitality? Simply send $18 (U.S. residents) or $20 U.S. (Canadian, Mexican, and other foreign residents) along with your name and address to: Frommer's Dollarwise Travel Club, Inc., Gulf + Western Building, One Gulf + Western Plaza, New York, NY 10023. Remember to specify which *two* of the books in section (1) and which *one* in section (2) above you wish to receive in your initial package of member's benefits. Or tear out the next page, check off your choices, and send the page to us with your membership fee.

FROMMER BOOKS   Date_____
PRENTICE HALL PRESS
ONE GULF + WESTERN PLAZA
NEW YORK, NY 10023

Friends:
Please send me the books checked below:

FROMMER'S™ $-A-DAY® GUIDES
(In-depth guides to sightseeing and low-cost tourist accommodations and facilities.)

☐ Europe on $30 a Day $14.95
☐ Australia on $30 a Day $12.95
☐ Eastern Europe on $25 a Day $12.95
☐ England on $40 a Day $12.95
☐ Greece on $30 a Day $12.95
☐ Hawaii on $50 a Day $13.95
☐ India on $25 a Day $12.95
☐ Ireland on $30 a Day $12.95
☐ Israel on $30 & $35 a Day $12.95
☐ Mexico (plus Belize & Guatemala)
   on $25 a Day. $13.95
☐ New Zealand on $40 a Day $12.95
☐ New York on $50 a Day. $12.95
☐ Scandinavia on $50 a Day $12.95
☐ Scotland and Wales on $40 a Day. . . . $12.95
☐ South America on $30 a Day $12.95
☐ Spain and Morocco (plus the Canary Is.)
   on $40 a Day. $13.95
☐ Turkey on $25 a Day $12.95
☐ Washington, D.C., & Historic Va. on
   $40 a Day. $12.95

FROMMER'S™ DOLLARWISE® GUIDES
(Guides to sightseeing and tourist accommodations and facilities from budget to deluxe, with emphasis on the medium-priced.)

☐ Alaska $13.95
☐ Austria & Hungary $14.95
☐ Belgium, Holland, Luxembourg $13.95
☐ Brazil $14.95
☐ Egypt. $13.95
☐ France $14.95
☐ England & Scotland $14.95
☐ Germany $13.95
☐ Italy. $14.95
☐ Japan & Hong Kong $13.95
☐ Portugal, Madeira, & the Azores . . . $13.95
☐ South Pacific. $13.95
☐ Switzerland & Liechtenstein $13.95
☐ Bermuda & The Bahamas $13.95
☐ Canada $13.95
☐ Caribbean $13.95
☐ Cruises (incl. Alask, Carib, Mex, Hawaii,
   Panama, Canada, & US) $14.95
☐ California & Las Vegas $14.95
☐ Florida $13.95
☐ Mid-Atlantic States $13.95
☐ New England $13.95
☐ New York State $13.95
☐ Northwest $13.95
☐ Skiing in Europe. $14.95
☐ Skiing USA—East $13.95
☐ Skiing USA—West. $13.95
☐ Southeast & New Orleans $13.95
☐ Southwest $14.95
☐ Texas. $13.95
☐ USA (avail. Feb. 1989). $15.95

FROMMER'S™ TOURING GUIDES
(Color illustrated guides that include walking tours, cultural & historic sites, and other vital travel information.)

☐ Australia $9.95
☐ Egypt. $8.95
☐ Florence. $8.95
☐ London. $8.95
☐ Paris $8.95
☐ Thailand. $9.95
☐ Venice. $8.95

TURN PAGE FOR ADDITIONAL BOOKS AND ORDER FORM.